ALEXANDER BUSTAMANTE
AND MODERN JAMAICA

Sir Alexander Bustamante, National Hero and first Prime Minister of Jamaica.

GEORGE E. EATON

ALEXANDER BUSTAMANTE
AND MODERN JAMAICA

© 1995 by George Eaton
First Edition 1995
Reprinted 1996
Reprinted 2000

10 9 8 7 6 5 4 3 2

Published by LMH Publishing Ltd.
7-9 Norman Road, Kingston CSO
E-mail: henryles@cwjamaica.com

ISBN 976-610-191-4

Printed by Lightning Print U.S.A.

To Kathleen — and our children

Gail, Dawn, George, Kevin, and Gerald.

CONTENTS

PREFACE

This book is not a popular interpretative work, as it would be, were it concerned essentially with the mere significance of the events and developments in the life and career of Bustamante as an outstanding trade union and political leader, or with his appreciation of, and reaction to, the social forces at work in Jamaican society. Such an approach would have made sense, had the official (government-sponsored) biography of Bustamante or other scholarly treatment of his life and times already been published. For then one could assume that readers either would be familiar with, or could be referred to, such sources for detailed background information. The fact is, however, that Alexander Bustamante remains a highly controversial and legendary figure even in his lifetime.

I have undertaken, therefore, to provide the reader with detailed and sometimes exhaustive accounts or background information when this seemed necessary or desirable to support analysis and interpretation or merely to set the records straight.

On the other hand, by conscious intent and design, this is not a purely academic work, as it would be, had it been originally presented as a doctoral dissertation or prepared as a textbook. This will be evident also in the very selective use of references and footnotes and identification of sources. This book is intended, then, as a serious and scholarly effort, but written, hopefully, in readable style and form so that it may appeal to a public of lay as well as professional readers in Jamaica, the Caribbean and elsewhere.

Of course, in analysing and assessing the role and contribution of Alexander Bustamante, one of the human instruments of political change in colonial Jamaica and a founding father of politically independent Jamaica, it is hoped that the reader will be afforded some insight into the politics of decolonization and of nation-building and modernization. Incidentally, if it appears that enough emphasis has not been placed on Bustamante's career as Jamaica's most famous labour leader, it is because this side of his career will be dealt with at length in my still-impending book "The Development of Trade Unionism in Jamaica".

As to the organization of the book, Chapters 1 and 2 provide historical and background information concerning the socio-economic and political milieu in Jamaica at the time of Bustamante's birth and upbringing, his personal and family background, travel overseas, his return to Jamaica and initial involvement in public affairs and agitational politics. Chapters 3 and 4 deal in much greater detail with the revolt of the labouring poor and the unemployed in 1938, the emergence of Alexander Bustamante and the other principal actors on the Jamaican labour and political fronts and their early relationships, the aftermath of the riots and conflicts of personalities and ideologies which were to have profound significance for the island's future.

Chapter 5 traces more selectively the development of political unionism in Jamaica as the Bustamante Industrial Trade Union was used by its leader to bring organized labour and the masses generally into the mainstream of organized politics, which in the process made the support of labour the yardstick of legitimacy for any political party that wished to survive or exercise political power. The Chapter also traces the forging of the two rival party and trade union blocs B.I.T.U./J.L.P. and P.N.P./ T.U.C. which has given Jamaican politics its distinctive flavour, and examines some of the consequences of this development. It is during this period that the dominance of Bustamante and Bustamanteism reaches its height.

Chapter 6 examines in broad sweep the increasing maturity of Alexander Bustamante as well as Jamaican politics and constitutionalism. Bustamante is won over to the cause of self-government, and constitutional reform goes forward steadily but gradually. He endures his first stint as Leader of the Opposition as his cousin Norman Manley and the P.N.P. take their turn at the helm of Government, thereby confirming the strength of bi-partism in Jamaican politics. Jamaica opts for self-determination within the wider framework of West Indian Federation but Alexander Bustamante reverses his earlier position and opts for Jamaica withdrawing from the Federation and going it alone. He successfully mobilizes the electorate to bring in a "no" verdict in the Referendum decided upon by Manley and the P.N.P., and in the ensuing General Election Bustamante achieves the pinnacle of political ambition when he becomes Jamaica's first Prime Minister. The factors and circumstances leading to the break-up of the West Indies Federation are therefore considered in some detail.

Chapter 7 describes Bustamante at the pinnacle of his career as the first Prime Minister of Jamaica and how failing health forces him to retire from the seat of power though not from the seat of influence.

Finally, Chapter 8 looks at Bustamante the man and the more personal side of his life and achievement, his retirement from active politics and the crowning of a life of hectic and vigorous public service by being named a National Hero.

I should like to acknowledge my debt to all those who accorded interviews and were helpful otherwise. I hope I will be excused, however, for mentioning only a few names. I am grateful to Sir Alexander Bustamante for interviews and visits and particularly to Lady Bustamante for generous cooperation and hospitality. I am also indebted to the Clarke family, surviving cousins of Sir Alexander, who still reside not far from Blenheim — for providing invaluable information about Sir Alexander's parents and his early boyhood. I wish to thank also the following for interviews accorded and very helpful insights provided: Mr. Edward Seaga, Member of Parliament; Mr. G. Arthur Brown, Governor of the Bank of Jamaica; Mr. Vivian Durham; and Mr. Bartholomew Kerr.

I have also drawn extensively on recorded interviews with other political and trade union leaders which were made earlier as part of my continuing study of "The Development of Trade Unionism in Jamaica", but it may be more appropriate to make those acknowledgments in that work. I cannot, however, avoid singling out, at this time, the late Rt. Honourable Norman Washington Manley, National Hero, for the individual insights provided in a series of interviews. Lengthy and spirited discussions with Mr. Frank Hill, journalist and radio commentator and former trade unionist as well as political activist, helped to clarify my own conceptions and approach to this work.

I am indebted to my colleague and friend Professor Rex Nettleford, Director of the Trade Union Education Institute and Director of the Extra-Mural Department — University of the West Indies, and to Dr. Louis Lindsay, also of the University of the West Indies, for agreeing so readily to review the manuscript and for their helpful suggestions. Certain chapters dealing with historical background were also reviewed by Mr. H.P. Jacobs, whose comments were as usual very helpful.

Finally, this is indeed one book which would not have been brought to fruition without the encouragement and active assistance of my wife, Kathleen, who served unfailingly as research assistant and critic.

G.E.E.
August 1972

Alexander Bustamante
née William Alexander (Aleck) Clarke

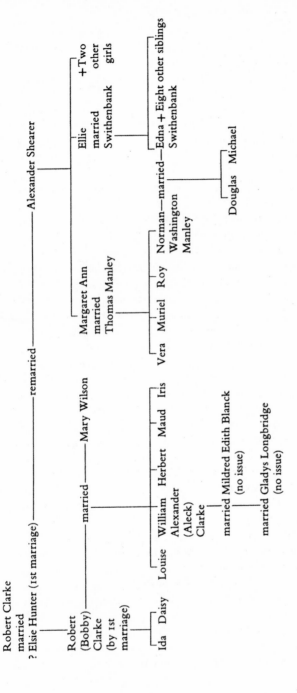

Robert Clarke
married
? Elsie Hunter (1st marriage) —————— remarried —————— Alexander Shearer

Robert
(Bobby)
Clarke —————— married —————— Mary Wilson
(by 1st
marriage)

Margaret Ann
married
Thomas Manley

Ellie
married
Swithenbank
+Two
other
girls

Ida Daisy

Louise William Herbert Maud Iris
Alexander
(Aleck)
Clarke

Vera Muriel Roy Norman—married—Edna + Eight other siblings
Washington Swithenbank
Manley

married Mildred Edith Blanck
(no issue)

married Gladys Longbridge
(no issue)

Douglas Michael

NOTES: 1. Alexander Bustamante and Norman Manley were cousins by virtue of their common maternal grandmother.
2. Alexander Bustamante and Edna Manley are cousins by virtue of their common maternal grandmother.
3. Norman W. Manley — Chief Minister (1955–9) and Premier (1959–62) — Leader of Opposition (1949–55 and 1962–9).
4. Michael Manley, Leader of Opposition (1969–72) — Prime Minister (1972).
Douglas Manley, Minister of Government (1972).

1 THE EARLY DAYS

The Right Honourable Sir Alexander Bustamante, Doctor of Laws (honoris causa), President General (for life) of the Bustamante Industrial Trade Union, Privy Councillor and first Prime Minister of Jamaica and the country's first living National Hero, was born William Alexander Clarke on the 24th February 1884. He was the second of five children, including sisters Louise, Iris and Maud, and a younger brother Herbert, born to Robert Constantine Clarke, familiarly known as Bobby, and Mary Wilson, his second wife. Clarke's first wife had died, leaving him with two young daughters, Ida and Daisy.

Bobby Clarke was himself the son of Robert Clarke, a white man, and Elsie Hunter, a coloured woman — coloured here signifying the progeny of white and black, or white and non-white, parents. Clarke senior died and his wife, who was still youthful, then married Alexander Shearer, also a white man of Irish extraction, and bore him four daughters. One of these, Margaret Ann, grew up and was trained to be a postmistress and while at Porus in the parish of Manchester in that capacity met and married produce dealer and farmer Thomas Manley, a near-black man and proprietor of a small property, Roxborough, located only four miles from Porus. The Manleys reared a family of four, including two daughters, Vera and Muriel, and two sons, Norman Washington and Roy. Both Norman and Roy saw active combat in Europe during World War I, but Roy did not survive.

William Alexander Clarke Bustamante and Norman Washington Manley were thus half cousins by virtue of having the same maternal grandmother — Elsie Clarke Shearer.

The researcher is hard put to present a consistent and complete account of the ethnic background or social and economic status of Bustamante's immediate family or even of his own upbringing and youthful experiences. Part of the difficulty is that William Alexander Clarke deliberately set out, in later years, to shroud his own background and upbringing and to substitute legends of his own making to serve his

1

own purposes, Thus, for instance, he initiated and has clung tenaciously to the story that at the age of five he was adopted by a Spanish mariner named Bustamante (hence his acquisition of a Spanish surname) and taken to Spain where he was brought up, schooled and lived, for nearly twenty years, venturing out as a young man to become embroiled in military escapades and adventures in Spanish Morocco and elsewhere. Let it be said that this is a colourful but highly imaginative story.

William Alexander Clarke or Bustamante, the surname he formally adopted by deed poll in September 1944, was born into a family which, by virtue of social and occupational status, fell within the plantocracy or planting class, an important and enduring segment of the ruling strata of Jamaican society. Other considerations, predominantly of race and colour, also contrived to make young Clarke a member of European Jamaica as distinct from African Jamaica. The two Jamaicas — the one European and white oriented, enjoying social, economic and political privilege and hegemony — the other, Afro-Asian oriented and black, and identified with poverty, ignorance, limited opportunities and political powerlessness — derived and owed their respective socio-economic and political forms and systems to the plantation economy, dedicated overwhelmingly to the cultivation of sugar-cane and the manufacture of raw sugar, the institution of slavery and British imperialism or colonialism, which provided the impetus for and shaped the development of the Jamaican economy and society.

Alexander Bustamante came into a world in which the sugar estate dominated the focus of rural life and activity. Such was the social prestige and economic importance of King Sugar that the sugar estate served as the operational model for other plantations, whether they were devoted to activities complementary to sugar, such as pen-keeping (cattle rearing), or to the cultivation of banana or to other minor staple crops, such as pimento (allspice), ginger, arrowroot and timber.[1] Yet, in spite of being the mainstay of the island's economy, the sugar industry was long past the golden era of economic grandeur. The heyday of prosperity had come in the eighteenth century. Then the West Indian planter was a familiar figure in English society. This was possible because of the institution of absentee landlordism, which meant that, as far as Jamaica was concerned, little of the wealth from cultivation and sale of sugar remained in the island.

The Europeans who then came to work or manage estates envisaged making a "quick" fortune to return to Britain, and once there "the planters' fondest wish was to acquire an estate, blend with the aristocracy, and

2

remove the marks of their origins."[2] They thus became members of the "nouveaux riches", their colossal wealth permitting lavish expenditures on the construction of houses or buying of seats in Parliament. The more competent among those who actually worked their estates in Jamaica earned their fortunes and left, and their children, who were sent to England for schooling, often did not return.

The West Indian interest also had constituted a powerful bloc in British politics. The strength of the planters was increased by large numbers of West Indian merchants who drew vast profits from the West Indian trade. This combined West Indian interest entrenched itself in the Lower and Upper Houses of Parliament and put up a determined opposition to any measures which threatened its sugar monopoly.

Despite sharp fluctuations of fortunes as the West Indian territories were caught up in statecraft between France and Britain, prosperity on the islands, including Jamaica, was maintained until the nineteenth century. But the foundations for the decline of the sugar industry had already been laid in the eighteenth century. The American War of Inpendence of 1776 struck the first real blow at the West Indian sugar émpire. American independence undermined the mercantilist system. Both the war and the post-war periods showed that Britain could increase production and wealth even when deprived of colonial markets, and free trade doctrines received considerable impetus as did the rising tide of dissatisfaction with the slave trade. The American War also left the British planters to face competition of the French sugar colonies. Santo Domingo (Haiti after 1804) experienced an astonishing development as a sugar producer.

By the end of the Napoleonic Wars in 1815, the European market virtually had been lost to British sugar interests. The Napoleonic Wars had given a stimulus to the production of subsidized beet-sugar in Europe, thus beginning the competition of the two sugars which has continued to the present day.

Bankruptcies became the order of the day in Jamaica. A Parliamentary Committee set up in England in 1807 concluded that the ills of the sugar industry were due to the condition of the foreign market and that production must be curtailed. To restrict production meant that the slave trade had to be abolished. The change in economic thinking, reinforced by a determined campaign on the part of a minority group of humanitarians, made possible the Abolition of Slavery Act of 1807.

The abolition of the slave trade, from the point of view of the planters, was a catastrophe. The supply of slaves could not be maintained and scarcity of labour developed in spite of resort to calculated breeding of slaves. Rising costs of production were to make competition difficult with producers like Cuba, Brazil and the British East Indies.

After the Emancipation of Slavery Act of 1833, it was but a matter of time before the eclipse of the West Indian sugar empire set in. The failure of the Apprenticeship Scheme designed to effect the transition from slave labour to wage labour and/or freeholders weakened the export potential of Jamaican planters. The British Act of 1846, providing for the progressive equalization of duties on British and foreign sugar, was an even more serious development, and a severe depression set in. Thereafter, only the most efficient estates could produce at a profit and Jamaican planters made attempts to reduce wages as a means of cutting costs.

Throughout the nineteenth century, planters nevertheless continued to cling to hopes of economic revival as the fortunes of sugar fluctuated. At the same time, the industry showed some resilience by attempting to adapt itself to the changing conditions, partly by amalgamation of estates and improvements in equipment, and partly by reducing wages. From the working classes there were, however, protests against destitution and wage depression and there were many petitions for redress of injustices and grievances which went unheeded. Thousands also began to seek relief via the route of emigration to Central America, but discontent was sufficient to produce the Morant Bay Rebellion of 1865 which was crushed with such bloody reprisals as to earn the distinction of being the bloodiest insurrection yet in the island's history.

Fluctuating prices and a serious outbreak of cane disease in the 1890's that ravaged plantations again gave rise by the close of the nineteenth century to widespread bankruptcies, and a Royal Commission was established in 1897. The Commission recommended the substitution of peasant cultivation for estates by a policy of land settlement and the introduction of new crops. The banana trade, already started in the 1860's, was expanded. The completion of the Rio Cobre Irrigation Scheme in 1876 ensured the successful growing of bananas under irrigation, making Jamaica the first country in the Western Hemisphere to claim this achievement.

The Jamaica into which Alexander Bustamante was born and spent his adolescence, therefore, no longer offered the prospect of fortune, power and fame to the planting class. Nevertheless, the Jamaican economy limped along, still tied to the mother country in its social and economic relations, and thus without hope or the will to effect any transformation in the structure of production. Arable lands remained divided up between sugar — for large plantations, dominated by British investment capital and characterized by absentee ownership — and banana — the basis for the existence of a class of small farmers and peasants, most of them the direct descendants of slave forebears and, in economic and political terms, not far removed from the conditions of their forebears.

In one sense, however, all Jamaicans, as producers of raw materials for British factories and the passive consumers of finished and manufactured products of that same industrial complex, were "hewers of wood and drawers of water". But the perpetuation of the traditional social structure, based on considerations of race, colour and class, reinforced by the pre-emption of certain economic activities and political influence, still made it possible for the plantocracy and their allies to maintain life-styles and delusions of grandeur, based not on on-going economic progress, but on the exploitation of privilege, for nowhere was the impact of slavery and the plantation system seen more clearly than in the social structure and social relations.

In the pre-Emancipation era, Jamaicans had been divided legally into three castes of free whites, coloureds (usually the progeny of white males and black slave women) and Negroes or blacks. This class structure carried over into the post-Emancipation period, the main difference being that social rather than legal sanctions and disabilities were relied upon to provide legitimacy and uphold it.

Skin colour largely determined social class and social mobility. At the apex of the social system were the whites, the British Governor and white officialdom, along with the native or creole whites engaged in commerce and large-scale farming. This was the primary political ruling class. In between, constituting the middle classes, came the coloureds — persons of mixed race — reflecting a wide range of occupational activities and an even greater range of shades or hues of skin colour and associated physical refinements. Social station tended to be fixed according to the darkening descent to black skin. Thus in descending order, there were near-whites or mustefinos, mustays of swarthy complexion but lighter than the brown-skinned mulattos, who in turn were subject to an almost endless variety of groups based on even further subtle and complex differentiations such as the extent to which white mixture was reflected in the quality of hair. Further down the social ladder, the lower echelons grew progressively darker, passing through "sambo" to black, at the base. At the base, then, stood the Negroes or blacks, the vast majority of the population characterized as much by homogeneity of colour as

5

by the poverty and ignorance which marked their lives.

As the class born in Jamaica, the coloureds were most Jamaican of the Jamaicans, exhibiting the strongest attachment to their island, but at the same time staunchly pro-British. Their patriotism and leaning toward British policies were the natural outcome of being the half-castes in Jamaican society. Even after legal discrimination had been abolished, the status of the coloureds, half-way between the two "pure" racial groups, made for the familiar psychological insecurity of the middle classes. "His [the coloured's] attempt to emphasize the European part of his social heritage made him reject the African part, but at the same time the local white refused to recognize him as a European and an equal. His insecurity, however, could be partly compensated by greater loyalty to Britain and greater loyalty to Jamaica."[3]

However, in spite of the tradition of tensions and antagonisms between the two upper segments of the society, arising largely from the attempts of the white ruling class to prevent the "brown people" from rising into their caste or, later, their class, the whites and coloureds emerged as natural allies. Both groups could claim to be the heirs and repositories of European culture in Jamaica. The people of colour, however, were very much conscious and proud of this heritage and, when it came to social philosophy and social policy, shared the attitudes of their white neighbours or social betters.

The Negroes or blacks, on the other hand, stood apart as a separate class, if no longer caste, not only because of their former status of slaves, but because their cultural heritage was predominantly African.

The only thing which linked the black population, sexual alliances apart, was common economic endeavour, but even so, there could be little consolation to the blacks, condemned, as they were, to relative poverty and degradation.

Nor was the socio-economic structure described above modified by the incursion of other minority racial and ethnic groups, such as the Jews, Chinese, East Indians and Lebanese, who continued to arrive as immigrants during the latter part of the nineteenth century. They were content to preoccupy themselves, as marginal social groups, with money-making and with maintaining some ethnic distinctiveness.

In the political sphere, the colony had reverted to Crown Colony government in 1865. The Morant Bay Rebellion had opened up the possibility of political reform, including extension of the franchise, a prospect which so alarmed the plantocracy and ruling classes that in one of the unique acts of history, the Jamaican House of Assembly thus voted in 1865 to ask withdrawal of the island's constitutional prerogative and the assumption of Crown Colony status.

The previous representative system had meant an oligarchy which, by its very nature and interests, had been incapable of improving the lot of the new freedmen. Under Crown Colony status, the imperial Government, symbolized by the "great white Queen or King", could at least restrain white oligarchies and give some consideration to the crying needs of the majority of blacks. There was virtual if not elected representation through the Governor.

In both the latter half of the nineteenth century and the opening decades of the twentieth century, a number of more "liberal" or progressive Governors successively took advantage of an increasingly more flexible interpretaion of the principles and norms governing British public finance to raise loans and undertake certain long-term or significant public and "development" works which could not be met from current or anticipated fiscal revenues.

While some of the development projects, such as the Rio Cobre Irrigation Scheme, were intended to bolster the flagging sugar industry and encourage a measure of agricultural diversification, the expenditures were prompted by concern to raise the island's backward public services to levels demanded by modern standards of civilization or to mitigate the more glaring excesses of the plantation economy, rather than to alter the structure of the economy and society.

Between 1884, the year of Bustamante's birth, and 1910, the Crown Colony system was modified to meet repeated demands for an elective element. In 1884, a new Legislative Council was formed, in which there were four ex-officio members plus as many as five nominated persons. To these were added nine elected members chosen under a limited franchise. For years after 1884, however, elected membership was composed of white persons, but by 1910 there were five coloured and one black in a total of fourteen. The non-whites did not immediately espouse constitutional change on behalf of the black and coloured sections of the population. However much they might resent the social disabilities imposed by inferior (non-white) status, they tended to think and act in harmony with the standards of the whites. The majority of the black population thus continued their existence outside the pale of political activity and decision-making.

Hanover, the parish in which Bustamante was born, is located on the western end of the island. In the closing decades of the nineteenth century, it was as remote as could be, culturally as well as physically,

7

from Kingston, the economic, social, cultural and intellectual centre. Economic, cultural and social activity in Hanover tended to centre around the plantation estate, which remained a self-contained but nonetheless complex organism, constituting in fact a microcosm of Jamaican society at large.

Within the three-tiered estate community, pride of place went to the proprietor, or in the case of the absentee owner — that scourge of Jamaica — to his planting attorney or representative. As a professional management group, the attorneys considered themselves vastly superior to the next in rank, the overseers. The overseer, in turn, was the chief operating official and the central authority figure on the estate. Responsibility for day-to-day administration and the maintenance of discipline and operational efficiency on the part of the labour force — white and black — lay with him. As such, the overseer had complete and autocratic control over nearly everyone on the estate.

Overseers, like the attorneys above them, were equally concerned to maintain social distance between themselves and the next and lowest rank of the managerial hierarchy, the book-keepers. In the pre-Emancipation era, the book-keeper had been the apprentice planter, the white proletarian of the planting society. In spite of his title, the book-keeper's duties could range from lending his physical presence in the field to see that work was actually done, to keeping watch in the boiler house or to issuing stores and supplies. But because his principal asset was a white skin, the book-keeper could hope to graduate after a five-year apprenticeship into the ranks of the overseers. Of course, in the post-Emancipation era, upward mobility was made much easier as the hierarchical structure of the ruling strata became more fluid.[4]

The social gradations in the plantation community found expression also in the physical lay-out of the estate. The proprietor or his representative, in the case of an absentee owner, resided in the most imposing structure on the estate, a commodious Great House which typically would be placed on the most convenient elevation or rise to take advantage of the breeze. In the absence of both proprietor and non-resident attorney — for attorneys often managed a number of estates — then the Great House would be occupied by the overseer as the effective administrator in charge and the principal white man in residence. If the overseer was not in residence in the Great House, he would be supplied with a spacious house near the Great House and with the appropriate retinue of servants. Finally, the subordinate white workers, including book-keepers, lived typically in separate barracks, not too far removed

8

from the Great House, but in much more modest circumstances than the overseers.

When, therefore, Elsie Hunter, a woman of colour, married Robert Clarke, a white man and property overseer, she was assured of a position of status and comfort however modest in Jamaican society.

For certain, one son, Robert (Bobby) Constantine, came of the union of Robert Clarke and Elsie Hunter. There was a second son born to Clarke who also grew up in Blenheim, but it is not clear whether this son was by his wife.

The death of her husband led Elsie Clarke into her second marriage to Alexander Shearer and to the next stage of her life and career. Also a white man and of Irish extraction, Shearer is reputed to have been book-keeper under Robert Clarke senior. He was referred to as "Jarman" Shearer by villagers, which would suggest that they considered him to be of "poor white" origin. The Seaford Town Settlement, in nearby Westmoreland, of poor whites of German extraction had evidently accustomed people to thinking of all poor whites as "Jarmans". Be that as it may, the Shearers moved up the social and occupational ladder when they leased Blenheim property from absentee owners and took up residence in the estate's Great House.

A relatively large property situated in hilly and mountainous terrain a few miles from the seaport town of Lucea, Blenheim estate lacked the flat or rolling expanses of arable land characteristic of the sugar estate, and at best it must have been a marginally viable operation. The Shearers resorted to sub-letting or tenancy to assure some income from the property, which was devoted to stock-rearing, cultivation of crops with a possible smattering of sugar-cane and timber. Labourers employed or attached to Blenheim who could be accommodated within the confines of the property were allowed to erect and live in traditional wattle and daub huts.

This was the environment in which Bobby Clarke, Bustamante's father, came to maturity along with his four half-sisters, the Shearer girls. His aging step-father, Alexander Shearer, began to suffer from failing eyesight, and as the administration of the estate devolved increasingly upon his mother, so she too began to rely more on her son for his assistance in the management of the property.

When tall and fair Bobby Clarke got married, it was to a white woman who bore him two daughters before she died. He then took as his second bride, dark-skinned (sambo) Mary Wilson, also of the same parish. Described by contemporaries as a tall, dark and handsome woman, who carried herself with dignity, Mary Wilson came from an established peasant or small settler family in Dalmally District not far from Blenheim. Alexander Bustamante always described his mother as being a descendant of the Arawak Indians, the indigenous inhabitants of Jamaica when the island was discovered by Columbus in 1494. Historians tell us, however, that the Arawaks were enslaved by the Spaniards and became extinct within fifty years of the Spanish occupation.

Bobby's choice of a second wife did not, however, please his mother, and as the mistress of Blenheim she ruled against Mary being accommodated in the Great House. A strong-willed and ambitious woman, Mrs. Shearer always encouraged the members of the family to "look up" and to seek to improve themselves.

Quite apart from her sensibilities about social class and social status, Mrs. Shearer was also a deeply religious person and a strict disciplinarian who expressed her conviction and displeasure in practical ways. Bobby had learned as a young man that she would not hesitate to bring the whip into play, if he was caught in dalliance or having an affair with a lower-class (and concomitantly dark) wench.

According to one published account, no one (including hired help) escaped her matriarchal fervour. "She used to get up at 5 o'clock or half past five in the morning and wake up everybody for prayers — maids and all. . . . After breakfast, with the family, or sometimes during break-fast, she would go out to the head of the stairs, Bible in hand, read a passage and pray for the labourers. No labourer would be allowed to work if late for prayers. 'Go home! Come tomorrow.'"[5]

Mary Wilson had two strikes against her. Not only was she darker than Bobby's first wife, but perhaps far more importantly, she was not "cultured". A surviving in-law of the Clarke family, a black woman also of peasant stock, who recalled with empathy her own childhood and adulthood relationships with Mary Wilson, helps us to appreciate Mary's ranking in the community at the time of her marriage: "But she go a bush — And she coarse, you know — she very coarse — she go all a ground you know and when you go all a bush, now you don't look so fine, so refined. But she go a ground — visit her ground."

The net result was that Bobby Clarke built himself a modest cottage on the side of a hill not far from the Great House but actually at a much higher elevation. When he walked a couple of chains from his house up to the brow of the hill, Bobby Clarke could look down at the main residence.

The first two or three of the new Clarke brood, including Aleck,

10

were born in the cottage. The remaining children, however, were born in more commodious surroundings, for within a few years, Bobby Clarke was to find himself in residence in the Great House. By then old man Shearer's eyesight had failed him and the responsibilities of managing Blenheim had become a burden on Grandma Shearer. Her attractive off-white daughters, all excellent horsewomen, had come of marriageable age and were going their separate ways. After thoughtful consideration, Grandma Shearer decided that the time had come to give up the lease and relinquish Blenheim property. A new lessee, Malcolm (Elder) Gordon took over the property, but retained the services of Bobby Clarke as overseer and Clarke, now a "busha" (overseer) in his own right, moved into the "backra house" (white-man house) with his dark-skinned wife and children. However limited or precarious may have been the economic rewards from managing Blenheim property, the Clarke family even in a condition of genteel poverty could now claim their niche in the social hierarchy, and a perch from which to view themselves in relation to others in the society.

Aleck Clarke grew up and spent his adolescence as a country boy in a rather rugged, hilly and isolated rural community. When the villagers of Blenheim and environs went to town, it was to the picturesque nearby coastal town of Lucea, making the journey by foot, donkey, mule, horse or buggy, depending on the economic and social status of the traveller. In any event, the roads leading to Blenheim were so steep and forbidding that it was unrealistic to expect the owner of a carriage-for-hire (or later an automobile) to venture into Blenheim, and a journey to Montego Bay could be contemplated only as a major event.

Aleck attended elementary school first at Cacoon and then at Dalmalley district. As a teenager he had his own horse, and not surprisingly his major recreational activity was horse-back riding. He thus spent many carefree hours meandering or racing with his cousins and other teenage companions in the neighbourhood. Meanwhile, the Shearers left Blenheim, but there is uncertainty as to their movements subsequently. Some of the family were of the impression that they had gone to live in the parish of Trelawny, reputedly the parish from which old man Shearer had come. Nor can the possibility be ruled out that the old couple may have gone, along with two unmarried daughters, on an extended visit to daughter Margaret Ann Manley at Roxborough in Manchester or to live nearby. What is certain, however, is that old man Shearer acquired, jointly with his son-in-law Thomas Manley, a property in St. Catherine called Belmont, "large and desolate in a district known as Guanaboa Vale, just ten miles out of Spanish Town on the road to Watermount in the St. Catherine hills".[6]

Again there is the possibility, also, that the Shearers might have gone directly from Blenheim to live at Belmont and to be joined three or four years later by daughter and co-owner Margaret Ann Manley and her four children, after the death of her husband.

When Manley senior died in 1899, (in his son's words) "having wasted his substance in litigious living", his widow, who was almost penniless, emigrated to the United States where she got a job as a postal-telegraph clerk in Washington. She found, however, that she could not support her four young children on her earnings and so returned to Jamaica. She then went to live at Belmont with her children, "a blind father, old man Shearer, an invalid sister, and yet another sister — a bright and lively woman — who left for England a couple of years after".[7] It must have been, then, that Grandma Shearer had died before her daughter and family moved to Belmont in 1902 or 1903. The late N. W. Manley could only recollect his grandfather living at Belmont and this has been confirmed by his surviving sister Dr. Muriel Manley.

Belmont, then, became the home of the Manleys and the surviving Shearers, as well as the second home of the Clarkes, including eldest daughter Maud (who had earlier been adopted into the Shearer family), Iris (who eventually emigrated to the United States), Louise and Aleck.

The twenty-year-old Aleck Clarke arrived at Belmont in 1904 to be trained as a junior overseer. It marked a sudden shift both in occupation and environment. Up to then, he had been working as a store clerk in one of the C.E. Johnston & Co. stores, on the island's north coast. Although an audacious young man, Aleck Clarke was not likely to be enthused at the prospect of being junior overseer at Belmont, even if only temporarily. "Belmont was a hard place to manage. It was quite undeveloped and like so many derelict places in Jamaica it carried on as best it could with a little of everything: logwood, sold after being cut into lengths of heart wood with the bark and sap chipped off; a few cattle; a few tenants; a little cocoa."[8] He was also a restless young man who was soon provoking concern and complaint over his frequent late nights out. Nevertheless, in the year that he was at Belmont, he developed a reputation as a young man of action, as his younger cousin Norman recalled. "I remember him vividly. There was nothing in those days to indicate the person he would become when he was fifty-odd years old, except his zest for life and a certain wildness and indifference for what others thought. I best recall the fact that he was a good horseman and the peasants from far

12

and wide would bring their animals to Belmont for him to 'break' as the word was in those days. Also, he played a fine game of draughts. I do not recall that I ever beat him, but he was twenty-plus to my ten years of age."9 His physical prowess and sporting were just the qualities likely to endear Aleck Clarke to his rustic audiences and one can imagine him occasionally biting the dust, but more often than not, hanging on to master his "bucking bronco" and earn the applause and admiration of estate labourers and peasants.

Aleck Clarke, however, soon bored with life at Belmont, began to yearn for excitement and adventure of a different kind — his thoughts having taken wings to nearby Cuba which beckoned him as yet it had many many Jamaicans. He talked of his wanderlust to David Mullings — a kind of upper-servant for the Manleys and their relatives — and struck a responsive chord. When Mullings, as general factotum, was not driving members of the home circle in the horse-drawn carriage, he was performing numerous other personal chores for members of the family. One of the more important of his responsibilities, and one which clearly established that he was no ordinary servant, was his special chore of reading for sightless Grandpa Shearer. In 1905, Aleck Clarke and David Mullings, two kindred spirits from widely differing social stations in life, made common cause when they packed their bags and decamped for Cuba, leaving the Manleys and Grandpa Shearer (in the case of Mullings) to bemoan the loss of a trusted and reliable personal servant.

When, therefore, in the year of his adulthood Aleck Clarke decided to leave the shores of Jamaica, it was to seek wider horizons and adventure and opportunity. Although heir to an upper-class tradition, it would seem he had concluded that being junior overseer at forbidding Belmont property, or even overseer at some other declining sugar estate, was not likely to take him much further along the road to fortune, fame or power.

In seeking greener pastures outside Jamaica, Aleck Clarke and David Mullings were following an escape route taken by thousands of their countrymen before and after them. The trek began in the late 1840's when, in the wake of economic depression, some 12,000 Jamaican labourers and tradesmen were attracted to the Panama Isthmus to find remunerative employment in construction of the railway linking Panama's capital city to Colon, its Caribbean seaport. The swell of Jamaican migration continued unabated for the next seventy years. The Panama-Colombia region continued to be the main lure as the building of the Panama Canal, in two attempts spanning the period 1879 to 1912, provided employment opportunities for as many as 75,000 Jamaicans. Indeed, many of the immigrants chose to remain in this new land of opportunity, to form a sizable Jamaican "colony" in Colon. Another Central American Republic — Costa Rica — opened up as another major migration outlet, only this time, the cultivation of bananas, or "green gold", rather than sugar-cane, was the lure which attracted 40,000 Jamaican workers as well as Jamaican capitalists seeking to establish banana plantations there. The same wave also took lesser numbers to Colombia, Nicaragua and Honduras for the same purpose, as well as to Cuba, where the familiar sugar-cane was being cultivated on a large scale. Finally, the United States provided yet another source for emigration of a more regular and orderly type.

Between 1850 and 1920, therefore, an exodus of close to 200,000 Jamaicans, drawn largely from the black under-privileged population, sought escape and economic advancement by migrating to Latin American republics washed by the Caribbean as well as to North America, particularly to the United States. Thus the alternative to protest and violence against throttling economic depression and social alienation lay in leaving the country, and there can hardly be any doubt that migration played a critical part as a safety valve in relieving the pressures of social discontent and protest, with the major exception, of course, of the Jamaican Morant Bay Rebellion of 1865.

By the time Aleck Clarke got to Cuba in 1905, then, the influx of Jamaicans seeking work in sugar fields and factories was promising to become a trek, and soon there were to be about 30,000 workers laying the basis for yet another Jamaican enclave in Oriente Province in the south.

Aleck Clarke fared well enough in Cuba. He got a job with a tramway company which operated both in Cuba and Panama. After two or three years in Cuba he was transferred to Panama and promoted to the rank of traffic inspector.

While in Panama city, he also met and courted Mildred Edith Blanck, an English woman and the widow of an English consulting engineer and father of her two sons. Along with Mrs. Blanck, who was in all probability his senior in years, Aleck Clarke, now turned twenty-six, returned to Jamaica in December 1910, and on the 12th day of that month, married Mrs. Blanck in a ceremony which took place at the Kingston Parish Church. The newly-weds returned to Panama shortly after and the bridegroom returned to his job. He remained in Panama, certainly until 1919, working for the tramway company, and reportedly returned to Cuba in 1919 or 1920, accompanied by one of his stepsons, Roy Blanck, a young man of twenty or twenty-one years. This stint in Cuba brought a change in occupation and he became a member of the Special Police

14

force under the regime of President Zayas. Bustamante himself later confirmed during a debate in the Jamaican House of Representatives, that he had been in Cuba during the Zayas regime, which incidentally lasted from 1921 to 1924. If further confirmation was wanted, Bustamante has insisted that he first met Marcus Garvey in Cuba, having been assigned to do security work. Garvey was in fact in Santiago, Cuba, in 1921.

The next glimpse that Jamaica got of Aleck Clarke was in 1922. Again, it was a short visit lasting only weeks, but it was long enough to show the former junior overseer in the role of a Cuban grandee or gentleman of affairs. This time he was elegantly and meticulously dressed and exuded an atmosphere of prosperity. He returned to Cuba, and Jamaica lost sight of Aleck Clarke for six years.

When he next returned to Jamaica in 1928, it was with the intention of staying and establishing himself. He ventured into the dairy business and again displayed the same capacity to lose himself in the role he had assumed. The late N.W. Manley recounted that he often saw Aleck driving his horse-drawn milk-wagon along the streets with the aplomb of a man who had been at it all his lifetime. But he could not make a go of the dairy business and he again sought haven in Cuba. Three years later Aleck was back in Jamaica, shortly before the regime of dictator Machado (1925–33) fell. According to some informants, he had continued as a member of the Special Police force during the Machado regime, but correctly read that the strongman's regime would not survive his unpopularity. Whether this was so or not, the fact is that by this time Cuba had been displaced as his Promised Land and the United States beckoned. Aleck Clarke returned to Cuba in 1932, only to ship out to New York. But when he turned up in New York, he was calling himself Alejandro Bustamanti, a cultivated white gentleman of Spanish birth. He appears to have been a hospital attendant at one of New York's better-known private hospitals.

Bustamante has not helped to make the picture any clearer. On his say-so, he would have spent a very considerable period of time in the United States. "I am a graduate dietician with ten and a half years' experience in one of the largest hospitals in New York which hospital was A-Grade."[10] According to Bustamante, he also found time while in New York to speculate on the New York Stock Exchange and to make his fortune that way. This, however, is one of the legends of which Alexander Bustamante is the only source and sole authority. Certainly when he returned finally to Jamaica in 1934, he did not, according to contemporaries, appear notably prosperous, and one wonders whether a man of his energy and dynamism would have limited himself to being a lender of money to "small people" had he made a "kill" playing the stock market as he claimed.

But perhaps what is more important is that in 1934 the *émigré* — now turned fifty — had decided that Jamaica was both home and haven. Indeed, in one of his unguarded moments, Sir Alexander once confided that he had left New York when he did in order to avoid having to establish his bona-fides to the U.S. Immigration Authorities. This might well have been the situation. In any event, America's loss, in this particular instance, was decidedly Jamaica's gain.

2

THE WANDERER RETURNS

In many respects, the Jamaica to which Bustamante returned in 1934 was not markedly different from the one he had left in 1905.

In the economic sphere, the plantation system remained structurally intact and socially dominant. In spite of its continuing secular decline, the almost exclusively British-owned and managed sugar industry continued to be the economic mainstay of the island and to dominate the island's social, economic and political life and thinking. The banana industry likewise continued to play second fiddle, although, in social terms, it had been perhaps more beneficial. In Jamaica, the moderate capital requirements for its cultivation had made banana ideally suitable for peasant exploitation, and its cultivation over seven decades had made possible the emergence of a peasant or small-farmer class which had helped to stabilize village life, building up the traditions of Afro-Jamaican folk culture — deeply conservative — around indigenized forms of religion, the family (concubinage or common-law conjugal relationships), fealty to the British Monarch — the great white protector — and acceptance, through conditioning, of the concomitant doctrine of superiority of the white race.

In the political sphere, developments of some significance had occurred and were still occurring. By 1920, the coloured and black middle classes, seemingly infected by incipient nationalism, had begun to voice criticism of the ineffectiveness of Crown Colony government and to espouse political advancement. In 1921 the elected members along with politically-minded supporters had launched the Jamaica Representative Government Association to promote constitutional reform and to make representations to Major Edward F.L. Wood, British M.P. and visiting Under-Secretary of State.

J.A.G. Smith, a black Jamaican, barrister-at-law and elected Member of the Legislative Council for the parish of Clarendon since 1916, presented, on behalf of the Association, a revised model constitution which called for a ten-man Executive Council, five members of which being elected,

17

with the Governor, as President, having a casting vote; a twenty-member Legislative Council with fourteen elected members constituting the majority, three-year terms, and abolition of residential qualifications; and finally, a separate nominated Legislative Council of eight members, which would not be able to introduce legislation. In 1922, Major Wood explained, however, that "neither in Jamaica nor elsewhere is there any demand for responsible government in the strict sense of the word, nor within a measurable distance of time would such a demand rightly be conceded."[1]

Notwithstanding, the Jamaican non-white members became more vocal in their criticism of the quality of the colonial administration. These criticisms on the part of the black and coloured, as well as middle classes, professional or propertied men of substance, were not, however, in the tradition of Robert Love at the turn of the century. Love, through his weekly newspaper *The Jamaica Advocate*, had argued in the 1890's that blacks should offer themselves as candidates for election to the Legislative Council. He went as far as to publish the list of names of prominent blacks whom he considered able prospective candidates. To the politically dominant whites, who were aroused by his political philosophy, Love rejoined: "Some are whispering that we are dangerous. We don't care if we are. We love the white man because he is a brother. We love the coloured man because he is a son; we love the black man because we must love ourself."[2]

The middle-class nationalism of the 1920's struck no such radical posture. The character of their nationalism was best exemplified by J.A.G. Smith in the role he adopted as critic and excoriator of the Crown Colony system. The "giant killer" of Jamaican politics of this era, he scathingly denounced the incompetence of colonial bureaucrats. But Smith, like his colleagues, was not at this stage espousing popular government or self-government. They were committed to working within the colonial structure they knew, even if they wanted to make it more effective and perhaps more responsive to broader social needs.

The upshot of Major Wood's visit and report was that the Colonial Office proposed that the Legislative Council should be restructured, to give the elected representatives a majority of four over the ten officials nominated by the Governor. Nevertheless, the Governor, as the representative of the British Crown, would retain a reserve power to overrule the majority vote of the council in a matter deemed by him to be of "paramount importance". The Colonial Office also proposed the creation of an Executive Committee, in addition to the Privy Council, to be an advisory body to the Governor, on which a number of elected members would serve. These proposals came before the Legislative Council in 1926, but the elected members found themselves hopelessly divided and the Council rejected the proposals. Thus the elected representatives were left with the existing legislative structure, within which they constituted half of the twenty-eight members reacting to the legislative initiatives of the Governor and his official slate, and in· effect were confined to negative and destructive criticisms. Their major constitutional prerogative was likewise obstructive. Under a power of delay, if nine of the fourteen elected members voted against a financial measure, the motion would be defeated. But even so, the Governor could declare the measure one of paramount importance and give it legislative effect.

These political niceties, however, were the concern and preoccupation of Euro-Jamaica or privileged Jamaica. The voting franchise, linked to carefully tailored income and taxation qualifications, ensured that the franchise remained restricted, so that government and administration remained in the hands of those best suited to rule. In a population of just under one million persons (with possibly half of them twenty-one and over) the island's electoral lists boasted no more than 40,000 electors, with some parishes having just about 1,000 each.

Nevertheless, in spite of the unbending nature and resistance of the economic and political systems to broader social change, the leaven of social ferment had been planted within the lowest strata of society, occasionally surfacing to show that the black labouring classes were not only becoming more conscious of their place and condition in the institutional scheme of things, but were seeking ways to escape its thraldom.

In the 1890's, skilled artisans in Kingston set about establishing craft unions such as the Artisans Union, but they were shortlived. There was little scope for craft unions in a small agrarian economy, subject to buffeting by every economic contraction in the metropolitan or industrially advanced economies.[3] Between 1907, when Kingston was devastated by the great earthquake, and 1908, printers led by one Marcus Garvey and tobacco workers resorted to strike action to enforce demands for better wages. The printers strike was broken by the Gleaner Company and Garvey was blacklisted, leaving him doubtful of the efficacy of the trade union as an instrument of social justice. Labour unrest of a more pervasive and sustained nature took place during 1918–20 in the wake of World War I and the economic dislocation it engendered. Returning soldiers of the West India Regiment were barely restrained from a mutiny.

19

In April 1918, a strike of sugar workers at Vere in Clarendon erupted into a riot which was quelled by police. Three persons were killed and a dozen wounded. Fire-fighters, dockworkers, railway mechanics and the match factory workers in Kingston and the banana workers and other categories in outports, in turn, resorted to strike action.

A. Bain Alves, cigar maker and founder and president of the newly launched Longshoremen's Union No. 1 of the Jamaica Federation of Labour, petitioned the Governor, Sir Leslie Probyn, to give official recognition to trade unions. Probyn, a Liberal, responded. The Trade Union Law was introduced into the Legislative Council in March 1919, given second and third readings in June, and was proclaimed on 25th October 1919. It conferred legal status on properly registered trade unions and protected them from criminal prosecution for conspiracy or as unlawful combinations operating in restraint of trade. It did not, however, release them from liability for suits for damages as a result of strikes, nor did it legalize peaceful picketing.

Strikes again occurred during July and December 1919, the most serious and protracted being among railway workers and shopmen who tried to derail the train by removing rails between Highgate and Albany.

A dispute between the tramway company and its employees also led to the establishment in January 1920 of the first conciliation and arbitration board in the island's history.

During the next decade and a half, labour unrest took the form of occasional strikes and riots.

The strike, as well as violence, usually emerging out of the protest demonstrations and invariably labelled as riots by the colonial administration, was well established, therefore, in the armoury of the deprived masses. But during the period of Bustamante's sojourn overseas, and especially from 1920 to 1934, working-class protest was muted, largely because the working classes sought escape from the harsh realities of life in Jamaica, through emigration, for those who were adventurous enough and could afford the passage to Central America, Cuba or North America, or through the apocalyptic transcendentalism of Bedwardism, and the more mundane but no less elusive back-to-Africa movement of Garveyism, for those who remained behind in the homeland.

Blacklisted and soured by his abortive venture into trade unionism, Marcus Garvey, at the age of twenty-three, left Jamaica, his homeland, and for two years travelled to Costa Rica, Panama, Ecuador, Nicaragua, Honduras, Colombia and Venezuela in pursuit of employment. Everywhere that he went, Garvey was struck and moved by the inferior social and employment status of the Negro. Emigrating to Great Britain in 1912, Garvey was inspired by the biography of the distinguished American Negro educator, Booker T. Washington, and in 1914 he returned to Jamaica to found the Universal Negro Improvement Association (U.N.I.A.), dedicated to "drawing peoples of the race together" and to working "for the general uplift of the Negro peoples of the world". Realizing, however, that Jamaica would not provide the support as well as scope for his activities, Garvey emigrated to the United States in 1916.

Within a few years, Marcus Garvey had created in the United States, and among Negro populations throughout the world, one of the largest mass movements of modern times. He appealed to the dreams of millions of Negroes throughout the world and he brought to them a sense of pride in race and ancestry. Especially in the new world, he made the Negro race feel proud at a time when they had little to be proud about. He "made them feel like somebody among white people who have said they were nobody". By enjoining pride of race and African nationalism, Garvey led Negroes to identify themselves with a vast continent where they could claim kinship with an ancient civilization which had had its moments of grandeur. Garvey's racial nationalism was so thoroughgoing that it extended into the sphere of religion and embraced the notion of a Black God. If man is created in the image of his God, then it is vital that pictures of God should be in the likeness of the Negro race, for, said Garvey, all religions tend to visualize Him in a likeness akin to their own race. To implement black religion, he saw to the establishment of a new African Orthodox Church in the United States in September 1921. Racial pride, spiritual redemption and return to the ancestral and promised land (one Aim, one God, one Destiny) were thus interlocking tenets of Garveyism.

Even as Marcus Garvey, the "Black Moses", beckoned from the United States to Negroes everywhere to escape emotionally to his visionary Republic of Africa, his poor and downtrodden countrymen were about to heed the call of the Revivalist Prophet Alexander Bedward, effectively the first in the line of "Saviours" in twentieth-century Jamaica, to escape via the route of Enoch to a new heaven and a new earth where importuning black hands would all become white.

Alexander Bedward who had travelled to Colon where he received his "vision", returned to Jamaica and was appointed successor Revivalist Prophet of August Town. His phenomenal rise to fame resulted from his prophetic vision that baptism in the Mona or Hope River, in a pool consecrated by himself, would bring healing to body and soul. In the quest for baptism in the pool, thousands of eager souls trekked from all over the island to the home of "Bedwardism", the Jamaica Baptist Free Church in August Town, over which Bedward presided as the ordained Bishop and "Shepherd" of the Church. Before long, Bedward's camp had become a veritable West Indian Lourdes, attracting Jamaican exiles and pilgrims from Cuba, Colon, Costa Rica and elsewhere in Latin America. As Bedwardite missions sprang up all over Jamaica and his sway grew, Bedward, then sixty-one years of age, decided that the time had come to shed the title "Shepherd", and announced his divinity.[4] "I myself am Jesus Christ," he declared. "I was crucified." Addressed as "Lord" from then on, he also declared that on the 31st December 1920 he would ascend into heaven, signalling the destruction of white people and the ensuing reign of Bedwardism on earth. Incredible scenes took place throughout Jamaica as the faithful, in anticipation of being "taken-up" with their "Lord" of August Town, began selling earthly possessions and separating themselves from unbelieving members of family.

Finally, on the appointed day, Bedward sat in a chair within full view of his followers to await the "happening". Nothing happened as far as Bedward was concerned, but at his prompting, a luckless disciple attempted to launch the heavenly flight from a tree only to land on the ground with a broken collar-bone. Bedward consoled that the time had not yet come. But in May 1921, while Marcus Garvey was on a speaking tour of the island, Bedward elected to march with his followers on Kingston, which he condemned as the modern-day Sodom and Gomorrah. Blocked by police on the outskirts of the city, the "Saviour" was arrested and committed to the lunatic asylum where eventually he died. Bedward, it may be noted, also injected a note of racial antagonism and determinism into his religious transcendentalism. "Brethren, Hell will be your portion if you do not rise up and crush the white man. The time is coming . . . There will be a white wall and a black wall, but now the black wall is becoming bigger than the white and we must knock the white wall down. The white wall has oppressed us for years. Now we must oppress the white wall."[5]

Alexander Bedward's immediate successor as "Messiah", turned out to be a competitor, Solomon Hewitt or "Brother Sal of the Cross" as he came to be known.[6] Active in Smith Village, a slum just outside Kingston, about the time that Bedward was at the height of his fame, Hewitt realized that he could not hope to be more than a minor prophet. So, following the tradition established by Bedward and followed by all Jamaica's modern heroes, Brother Sal shipped out to Panama to acquire "foreign experience". He was an instant success among the Jamaican colony there. On hearing of Bedward's confinement, he returned to Jamaica and erected his church in Smith Village. A nimble dancer and attractive personality, the illiterate Brother Sal attracted many of Bedward's shepherdless flock and developed an even stronger following than Bedward had among the womenfolk. Moved by the adoration of his female followers, including a Black "Virgin Mary" and Black "Mary Magdalene" who addressed him as "Father", and possibly by the realization that he had yet to achieve the island-wide eminence of Bedward, Brother Sal hit upon the idea of a spectacular crucifixion to establish his messianic purpose. He would, presumably, be resurrected from the dead. When, however, the chosen Good Friday dawned and he was about to be nailed to a wooden cross, Brother Sal of the Cross suggested that tying with rope would serve just as well. Unfortunately, he suffered the further indignity, after a few hours on the cross, of a fainting spell. From then on, abandoned by his followers, he was left to bear in ignominy his cross of ridicule and shame.

Back in the United States, Marcus Garvey, the international crusader of the Negro race, had run afoul of the postal authorities and was indicted and convicted in 1923 for fraud — specifically for causing promotional material relating to the establishment of the Black Star Line to be sent through the mails. He began serving his five-year term of imprisonment in an Atlanta penitentiary in February 1925, but was released and deported to Jamaica in December 1927. This time, on his arrival in Jamaica, Marcus Garvey was given a hero's welcome by thousands of his countrymen who lined the quay and streets of Kingston. Garvey immediately launched a vigorous island-wide membership drive and established U.N.I.A. branches throughout the island.

Through regular meetings, mass rallies, plays written by Garvey himself and spectacular events such as the U.N.I.A.'s Sixth International Convention held in 1929 which featured a mammoth procession in Kingston as well as a court reception attended by 10,000 persons at Edelweiss Park, the U.N.I.A. played a vital role in politicizing the masses, especially between 1928 and 1935.

Relegated by restrictive franchise qualifications to being passive objects of, rather than participants in, the political processes of the country, the working classes of Jamaica were given a political and organizational experience of their own by the U.N.I.A. It served as the means for throwing up working-class orators and spokesmen.

Marcus Garvey himself attempted to participate directly in the political affairs of the country, but operating as he did within a colonial political structure, his ventures into Jamaican politics were only moderately successful. In 1929, he was elected a councillor of the Kingston and St. Andrew Corporation, even while serving a three-month prison term for contempt of court. His seat was declared vacant, but Garvey was again re-elected upon his release. His attempt to launch a political party — the Jamaica People's Political Party — in 1928, as well as a worker's movement — the Jamaica Workers' and Labourers' Association — in 1930, both proved abortive, as was his attempt to win a seat in the Legislative Council in January 1930. When Garvey left Jamaica for the last time in 1935 to become an exile in London, his black, downtrodden, but racially aroused, countrymen were forced to shed their preoccupation with distant Africa and to contemplate, with growing disillusionment, their immediate and depressing lot at home. Disillusionment was further heightened and embittered by the invasion of Ethiopia by Mussolini and that country's abandonment by the League of Nations. The black man appeared to have been sacrificed once more on the white man's altar of expediency.

Through Garveyism, therefore, black Jamaicans had not only been made aware of themselves as a race and the place they occupied in the Jamaican scheme of things, but had been given an institutionalized forum for talking about their problems, hopes, and aspirations. Garvey had challenged openly one of the traditional social values and fundamental organizing principles of life in Jamaica — in itself a justification for pre-servation of the status quo — that failure of the black population to rise above poverty was due to the innate incapacity and inherent inferiority of the Negro race. He had demonstrated both in the United States and Jamaica the capabilities of the Negro for complex organizational activity and economic endeavour. In March 1921, he had visited Jamaica aboard the S.S. *Kanaha*, one of the ships of his celebrated Black Star Line — launched to link the coloured peoples of the world in commercial and industrial intercourse. He had also given his black underprivileged countrymen a taste of organized political and social life.

For while he had continued between 1927 and 1935 to sustain his sense of world mission and to dream of a Negro empire in far-away Africa, Garvey had not neglected to spell out, and seek organized support for, an electoral manifesto which embraced self-government, protection of (native) labour, minimum wages, land reform, and establishment of institutions of higher education and training. He also saw the necessity of proceeding simultaneously on both the political and labour fronts, and accordingly he founded a political party and a labour union. In the latter case, Garvey had come full circle from blacklisted unionist to international crusader, business promoter and shipping magnate and finally to trade union founder.

Of course, of the two organizations, union and party, the labour union as a basically working-class phenomenon offered the better prospect, not only of achieving immediate improvements in the economic well-being of those fortunate enough to be employed, but also of increasing the involvement of workers, and the lower classes generally, in the political processes. Effective trade unionism did not depend upon extension of the franchise, whereas effective political action certainly did. This had been the experience of the working classes in Great Britain and other European countries which had embarked upon industrialization during the eighteenth and nineteenth centuries.

The dynamics of trade unionism and collective bargaining, involving the use of weapons — the strike, go-slow, mass picketing and even sabotage — all of which are highly disruptive and often transform labour-management conflict into social disorder, would be also more in keeping with the traditional means of protest used by the Jamaican agro-proletariat since the time of Emancipation. Another practical consideration was that a form of trade unionism had existed continuously since 1918 among Kingston waterfront and hotel workers. When, however, Garvey found himself harassed through the courts and isolated by the black and coloured middle classes, he chose to exile himself in England and to languish within reach and sight of the seat of imperial power, rather than to embark upon direct action and mass protest, the traditional responses of Afro-Jamaicans to perversion of justice and legitimated intimidation. His departure left the U.N.I.A. without black leadership of national stature and thus working-class protest, when it erupted two years later with violent intensity, lacked organizational direction.

In a sense, however, Garvey's mantle of leadership had been merely laid aside, waiting to be taken up by others who by virtue of personal or other circumstances might be able to surmount the constraints and limitations imposed on political and industrial leadership by colonial Jamaican society.

As it turned out, Alexander Bustamante emerged as Garvey's successor and champion of the Jamaican masses because he was able, first of all, to achieve an emotional identification with the black populace similar to that forged by Garvey, and secondly, to provide leadership which fitted readily into a more easily understood institutional framework

25

for managing labour protest — trade unionism — and was more in accord with the mood of the common people. Trade unionism, in its formative and youthful stages, calls for militant, fearless and astute leadership, both to mobilize worker support and solidarity and to withstand opposition of the employer as well as of the state, particularly in situations where the employer invokes intervention of the "forces of law and order" to protect his property rights and/or to break up picket lines.

In the case of Jamaica, however, a plantation economy provided little scope for conventional craft or industrial unionism and the gainfully employed labourers and artisans were not far removed from either the condition or status of the unemployed. In the absence also of established machinery for the orderly processing and resolution of grievances, conventional unionism had to give way to a more volatile mass labour (or even populist) movement which would agitate, not just for improved wages and working conditions for those gainfully employed, but also for a measure of relief for the unemployed and land-hungry peasant-cultivators living barely at subsistence levels. Stirred by emotional appeals, admonitions and unfulfilled hopes during the 1920's and early 1930's, the mood of the Jamaican populace was changing. They were no longer prepared to wait for a better life in Bedward's heaven or Garvey's Africa. More importantly, the agents and instruments of oppression and frustration were at hand in Jamaica and could be made to feel the force of working-class resentment and displeasure.

When Alexander Bustamante showed that he was prepared to go beyond words and journalistic polemics and join in labour protest — in the streets and at the work place — he was welcomed, then acclaimed, as labour leader by militant masses who admired his style of leadership or "brinkmanship". Less susceptible to police harassment or brutality by virtue both of colour and economic status, Bustamante boldly "led them along the streets of Kingston and through sugar estates and his offer was their demand, a better life, here and now, in a country of which they formed the majority but from whose society they had hitherto been excluded".[7]

Alexander Bustamante, therefore, helped to bring to fruition the seeds of social ferment which had been sown by others. When he returned in 1934, the black masses had been steadily undergoing a process of politicization, more directly through Garveyism and the U.N.I.A., only indirectly through the formalized system of politics, all of which could not help but enhance racial awareness and class awareness on their part.

In fact, the inter-war period witnessed a surprising amount of civic and political organization and activity. Citizens' and rate-payers' associations flourished in nearly every parish and major town in the island. Federations provided wider regional links. Reform clubs and rudimentary political parties were formed, lasted for short periods or longer periods, then disappeared. Although municipal and national politics were primarily middle-class concerns, increasing numbers of the urbanized and rural urbanized agro-proletariat were being drawn in beyond the stage of disenfranchised listeners to become political touts and henchmen.

The influx of returning *émigrés* during the 1930's, spurred by the enactment of discriminatory and restrictive immigration laws in many of the traditional host countries, beginning in the 1920's, and the Great Depression which helped to intensify popular feeling against Jamaicans competing against natives for jobs in many of these same countries, brought back to the Jamaican scene a politically more aware and more vocal group.

As one such returning *émigré*, Alexander Bustamante decided to set himself up as a person of independent means. This was the expected thing to do. He had spent nearly thirty years abroad, albeit punctuated by four or five visits to Jamaica, all of them (with one exception in 1928) very brief. He had worked overseas, had acquired foreign experience and should have made good, that is to say, brought back some savings, however modest. He opened up his office at 1a Duke Street, at the corner of Water Lane in downtown Kingston. His office was small, modestly equipped, but bore no name-plate on a street which was, at that time, as it is now, the main location of the more important legal firms and financial and insurance houses and agents. Bustamante, however, could do without the name-plate, for in his type of business — money-lending — his clients could be expected to seek him out. Moreover, the clients he had elected to cater to were drawn, not from the echelons of the more comfortable but opportuning classes, but from the ranks of minor civil servants, local government subordinate employees, and the working poor. His money-lending business grew steadily, the high-risk element attendant on the occupational and income status of his clientele being offset by the correspondingly high rates of interest charged for such types of loan.

Before long, he also acquired a private secretary in the person of Gladys Longbridge who became his most trusted assistant, confidante, and devoted companion. An attractive brown-skinned girl, Miss Longbridge worked as a cashier at the Arlington House restaurant where

27

Bustamante lunched frequently. Their awareness of each other began, however, on one memorable Sunday morning, when on her way from the Moravian Church at the corner of Duke and North Streets (where she attended on Sundays with unfailing regularity as befitted an ardent church-goer) she was stopped and greeted by Bustamante. This Sunday morning encounter between the young, shy and retiring young woman from Westmoreland, and the mature but debonair and elegantly dressed Bustamante — cutting a dashing figure as a worldly man of affairs, with charming if exaggerated manners and a clipped foreign accent — became a regular "happening" in the months that followed.[8] When Bustamante decided that he warranted a private secretary, the choice — by the process of natural selection — fell on Miss Longbridge. The seal of their romantic interest did not come, however, until over three decades later, when in September 1962 Gladys Longbridge became Lady Bustamante, the wife of Jamaica's first Prime Minister.

Meanwhile, back in the 1930's, Bustamante showed no anxiety to disclose that he was Jamaican-born William Alexander Clarke.[9] The members of his family had gone their separate ways. One sister, Maud, who had been adopted by the Shearers, was married to dark-skinned Methodist clergyman Austin Evelyn. Her son later became a full Professor of Physics at McGill University in Canada, an achievement which has been a great source of pride to Bustamante. Another sister had married a Grenadian, Bertie Purcell, and together they had founded the Purcell Home for boys in Highgate, St. Mary. Their son also became a successful mechanical engineer in the United States. Yet another sister, Iris, had emigrated to New York City to qualify as a nurse, while younger brother Herbert had settled in Boston. He returned to Jamaica for the first time in 1962, to witness the achievement and celebration of Jamaica's political independence, but died shortly after his return home to the United States. Bustamante's half-sisters, Ida and Daisy, had settled in Kingston, and Daisy had become Mrs. Cotterell.

His parents, Bobby and Mary Clarke, when they left Blenheim, retreated to Cacoon, a village nearby, where father Bobby owned a small property. They next moved farther east along the north coast, possibly to Annotto Bay, but finally ended up in Kingston, where they lived in a home bought for them through the generosity of their daughter Iris, then in the United States. Bobby Clarke died in 1924. Iris, out from the United States for the funeral, decided in consultation with her mother to sell the home in Kingston so that mother could be relocated in the country where she preferred to be. She was settled on a small farm in the hills of Portland, Jamaica, but became seriously ill in 1934, the year of Bustamante's return. She was then taken by daughter Louise to reside with her at the Purcell Home, but never recovered. She died the following year and was buried in Annotto Bay. William Alexander Clarke Bustamante was not at the funeral. But in any event, he was little concerned with family affairs.

Indeed, even his money-lending business could no longer be said to be the focus of his full concern and energy. For he had decided that the time had come for him to broaden his interests and become involved in public affairs. He began with a letter to *The Daily Gleaner*, the island's century-old and sole daily newspaper and secular bible. This first letter in April 1935, however, contained strong political overtones. He defended the right of the unemployed to carry out a planned demonstration, contending that the demonstration "is a proper method of calling attention to conditions or grievances". "Hungry men and women and children have the right", he asserted, "to call attention to their condition and to ask of people fulfilment of promises made to them, as long as they do so without using violence or behaving disorderly." If demonstrators were cautioned against irrational resort to violence, the Government also was ticked off for being so readily predisposed to use force against the aggrieved: "It is no good telling people that government is not concerned with them, for government tells them what to do and what not to do, where to buy and how much to pay for it. Government poses as a paternal government and as one looks to one's natural parents, so the people look to government when they are unable to help themselves.

"What is also wrong is that when people seek the right of self-expression, that force should be employed, not to assist them as is done in other countries, to carry an orderly demonstration and to protect them, but to intimidate. Force is a dangerous thing, it does not always protect, but when used to intimidate sometimes irritates and becomes the author of disorder. Those who possess force should be careful how they use it."

With this thoughtful and reasoned letter, Bustamante was well launched on his career as letter-writer and polemicist. He was revealed as a person with a vigorous and original style and an advanced social conscience evidenced by his concern for the underprivileged.

The immediate reaction of the more liberal among *The Daily Gleaner's* readers was extremely favourable, and Bustamante, who must have taken pains to move around and take a reading on the day his letter appeared, decided to press home his advantage. He returned to his office and dictated his follow-up letter that same day. In it he decried the tendency of many employers, some because of selfishness, others because of greed, to cut down expenses by dispensing with employees. He drew attention to the action taken by the British King George V in setting up, as part of his Silver Jubilee Celebration, a fund for carrying out useful projects, and proposed that every employer of labour "employ one extra person, however small the wages might be, when we are able, and give this a try for, say, six months as the start of Jamaica's Silver Jubilee Employment Campaign". Of course, this rather novel proposal fell on deaf ears, but then again it pointed up Bustamante's assumption of the role of champion of the oppressed and underdog.

Having found an outlet for his seemingly endless energy, Bustamante kept up a spate of letters which touched upon a wide range of public issues. Between April and November 1935 over twenty letters were despatched to the editor of *The Daily Gleaner* alone. In May, he attacked a bill before the Legislature designed to protect native industries by restricting imports, but which at the same time would create local monopolies. Bustamante displayed a strong philosophical bias towards economic individualism. "The result of monopoly is always increased suffering of the unfortunates. Industrial dictatorship suits but two classes who are much in the minority, viz., a few large privileged capitalists and some smaller traders who have already established themselves in some form of industry and would rather bear the punishment of the devil destroying the entire world than to have their own countrymen start similar industries." He next joined in a vigorous controversy over a proposal to impose a quota on the shipment of bananas by the Jamaica Banana Producers Association (J.B.P.A.) to the United Fruit Company. He assailed the suggestion that competitors of the J.B.P.A. were out to destroy it and held to the middle-of-the-road between the competing claims of farmers and the giant company. "Notwithstanding all that has been said about the activities of this magnificent octopus, it cannot be gainsaid that this company, aside from definitely placing Jamaica on the map, has done more than any other company to develop the island's resources and to improve the condition of labouring people by instituting medical services, better houses and living conditions and at the time when this was sorely needed. There might not have been the large class of peasant proprietors that exist today had it not been for the activities of this company.

"The Jamaica Banana Producers Association was formed as a cooperative movement among the farmers themselves, and as a native concern and to create competition so as to prevent the business falling entirely in the hands of the foreign concern and it is therefore right that it should consider to preserve its existence especially that the Jamaica Banana Producers Association is guaranteed by tax-payers' money.

"Care should however be taken that in such actions the claim of the United Fruit Company should be considered and that one monopoly should not be destroyed for the setting up of another."

Sympathy for the poor and the unemployed, criticisms for the rich and uncaring, no hesitation in attacking the colonial administration, a strong attachment to economic liberalism with a corresponding marked antipathy for monopolies, forthright language rich in biblical imagery — these were the qualities and attitudes which had emerged clearly as Bustamante sought, in 1935, to make his impact on the Jamaican reading public. Curiously enough, what proved to be the first wave of labour unrest, and a "dress rehearsal", so to speak, of the working-class revolts which took place in the West Indian territories including Jamaica from 1937 to 1938, passed by without Bustamante becoming involved. In Trinidad in July 1934, hunger marches precipitated strikes in the oil fields. In January–February 1935, St. Kitts had its turn as striking sugar workers were insistent and threatening in their demands for higher wages. The Governor summoned a warship from Bermuda as well as police reinforcements from Antigua. The ensuing clash between police and strikers left three dead and eight wounded.

Jamaica was next, and then later in the year there were strikes in British Guiana, a serious disturbance (riot) in St. Vincent and a coal strike in St. Lucia.

In Jamaica, at the outport of Oracabessa in the north-coast parish of St. Mary, banana workers became incensed over the introduction of workers from the nearby town of Port Maria. On the 14th May 1935, they paraded in protest with sticks and other makeshift weapons. They were quelled by police action and Government officials accused "outside" agitators of inciting workers. One week later, violence flared in Falmouth and other outports. At Falmouth, wharf workers tied up traffic to forestall strike-breakers being brought in. One died in the collision with local police. These incidents did not make the impact they might have, because they were localized and did not extend to Kingston.

Bustamante's non-involvement is also understandable. Although he had begun to travel to country parts to make his own assessments of the mood of the country, yet, outside of Kingston he was still relatively unknown, other than as a letter-writer with a foreign name. In July 1935, while the banana quota controversy still raged, he was given his opening by a J.B.P.A. defender who wanted to know who this Bustamante was. Bustamante readily obliged, publicly stating for the first time the legend of his early years. "I was born in Hanover. At a very tender age, Spain became my home. I served in the Spanish Army as a cavalry officer in Morocco, North Africa. Subsequently, I became an Inspector in the Havana Police Force. Recently, I worked as dietician in one of New York's largest hospitals. Bustamante is a lonely fighter; he belongs to no organization or club. He fights on the side of fairplay. Not only that, he fights on the side of his enemy if he is on the side of Justice, without fear of any consequence whatever. It is characteristic of him to always put his address with his name when writing to the Press. . . .

"Bustamante enjoys the privileges of possessing an irreproachable character, excellent health and a fair amount of wealth. He pays taxes and licence and does not work for anybody. . . .

"With regard to my authority for making the statement I did in a previous letter, I did not get it by sitting in my office at No. 1a Duke Street, but spending my money travelling by motor-car from Port Morant to Negril Point investigating the conditions of the island in which I was born." The members of the Clarke family could be excused if they were left wondering whether this was in fact their errant brother Aleck.

For the remainder of the year, Bustamante displayed considerable versatility in the topics he touched upon. His nationalist fervour also came through strongly. Thus he objected to the importation of foreign personnel when there were suitably qualified Jamaicans available at home, took strong exception to the use of the word "bastards" to describe Jamaican children born out of wedlock, and praised the virtue of Jamaican women and the courtesy and hospitality of the country's motorists. He assailed and labelled as monstrous a suggestion that because of high costs the use of drugs should be curtailed at the public hospitals, the greater proportion of the clients of which were the poor, and spoke of his years of experience among doctors (presumably as a dietician). He defended the Pope against an allegation of complicity in Mussolini's invasion of Ethiopia; defended small businessmen; defended or attacked, respectively, deserving or undeserving elected Members of the Legislative Council; supported the candidacy of those aspiring to public office who had earned his approval; and emphasized that agriculture should be given top priority in the allocation of public expenditures.

By 1936, Bustamante's fame as a letter-writer was well founded. *The Daily Gleaner* and other weekly newspapers continued to be liberal in publishing his regular flow of letters. Displaying a lively and original wit as well as a courtly regard for his adversaries, he continued to widen the net of his public concern. He commented on the location of the Tuberculosis Sanitorium; made an appeal to dark-skinned women to take a more active role in sports; attacked the Jamaica Public Service Company, which operated the trolley-car service, for being an inefficient monopoly; protested against the impending dismissal of H.H. Coote, expatriate Bee Instructor; challenged the suggestion that the United States had no choice but to defend Jamaica in the event of war and asked what was wrong with good Old England; supported the right of those who wanted to demonstrate against Lloyd George (holidaying in Jamaica); commented on the Spanish Civil War; and pleaded on behalf of Jamaican needle workers, for protection against Japanese textile imports.

While Bustamante was concentrating on the power and efficacy of the written word and making jaunts throughout the island to supply the raw material for his polemics, important organizational activity was being carried out among employed workers. The labour unrest in Oracabessa and Falmouth in May of the previous year, had pointed up the dire need for more workers' organizations to facilitate the management of labour protest and the processing of grievances.

A new initiative at trade union organization was taken by A.G.S. (Father) Coombs, among others. Allan George Coombs, a man of peasant stock, served first in the Police Force for about three years and then in the West India Regiment for about five years. When he left the Regiment in 1927, he had attained the rank of Lance Corporal. In 1936, Coombs formed the Jamaica Workers and Tradesmen Union (J.W.T.U.), a blanket type union into which all categories could be organized without too much concern for occupational identity. The J.W.T.U. derived its support initially from artisans and their helpers, as well as waterfront workers, who were still being served principally by the Longshoremen's Unions Nos. 1 and 2 of the Jamaican Federation of Labour, originally founded in 1919 by A. Bain Alves, cigar worker and municipal politician. But soon, Coombs, an austere man with a forceful personality, attracted a modest following and the union expanded slowly into St. Catherine, St. Mary and St. James, attracting dockworkers and agricultural labourers. As his union was not financially viable, Coombs supported himself working for the Public Works Department as a road contractor.

Coombs' trade union activity was timely, for the next year, 1937, saw the beginning of the second wave of labour unrest which was to culminate in a social upheaval and mark the beginning of Jamaica's modern era. During January and February there were frequent reports of hunger marches, strikes and sabotage by discontented workers throughout the island. The J.W.T.U., led by Coombs, expanded organizational activities and the ranks of membership swelled. It was claimed that in one section, in Spanish Town, membership had climbed to the respectable total of 2,000.

Bustamante's spate of letters to the press began to subside perceptibly, as he turned more of his time and energy to travelling through the countryside, holding small meetings, fraternizing and making himself more widely known. His final letters as one of the country's leading letter-writers allowed him to expand the legend of being a trained dietician, even as he compared the quality and cost of food in hotels in Jamaica and the Canary Islands. He came to the defence of *The Daily Gleaner* whose monopoly appeared to be threatened by the launching of a vigorous and less conservative new daily, *The Jamaica Standard*. He also had a kind word for Lady Denham, wife of the Governor.

The quickening tempo of Jamaican society called for action, not words. In March, sugar workers at Gray's Inn sugar factory began to show signs of restiveness and expressed themselves in what now seemed to be the only acceptable manner. The police were called in to maintain order. Within the next few months, labour discontent began to build up in Kingston. In August, ex-servicemen from the World War I clashed with the police as they tried to march on King's House to protest low wages and unemployment. They were dispersed by the police and twenty-three of the marchers were arrested. Banana workers at the outports of Montego Bay and Oracabessa brought loading operations to a halt. And all over this hung the prospect of new municipal and parochial elections.

In Kingston, the waterfront was soon tied up by a strike of stevedores, and the major fruit companies announced pay increases in an effort to mitigate the discontent. The strikes continued, however, and before long throughout the island crowds of labourers armed with machetes and sticks faced heavily armed police squads. Estates took on the appearance of armed camps.

Bustamante appeared on platforms in Kingston making fiery speeches in which he claimed an attack had been made on his life because of his association with the cause of the working man. In the trade union field, Coombs sponsored a number of meetings in the hope of establishing effective unionism, but no satisfactory formula to restore peace could be found. Bustamante associated with Coombs on the platform of these public meetings and, appreciating the opportunity for contact with the masses, accepted Coombs' invitation to become Treasurer of the J.W.T.U.

Early in September 1937, Bustamante, Coombs and L.W. Rose (a Garveyite and Secretary of the Spanish Town Division of the J.W.T.U.) were accorded a tumultuous welcome at a public meeting in Montego Bay. From press reports it was clear that Bustamante was a major drawing card. In a letter published in *Plain Talk* on 11th September 1937, Coombs paid tribute to Bustamante as "a man with a human heart".[10] He traced the founding of the J.W.T.U. in May 1936 and explained that he had invited Bustamante, whom he knew only by reputation as a letter-writer and speaker on public affairs who was reportedly a rich man, to support the Union and the cause of labour. Bustamante had come forward when other capitalists had not and his name was helping to swell the ranks of union membership.

The J.W.T.U. seemed poised at this time to play a significant role as well in the pending municipal elections in Kingston. Prospective candidates angled behind the scenes for Coombs' support. Bustamante dashed off a letter to *The Daily Gleaner* in which he cautioned: "The leaders of the union should not use any influence whatsoever with their members to vote for any candidate who is either afraid or ashamed or has not enough interest in labour to fight for the union openly."

The reaction to this letter whetted Bustamante's appetite for a more significant role in the new trade union — his first contact with a labour organization. He put a delicate proposition to Coombs: If he would turn over the presidency of the Union to him, he [Bustamante] would finance a vigorous campaign out of his own pocket to establish the Union on an island-wide basis. Attracted by the financial implications, Coombs allowed his hesitancy to be overcome. In a letter dated 12th October 1937, addressed to the editor of *Plain Talk* (now regarded as an important labour weekly), Coombs proclaimed that he had voluntarily relinquished the presidency to Alexander Bustamante and would become first Vice-President. Members of the Executive Committee, however, soon began to have second thoughts. Moreover, Bustamante found a formidable contender in the person of Hugh Buchanan, General Secretary of the Union and a long-time Marxist, whose ideological fastidiousness was revolted by the idea of a money-lender leading a workers' union.

Buchanan had joined hands with Coombs to help organize the J.W.T.U. He had also teamed up with a printer, Stennett Kerr Coombs, to publish the openly Marxist *Jamaica Labour Weekly* on luridly coloured newsprint. With the growing disenchantment over Bustamante's presidency of the J.W.T.U. and with Coombs having second thoughts as to whether he had made a good bargain, Buchanan organized a counter-coup which ended in Bustamante having the traumatic experience of being expelled from the Union.

Throughout November and early December of 1937, *The Daily Gleaner* and other weeklies carried letters of recrimination between Coombs, Bustamante and other trade union colleagues and well-wishers. Bustamante alleged that he had resigned from the presidency because of irregularities in the Union's financial affairs. Union officials replied that he could not have resigned from a post in which he had not been confirmed, and accused him of exacting his "pound of flesh" for his financial contributions.

Meanwhile, social unrest was visibly quickening. Spontaneous "mini-strikes" were mushrooming in lightning fashion among banana workers on various estates. The infection began to spread to white-collar groups. Hotel employees formed their own organization and registered the Jamaica Hotel Employees Association on 1st December 1937. The city's retail clerks, euphemistically called "shop assistants", restive over un-satisfied demands for minimum wages and shorter working hours, flocked into a new clerks' association organized by a trio of professional middle-class leaders: Florizel Glasspole, a city accountant (and later to be one of the island's outstanding trade union leaders), Erasmus Campbell (an aggressive barrister who had resigned his job as an industrial chemist in the government service and had gone off to Britain to qualify) and Ernest Rae (who had achieved national repute as a Test Cricketer and who was also helping to organize citizens' associations to bring reform to municipal politics). The clerks were planning to close the retail shops during the Christmas shopping season. A lean Christmas was narrowly averted when the Legislature bowed before their militancy and passed a Shop Assistants Law which prescribed and limited working hours and allowed for a weekly half-day holiday.

During his brief honeymoon with Coombs in the Jamaica Workers and Tradesmen Union, Bustamante had attempted, in one of his letters, to spell out his conception of trade unionism. "The objects of unions are: to get the people to unite in masses to contribute their little money for cases of emergency so that in the time of this and the time of that the union will have money to work for the interest of the members the way the Executive Committee thinks best; that there should be labour representatives who will represent the cause of labour not alone to their employers but to Government; to work for better understanding between

Labour and Capital; to work for better wages, better working conditions, and to work in the interest of the unemployed to seek ways and means to obtain them work.

"A labour union is nothing more than the working people's club where they can unite for one common good, for one common cause, so that they can bring their grievances to their officers. Union members, if you want to be successful, you must remember that you must follow your officers and must not expect them to follow you, and for that reason the officers should be men of intelligence, honesty and reliability. You, the workers, are seeking justice from your employers, then to accomplish this you must also measure out justice and fairplay to them, however cruel they may be.

"You must never even (go to) strike against them without first bringing to their notice, through the right channel, that you are dissatisfied, and even when capitalists may refuse to do anything, it is your duty to persist in an amicable way to gain your ends before you resort to strikes. Strikes must be the last thing on your minds; they must only come about — if they have to come — after we have exhausted every arbitrary method with capitalists and Government and both turn their backs on us; then and only then it is time for us to make up our minds not alone to starve for one common cause, but if needs be to die for it with a smile upon our quivering lips. I do not agree with these strikes that have been going on here and there; it might help a little section, but it will prevent progress of the union, and I want the workers to know that if they want my help they will have to follow my advice. I do not intend following theirs."

Bustamante at that moment was, however, at odds with the temper of workers when he exhorted them to exhaust orderly procedures of grievance administration before resorting to strike action. The masses once aroused and set in motion have a mood, not a mind. It was clear that disorganization had already set in. Workers remained confused, inarticulate, and without effective accredited representatives. The year ended ominously with a strike of agricultural labourers on the Serge Island Sugar Estate in St. Thomas on the eastern end of the island.

3

THE CALL TO LEADERSHIP

The year 1938 marks the beginning of Jamaica's modern era. It is the year in which the labouring classes rose up in revolt and protest against crushing poverty and moral degradation. The social upheaval they precipitated gave birth, simultaneously, to a trade union as well as a political movement. The early expectations of those who emerged as leaders were that both movements would complement each other, serving as two facets of a single process aimed at achieving economic betterment for those gainfully employed, as well as self-government, political independence and social reconstruction for Jamaicans at large.

Within five short years, however, Jamaica had ended up, not with a single unified labour movement and a single party at the political level, but with two rival trade union blocs and two contending political parties, both drawing on their respective trade union wings for grass-roots or mass support. Alexander Bustamante emerged as the key figure in this development. His increasing and direct participation in the critical events of the period began early in 1938.

The strike of sugar workers at Serge Island estates, which had ushered in the New Year, produced not settlement but impasse. One thousand striking cane cutters remained adamant in their refusal to return to work at the existing rate of $10\frac{1}{2}$ d per ton for cutting cane and demanded 2/– per ton. They were, however, dispersed by police with flailing batons, and patrols were reinforced. On the 5th January 1938, some 1,400 workers armed with machetes and sticks staged hostile demonstrations, blocking carts and wagons from entering or leaving the estates, and a virtual state of siege prevailed. At this stage, Alexander Bustamante appeared on the scene to address workers. He asserted that the existing rate for cutting cane was inadequate, and the proprietor of the estate felt constrained to make an offer of 1/– per ton from the same platform. Enraged workers rejected the offer and the speakers, including Bustamante, left the platform under police escort. Police reinforcement arrived from Kingston and the inevitable clash ensued: thirty-four strikers and one policeman were injured while sixty were arrested. A week later, fines and prison sentences were meted out to twenty-one of the sixty workers. By this time, cane cutters had begun trooping back to work, albeit reluctantly, with the new rate of 1/– per ton for cutting cane in force. An uneasy calm settled over the estate area, a mere six miles from the stamping ground from which Paul Bogle had launched the Morant Bay Rebellion nearly three-quarters of a century before.

Meanwhile in Kingston, Governor Sir Edward Denham was preparing his annual report to the Legislative Council on governmental activities for the fiscal year 1937. Two months later, in March, he delivered a message to the Legislative Council which exuded optimism, although some concern was expressed at the level of unemployment. The Government had ended the fiscal year with a budgetary surplus of £145,000. Moreover, the threatening unemployment situation was not without its silver lining. Tate and Lyle, a British sugar firm operating in Jamaica as the West Indies Sugar Company, had acquired a number of properties in Jamaica and planned to centralize operations at a huge factory to be built at Frome — a large sugar holding in the western parish of Westmoreland. The Company announced plans for construction of modern cottages for employees, as well as the facilities of schools, churches and a hospital, to be made freely available to labourers and their dependents. Total expenditure was to be in the vicinity of half a million pounds.

Labour agitation continued nevertheless. Seemingly, the "infection" of Serge Island workers could not be prevented from spreading throughout the island. Governor Denham announced on the 29th March 1938 the appointment of a commission to inquire into and report upon wage rates and conditions of employment of field and day labourers in receipt of not more than thirty shillings a week.

During April, Bustamante became a familiar figure on platforms in Kingston, directing a personal attack on the Governor and elected Members of the Legislative Council. He complained about the lack of relief work and the failure of institutional measures to relieve unemployment. He found time, however, to write a spirited letter to *The Jamaica Standard* captioned "In defence of money-lenders". The newspaper's editor, W.J. Makin, in a leader article on "Poverty in Jamaica" had charged that the poverty and distress so prevalent in Jamaica could be attributed to the existence of the money-lender. Baiting Bustamante, Makin invited him to suggest a remedy "to rid ourselves of the incubus". Bustamante argued in defence, that low wages lay at the root of working-class poverty and that without the money-lender to bail him out of emergencies, the impoverished worker would probably end up in debtor's jail.

On the 20th April 1938, events shifted dramatically to Frome when a gang of some 1,000 strong, equipped with the usual sticks and cutlasses (machetes), went on the warpath and attacked the West Indies Sugar Company pay office, protesting against arbitrary deductions ranging from 3d to 6d per day and demanding removal of the pay clerk. Their demands extended to "no more barracks, no sleeping under trees in hammocks, and a daily wage of 4/– (one dollar)" which they claimed the company had promised to pay. The situation quickly deteriorated and on 2nd May the police judged the situation sufficiently serious to open fire on "a mob" estimated by them to be over 1,000 strong. Rifle volleys were followed by bayonet charges. Four died, one a pregnant woman; thirteen were injured, including innocent bystanders; and more than a hundred were arrested and charged with rioting. Bustamante arrived at 5 o'clock the next morning, identifying himself with the cause of labour and equipping himself with first-hand observations.

The causes of the flare-up, which was the subject of investigation by a commission, included: inadequate organization and administration on the part of the company; insufficient housing for the employed; attraction of too large a labour force, so that many job-seekers were disappointed and frustrated; and dissatisfaction over delays in payment of wages, rates of pay, employer deductions from wages, and so on. The main slogan of workers had been the magical "dollar a day" (four shillings) — interestingly enough, the same wage norm which had captured the imagination of strikers in an earlier period of labour unrest, 1918–20.

Just when the situation at Frome appeared to be quieting down, demonstrations began in Kingston as the government-appointed Unemployment Commission held its first sitting in Kingston. At Victoria Park, St. William Grant, popular orator and follower of Marcus Garvey, and a spokesman for aggrieved labourers, addressed a milling crowd of 500 workers.

The Frome affair echoed in the British Parliament and the Governor, in response to an inquiry from the Secretary of State for the Colonies, replied that "the disorders of Monday . . . gave no basis for reports that dissatisfaction was rife throughout the West Indian colony." The House of Commons was also told of the Governor's denial that many native children were suffering from undernourishment and that disaffected labourers were contemplating a hunger march in Kingston.

Actually, the cause of the concern in the House of Commons could be traced back to two letters sent by Bustamante to Labour M.P.'s George

Griffiths and Clement Atlee, the latter then Leader of the Labour Opposition. In his letter to Griffiths dated 26th January 1938, Bustamante painted a grim and explosive picture of unemployment and hunger: "Thousands of children run the villages not being able to go to school from the lack of food and clothing; some are weaklegged and bow-legged from the want of nourishment. . . . I estimate 100,000 people starving and on the verge of starvation, the population is being wasted away by tuberculosis chiefly from the lack of proper food caused through unemployment and sweated labour wages."

According to Bustamante the situation could be sized up thus: "unemployment rampant, starvation wages, taxation destroying us, the captain at the helm of this ship never seem(s) to have sufficient control of the rudder, each day it appears to be slipping more and more out of his hands; the situation is critical, it needs a specialist, but there is *none* in Jamaica."

To Bustamante, it seemed that "the duty of our Mother Government is to send a Royal Commission to investigate and not just to treat the people of this country as if they were merely squatters in British territory." The second letter written to Major C. Atlee, dated 16th March 1938, expressed "Busta's" concern that those who agitate for labour tend to be classed as undesirables. He repeated the call for a Royal Commission.

Meanwhile in Kingston, during the latter part of April and first week in May, J.W.T.U. President Coombs was busy interviewing managers and labourers seeking to ameliorate labour discontent. Bustamante, accepting any platform which enabled him to deliver impassioned addresses, appeared under the auspices of the Reconstruction League and the Jamaica Protective League and spoke to a crowd of 7,000 workers. He did not allow his audience to forget "the Frome Affair". He described how he saw "poor defenceless men and women writhe in agony and pain and die — through murderous police action". "Why did not the police aim at the feet of the people if they wanted to restore law or order as they say? No — they aimed deliberately at the hearts of the people who were agitating for their bread. . . . I saw one woman who would in the next four or five months become a mother suffer and die from a bullet in the forehead." Actually, Bustamante had arrived at Frome after the shooting incident, but this did not apparently lessen the impact of his graphic presentation. He also charged that the elected Members of the Legislative Council, who applauded when the Governor reported the action taken to quell the riot, were cowards, traitors and subjects in the Governor's hands. He declared that the Commission appointed to investigate unemployment had achieved nothing but instead was a farce.

On 10th May, token strikes began in St. Ann's Bay and in Kingston on the waterfront, but were quickly settled. Marches then began throughout the city, often led by St. William Grant, and the reports of these activities filled the press. On the 13th May, one mob of job-seekers laid siege to Headquarters House (Executive Office of the Colonial Administration), while in Trench Pen a crowd also menaced a contractor and his work gang. Bustamante again appeared to address the workers, calming them somewhat, but in the process made the allegation that the elected Members of the Legislative Council believed that they constituted "a Black Royalty". He continued to address huge audiences, and at a meeting held on 16th May clashed with his former associate Coombs of the J.W.T.U. Bustamante asked the crowd "if they had not had enough of that insincerity in the past — away with Coombs. Better to be a flock without shepherd than to have blind leaders." As restiveness grew, the British Secretary of State for the Colonies, Malcolm McDonald, replied to criticisms in the House of Commons that "no useful ends would be served by an enquiry into the situation in the West Indies. It was a disequilibrium between demand and supply of sugar."

A sympathetic Dr. Oswald E. Anderson, Mayor of Kingston, summoned employers and wharfingers of the city wharves to a conference to discuss ways and means of providing work for the unemployed. On the 17th May, Trench Pen workers staged another jobless march and Bustamante, addressing a crowd of about 2,000, protested against their too ready recourse to violence. Two days later, waterfront workers again struck and were urged on by Bustamante and Grant to stick out for higher wages. By the next day 400 strikers were being supported by 6,000 demonstrators.

On 23rd May 1938 began the social upheaval ignited by a revolt of the working classes which, before it subsided three weeks later, gave Jamaica a new sense of direction and national purpose.[1] Preparing dockers for the fray in a fiery speech on 23rd May, Bustamante observed: "This is not a military revolution — it is merely a mental revolution. . . . I say and I shall repeat that if there is going to be a master of this field (labour relations) in Jamaica, if there is going to be a dictator, then I am going to be that dictator."

Addressing a throng of several thousand on Harbour Street, Bustamante and Grant refused to disperse when requested to do so by police. But the crowd was eventually scattered by a baton charge. At another venue in Victoria Park, Bustamante climbed the statue of Queen Victoria to address a crowd estimated at 8,000, but this time police aided by British troops — the Sherwood Foresters — dispersed the crowd. By the end of the day, all services and business activities had been brought to a standstill by marauding workers. Kingston lay in the hands, and at the mercy of, the discontented and the disenfranchised.

At 9 o'clock the next morning, Bustamante and Grant attempted to address a crowd at Spanish Town Road, but police intervened and broke up the meeting. An hour later, both men found themselves at the Headquarters of the Fire Brigade at Highholborn Street where fire-fighters, although restless, hesitated to join the ranks of strikers. Expressing sympathy for the demands of the firemen, Bustamante, accompanied by St. William Grant, set out for the office of the Mayor of Kingston to plead their cause. Striding past the police headquarters, Bustamante was accosted by a police officer and contingent and placed under arrest. Grant, at this moment, made a bid to escape but was caught and clubbed to the ground. As the beaten, bruised and helpless Grant was hauled to his feet, a furious Bustamante submitted to arrest without resistance, but warned, "Don't you dare touch me with your clubs."[2] With Bustamante and Grant immobilized, "Busta's" cousin Norman Manley, K.C., Jamaica's leading criminal lawyer, indicated to the Governor late that night that he was ready to represent striking dockworkers and other groups in negotiations with employers. As Denham eagerly accepted the offer of assistance, Manley notified the press of his intention to intervene and the announcement was headlined in the daily newspapers.

On Wednesday 25th May, Manley became active as a mediator and outlined to dockworkers the nature and scope of his role as well as the terms of settlement proposed by the steamship companies. He was greeted with the ultimatum "No work; we want Bustamante". Bustamante and Grant were, however, held in custody as the acting Resident Magistrate for Kingston, Mr. S.T.B. Sanguinetti, denied the application for bail made on their behalf by barrister J.A.G. Smith, instructed by Solicitor Ross Livingston. As disorder and unrest became widespread and more pervasive throughout the island, a second application was made by Bustamante's lawyers — this time before a Judge of the Supreme Court. The police opposed bail, intimating that four charges would be laid against Bustamante — two for sedition, one for inciting to assemble unlawfully and one for obstructing Inspector-in-Chief of Police W.A. Orrett in the execution of his duties. On the 27th May, Mr. Justice Seton upheld the Crown's contention that it would not be in the interest of public order and safety to release Bustamante and Grant. It was thus to be left to

Norman Manley to secure Bustamante's freedom. On the day following Bustamante's arrest, Manley had suggested to Denham that Bustamante be freed, but the Governor could not be persuaded. What if he should secure Bustamante's release only to find that trouble grew and that Bustamante would do nothing to calm the situation? Would he not be condemned on all sides for irresponsible conduct? By the 27th May, only three days after Bustamante's arrest, the newly appointed Conciliation Board, working in conjunction with Norman Manley, had got the shipping companies to agree to all demands made by waterfront workers. When, however, Manley made it clear to members of the Board that no settlement would be accepted by workers while Bustamante was detained, they also added their plea for the labour leader's release. Finally, having been prevailed upon by Manley that the longer Bustamante was detained the more explosive the situation would become, Sir Edward Denham agreed to Bustamante's release, providing that Manley would be willing to vouch for Bustamante's good behaviour. Manley agreed to give evidence on his cousin's behalf, but indicated that he would first have to seek and receive certain assurances from Bustamante personally.[3]

At 11 o'clock that night, Manley conferred with Bustamante in jail. When they met, it was the first time in four years that they were speaking to each other. On his return to Jamaica in 1934, Bustamante had kept aloof from the members of his immediate family. Apparently he had not been sure that he would find his niche in Jamaica and thus had wanted to preserve his image as a foreigner in the event he again had to seek his "place in the sun" elsewhere. Norman Manley, who felt deeply about the duty to respect one's family obligations, expressed his disapproval by treating Bustamante as a stranger and for four years they passed each other on the streets, going their separate ways without speaking.[4] But on the 27th May 1938, family feuds were forgotten in Jamaica's moment of crisis and Manley was able to report personally to Denham that Bustamante and himself would make common cause to restore order and save Kingston from imminent disaster. Assuring Manley that if a new application for bail could be filed the next morning, Bustamante would be released, the Governor then followed through with a telephone call to Mr. Bertram Burrowes, Justice of the Supreme Court (who would hear the application), and instructed him that he should grant Bustamante's application for bail.[5] At 11 o'clock in the morning on the 28th May 1938, supported by Manley's evidence and affidavit, William Alexander Bustamante and St. William Grant were both granted bail and bound over to keep the peace. Thus occurred one of the few occasions in Jamaican

Labour leaders Alexander Bustamante and St. William Grant leaving the General Penitentiary on 28th May 1938, after Norman Washington Manley had intervened to secure bail. Beside Bustamante is his counsel, Hon. J.A.G. Smith, and behind him is his solicitor, Mr. Ross Livingston.

history when the workers of Jamaica, by refusing to work unless their chosen leader was released, imposed their will upon the Colonial administration. By 3 o'clock that same afternoon, some 3,000 jubilant waterfront workers had assembled at No. 1 Pier to hear Bustamante, his lawyers, St. William Grant and Norman and Edna Manley.

Bustamante was in an expansive mood. "I was glad that Mr. Manley came down to enter the breach. I was glad that he tried to do something to help you but I was more glad when I heard that you all refused to work. When you did this, you gave definite proof that you respect your leader, and that you accept but one leadership. Yet, my friends, Mr. Manley meant well and he came at a time when I did not ask him to come, but when I really needed his services. He volunteered to help in getting me out of the Penitentiary and I appreciate it sincerely. If he had waited until I asked him, I would not have appreciated it, and when he told me that Mrs. Manley, his wife, was doing something to help you, I was overwhelmed." Bustamante was even more overwhelmed by the loyalty given to him by workers. "I did not expect such an enormous amount of loyalty," he declared, and asked them to be patient until he met with the Conciliation Board.[6] Later that afternoon, Bustamante, Grant and Manley met with the Conciliation Board and the labour leader agreed to accept, on behalf of workers, the settlement worked out by the Conciliation Board and Manley.

That night, a vast throng of about 15,000 workers greeted Bustamante and his colleagues. Having thanked his friends for their devotion in helping secure his release, Bustamante reportedly went on to add: "I have been out of jail only a few hours but I have got everything for you." Pandemonium broke loose and amid tumultuous and delirious cheering, Bustamante stood receiving acclaim, without having to say another word. When he left the waterfront, the vast crowd went after him, leaving Norman and Edna Manley behind to contemplate the awe-inspiring demonstration of the utter and incredible devotion of the masses to "Busta" the "Chief". "I'll never forget, as long as I live," mused Norman Manley at the twilight of his life and career, "the echo of the feet on the boards of the wharf as we walked from the deserted place."[7] It was not long after that Jamaica was to be filled with the refrain — "we will follow Bustamante, we will follow Bustamante 'till we die."

That night, therefore, was Bustamante presented with his great moment — the call to leadership — in which an emotional link had been established and a hero was born. He sensed, with an intuitive yet profound grasp of mass psychology, the nature of that call. He was being cast in a

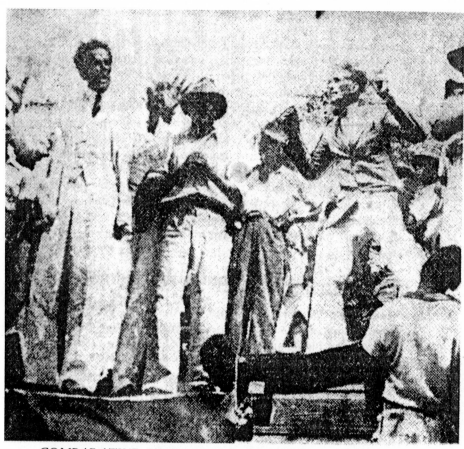

COMPARATIVE GESTURES: *Norman Washington Manley (left) and Alexander Bustamante (right) addressing a vast throng of labourers at Trench Pen, from the top of the Corporation's Pay Office, on 30th May 1938, during the social upheaval.*

new and momentous role — the "Messiah" or "Saviour" of the working classes of Jamaica.

How was it that William Alexander Clarke, who returned to Jamaica in 1934 with a foreign-sounding name (Bustamante), foreign mannerisms and a foreign accent and who, before 1937, was hardly known to the masses in person, could, by 1938, command such devotion and loyalty from the masses? The answer lies in the fact that social forces and influences which were at work in Jamaican society converged and came to a head in 1938 and Alexander Bustamante, by force of personality and character — as well as understanding the role which he was called upon to play — became the focal point of the social ferment which resulted. These social forces already have been alluded to: bankruptcy of the Colonial administration; return of *émigrés*; Garveyism; and race consciousness and increasing politicization of the masses. Of course the example of the other West Indian colonies which successively resorted to direct action was not lost upon Jamaica.

BANKRUPTCY OF THE COLONIAL ADMINISTRATION

The riots (or "disturbances" as they are called in the polite language of Colonial administration) which shook Jamaica and the West Indies in 1938, marked the beginning of the end of the Colonial era. They represented a profound revulsion against the thraldom of poverty and despair — and a forceful protest against deterioration in the quality — albeit marginal — of life. The promise of the free society created by the Emancipation Act of 1833, had not been realized a century later. Apart from substituting labour-market relationships for slave-labour, the plantation system, dominated by a white plantocracy and the coloured middle classes who identified with them, had continued much as it had before.

In 1938 (as in 1833 and 1865), to be black was to be poor; to be black was to be working class and socially and racially inferior; to be black was to be illiterate, unskilled and underprivileged; to be black was to be unemployed or part-time employed. The plantation economy, administered albeit by a benevolent colonial administration, had proven incapable of satisfying the rising tide of expectations. Yet, as far as the descendants of freedmen were concerned, the hope of a "good life" was not just an ideal in Jamaica. There was the planter or estate manager, the man of leisure, who did not have to soil his hands, but for whom they laboured. True, he might be given to human excesses and might not be

48

too concerned about moral scruples. But he was white and it seemed that the institutional order of things continued to reserve the best opportunities for those who were white or closest to white in complexion.

The West Indian (Moyne) Royal Commission appointed to investigate the strife in the West Indies in 1938 observed: "The discontent that underlies the disturbance of recent years is a positive demand for the creation of new conditions that will render possible a better and less restricted life. It is the coexistence of this new demand with the unfavourable economic trend that is the crux of the West Indian problem of the present day." The economic conditions, then, provided little hope that mounting aspirations would be met. But at the same time, as an offset to this demand for a better life, reinforced by "the cumulative effect of education, the press, wireless, the spectacle of standards of living of white people and reports of West Indians who have lived abroad, particularly in the U.S.A.", the Colonial Office had not offered constructive measures of sufficient scope. The stipulation of Colonial fiscal policy that each administrative unit, however small, stand on its own feet financially, imposed a major constraint on the local House of Assembly's capability, already inhibited by economic and social theories prevailing in Jamaica, to deal with endemic economic and social problems. By 1938, the bankruptcy and sterility of the Crown Colony system had become abundantly evident. Caught between the unremitting intransigence and obstructionism of the white planter class on the one hand, and the ambivalence of the black and coloured Jamaican élite on the other hand, the Government of Jamaica merely limped along like a tired, old, battle-scarred veteran.

The plantocracy had repeatedly demonstrated how they could, by pursuing a policy of calculated obstruction at the level of the individual estate and in the House of Assembly, successfully thwart or frustrate political and social change. In 1830, alarmed at the prospect of Emancipation, they had launched a separatist movement and talked of joining the United States. Permitted to attend protest meetings, slaves listened to intemperate remarks and threats made by their masters. They came to realize that while sympathizers in Britain were working to win their freedom, these efforts were being strongly opposed by local planters. The result was the so-called Baptist War or Slave Rebellion of 1831 instigated by Sam Sharp, a literate domestic slave and Baptist deacon in Montego Bay. In the post-Emancipation period, the Apprenticeship Scheme, designed to effect the transition from slavery to wage employment, foundered on planter intransigence and had to be terminated within five years. What was intended to be an experiment in training and reorientation of freemen was converted into a system of coercion as brutal as slavery itself. By 1865, the Government of Jamaica had established a record of ineptitude and maladministration. Governor Eyre and the Assembly had dissipated their energies in a series of quarrels. Disputes about land and use of land had become widespread; relations between planters and rural labourers had not improved after the inauspicious start at Emancipation. When Paul Bogle and his followers came down from the hills to the square in front of the Morant Bay Court House, it was to protest against the abuse of authority by the Judiciary and Vestries (local government) which made them despair of ever obtaining fair play and justice. The courts had become the means of enforcing the rule of the plantocracy. Denied legitimate redress, Bogle and his followers responded to provocation by resort to violent protest and thus began the Morant Bay Rebellion.

Thus again in 1865, faced with the prospect of political and social reform, the Jamaica Assembly voted to abolish itself and permit the return to Crown Colony government. While this system of bureaucratic administration brought the advantage of legal protection to the black population against physical domination by the plantocracy, it was inhibited by contemporary social theories from acting to improve the welfare of the black working-class population. The system could, however, always be manipulated by the plantocracy to protect economic privilege. To do this, they constantly had to be predicting impending economic collapse of the sugar industry and later of the banana industry as well. The Governor or the official administration could always be accused of betraying Jamaica's true interests if they opposed planters' demands. Thus, as late as the 1920's, Governor Sir Leslie Probyn could be quickly discredited by planter interests and the local press, because he promised, in the wake of widespread labour unrest and trade union organizational activity during 1918–20, to establish a Labour Department and thus provide formal machinery for the processing of workers' grievances.

Equally in 1937, when there were already abundant signs of social disillusionment, reorganization of the banana industry was undertaken by the Government with the avowed purpose of helping the small man. One of the major advantages claimed for the new agreement between the banana companies and the reconstituted Jamaica Banana Producers' Association, was that it would increase the purchases from small producers. Banana carriers and peasant workers, especially along the north coast of Jamaica, were held out the prospect of growing bananas themselves

50

on small holdings. To the landless labourer, on the other hand, the only hope of becoming an independent proprietor or of making money lay in acquiring a plot of land. The promised benefits did not filter down, however, from planters to peasants and workers. If anything, the situation served to intensify the hunger for land even as the fluctuating economic fortunes of the industry added to the frustrations of workers and peasants. It is no wonder that banana workers constituted the most militant element among strikers in 1938.

If the white planter class was the Scylla or hydra-headed monster which exhausted the energy and imagination of the Colonial administration, the black and coloured middle classes constituted the Charybdis or whirlpool, albeit much less perilous, which the administration also had to navigate. Although torn between loyalty to the British government and identification with Jamaica, they too, for different reasons, began increasingly to voice criticisms of the ineffectiveness of modified Crown Colony government. Their demand and representations for constitutional advance in the 1920's were noted earlier.

The coloured and black bourgeoisie and professional classes were not wholly indifferent to the plight of the working classes. The problem was that they were happy to accommodate themselves to a political system which, for *all* practical purposes, was incapable of solving or easing the burden of the masses. As both liberal and conservative upper and middle classes continued to belabour the ineffectiveness of the Crown Colony system, each class for its own ends, they contributed to a more general dissatisfaction which began to manifest itself throughout the island as early as 1932.

THE RETURN OF THE ÉMIGRÉS

Emigration, a dynamic factor in the economic and social adaptive processes, was drastically reduced and Jamaica's social safety valve thus was closed. The returning *émigrés* brought back ideas and experiences to which they had been exposed: of Garveyism or race consciousness; of trade unionism; of liberal democracy; of republicanism; as well as revolutionary ideology and politics. To the many thousands who had worked in Latin American Republics, where governments were toppled and changed frequently by palace revolutions, the British monarchy and imperial power, as well as the local Governor and administration, were no longer sacrosanct persons and institutions, insulated against criticism. The inarticulate black masses were being provided with spokesmen of their own, who could hold forth at street corners and

51

under shop piazzas and within the bars, espousing their cause.

Furthermore, contact with white proletariat also served to deepen awareness of the privilege attached to colour in Jamaica. Even when they remained based overseas, politically-minded and astute Jamaicans began to preoccupy themselves with Jamaica. The Jamaica Progressive League was formed by such a group in New York in 1936 to promote the idea of self-government for Jamaica. By 1937, leading spokesmen of the League such as W.A. Domingo, Adolphe Roberts and Rev. Ethelred Brown were conducting lecture tours in Jamaica.

They were provided with a forum and an organizational base in Jamaica with the founding of a new weekly, *Public Opinion*, in 1937. Managed by O.T. Fairclough, later one of the founders of the People's National Party in 1938, H.P. Jacobs and Frank Hill, all "avowed" Fabian-type socialists, *Public Opinion* took up the cry of self-government for Jamaica, allowed for middle-class and intellectual criticism of a more radical nature to be brought to bear on the Jamaican scene and served, at the same time, as the rallying point for a critical new breed of Jamaicans, most of whom later became adherents of the Manley-led People's National Party.

The 1930's therefore provided fertile soil for the seeds of agitation, as Bustamante, the letter-writer and polemicist, soon found out. Once he had decided that his sympathies lay with the working classes and the small man, Bustamante was able to utilize a variety of public platforms — citizens' associations, Coombs' J.W.T.U. and Garvey's Universal Negro Improvement Association. As a near-white Jamaican and budding capitalist, although somewhat tainted by the disreputable aura of the money-lender, Bustamante could have made his way into the ranks of the privileged. Instead, he chose to array himself on the side of "have-nots"; and in the attacks which he mounted against the Colony's administration, reserved the harshest criticisms for the black and coloured Members of the Legislative Council whom, in 1938, he dubbed "Black Royalty".

In a letter to *The Daily Gleaner* in 1935, Bustamante asserted that it was not because of limited constitutional powers that elected M.L.C.'s were ineffective. "Disaster is facing us, not through our constitution, but through most of the elected Members. It would seem to me that instead of the people of this island being blest with the right kind of people to represent them, we are being suffocated by most of them." In other letters in the same year and in 1936, he maintained this theme, accusing the Members of the Legislative Council of being insensitive to the needs of their constituents and of bringing sorrow to the island. In 1937,

Bustamante flirted with the idea of running as a candidate for election to the Kingston and St. Andrew Corporation but finally decided against it. It was fortunate for him for, had he been elected, he may have had to compromise and make his peace with the Jamaican middle classes towards whom he developed a strong antipathy which, incidentally, he retained throughout his entire career. In November 1938, when giving evidence before the West India (Moyne) Royal Commission in Jamaica, Bustamante savagely attacked the elected Members of the Legislative Council, whom he described as "no good" and "imbeciles", as well as the nominated Members whom he referred to as "yes-men". Jamaican civil servants or bureaucrats did not escape his wrath. He alleged that as soon as the local bureaucrat obtains a high position, he seeks to grind down his fellows. Equally fierce was his denunciation of Jamaican police officers. "We have had more justice from imported whites than from our coloured and Negro bosses. Even in the police force." Of course it is not impossible that Bustamante's hostility to the police may have been influenced by his own activities as a member of the Police Force in Cuba under two dictators.

GARVEYISM AND RACE-CONSCIOUSNESS

Alexander Bustamante, on the night of the 28th May 1938, came to inherit, as well as embody and confirm, the yearning of the Jamaican working classes for a "Saviour", a yearning which had made them turn to Alexander Bedward as well as Marcus Garvey. Unlike the Black Christ, Alexander Bedward, who would have relieved his followers of the burden of temporal poverty and ignorance by ascending into heaven, and Black Moses (Marcus Garvey) who enabled black toilers to bear their lot with fortitude and dignity even as they contemplated his distant but equally elusive new Black Jerusalem, Alexander Bustamante, a near-white "Moses", translated his concern for the oppressed and black population into mundane and practical action which would improve their material and spiritual well-being here and now. For Bustamante encouraged workers to unite and strike if need be, in order to secure redress of grievances and improvements in working conditions.

In the upsurge of race consciousness, which peaked in Jamaica in the 1930's, one might expect that Bustamante's colour would have been an obstacle to his acceptance by the masses, and indeed when he was first introduced as a guest speaker on a U.N.I.A. platform, his sponsor St. William Grant, felt obliged to apologize for Bustamante's complexion.

53

But once Bustamante had established that he was on the side of the common man and that he was prepared to incur the approbrium of the privileged and ruling classes, both white and non-white, then paradoxically, his colour became an advantage.

After close to two centuries of physical enslavement with its supporting racial theories which postulated the inherent inferiority of the Negro slave and the inherent superiority of his white master, and after a century of post-Emancipation existence in which the white bias and concomitant economic hegemony had been carried forward and reinforced by a colour-class structure, which confirmed for the black majority the association of colour and race with low social and economic status, the Jamaican working classes had been conditioned to doubt their own capabilities for leadership. It might be too harsh a judgment of history, to say that workers in 1938 were unwilling to let anyone from their ranks rise to prominence and leadership, because they were convinced, as a group, that they were truly inferior. Let us say, then, that in the context of the times, it would have been a natural instinct for workers to turn to someone who, seemingly, had all the attributes of leadership needed to overcome the psychological barriers which would make bargaining between rank and file and employers difficult. From this point of view, Alexander Bustamante satisfied the requirements for leadership. As he strode through the streets of Kingston and major rural towns, tall, gaunt, with high cheek-bones, flashing eyes and unruly hair, he was the warrior knight, the St. George, breathing denunciations and threatening to slay the offending dragon. On public platforms, he displayed even greater flamboyance and melodrama, gesticulating, baring his encased dagger, occasionally brandishing his revolver, especially when reporting alleged plots against his life because of his identification with the cause of the common man. He spoke in short, clipped phrases, repeating his points as if to hammer them home into the consciousness of his listeners. He spoke English as though he had had to learn it as a second or foreign language. But even so, was this not compatible with years of residence and travel in Spanish-speaking countries? Already in circulation were the legendary and romantic stories of his being adopted and taken to Spain, being educated there, and seeing military service in the Spanish Army in Casa Blanca and Spanish Morocco. As the capstone to a full life of adventure, there was the claim of having acquired a fortune by playing the stock market and beating Wall Street. His occupation as a money-lender in Jamaica, instead of being a handicap, served merely to confirm to the hopeful and expectant masses that he was a man of affairs, a man with "foreign experience" who would not be outwitted by "backra" or the white boss-man. He was every bit as good as the bosses were.

Just as he displayed demagogic powers to arouse to fever pitch the large crowds that increasingly assembled to hear him, so Bustamante displayed great personal courage in many tense confrontations between workers and police. Although Bustamante was allowed by police to circulate freely and without being touched (until his arrest on Tuesday 24th May 1938 — and this goes for St. William Grant too), he often intervened to escort to safety ragged and barefooted women and men who were being mauled by police. Bustamante's actions were tempered by his concern to prevent indiscriminate bloodshed and loss of life. Typical of his prudent concern was his encounter with the police which has since been embellished and made into a legend. "Come on you black bastards! I'll knock hell out of you!" — waving his baton, a white Jamaican Inspector invited a tough crowd to rush. Behind him were his men, ready to level their rifles and fire at any such rush. Bustamante, tense and pale with excitement, stood at a street corner. A little group surrounded him. "There'll be no shooting," he shouted aloud. "Then tell that mob to get to hell out of here." Bustamante turned to the crowd, the fierce black faces, the ragged, ill-kept figures, the hovering amazons in the background — "All right comrades. Follow me." "They turned and followed him docilely."[8]

A man of great personal charm and generosity, Bustamante also retained the earthiness of his rural background and upbringing which made it easy for him to establish an easy affability and emotional link with the illiterate peasants and workers who not only believed in him, and revered him, but were prepared to die for him. Of course, there was no firmer believer in Bustamante than Alexander Bustamante himself. It was reflected in a powerful egotism and an unerring instinct for power which made it very evident to Coombs, as well as to others, that he would play second fiddle to no man. With his arrest on 24th May 1938 and release four days later, the labour leader and agitator was accorded instant martyrdom and was well launched on his way to becoming the authentic prison graduate in a colonial polity.

With the dock strike having been called off by Bustamante on the 28th May, Kingston began to return to normalcy, but strikes, rioting and violence grew more intense in the rural areas, reaching a peak on the 6th June and then quickly subsiding by the 8th June 1938. Bustamante appealed in the name of "Manley and myself" for a return to law and order, and by 12th June the revolt had spent itself.

Alexander Bustamante and Norman Manley became a familiar two-some in the weeks that followed. Indefatigable, they toured the island, calming aroused workers. It is to the disposition and willingness of these two men, as also Coombs and Grant, to work within the existing frame-work of society and to compose protest by seeking immediate improvements in wages and working conditions, that we must attribute the relatively very small loss of life which occurred. Another factor, of course, is that the major upheaval took place in Kingston where the urban working class were considerably less militant than their counterpart in the rural area where the interests of peasant-cum-agricultural wage-earners were reinforced by an element of land hunger. This became evident when Bustamante and Manley addressed banana and outport workers at Port Maria and Annotto Bay on the 31st May and found that the promise of higher wages was not sufficient to induce them back to work. If anything, militancy grew, leading to the clash at Islington on 3rd June 1938 in which four workers were killed and three wounded by police while attempting to disarm a hostile crowd of their sticks. This one incident accounted for half of the total number of lives lost during the period of disorder of May–June 1938.

The growing intensity of the hunger for land on the part of the agro-proletariat, especially along the north coast, was correctly grasped and nipped in the bud by the Acting Governor Mr. C.C.Woolley, when he announced on 5th June 1938 that the Government would spend half a million pounds on a land settlement scheme for peasant farmers.

The element of spontaneity and lack of organizational direction so apparent in the 1938 upheaval sets it apart from the Morant Bay Rebellion. For whatever were Paul Bogle's original intentions, once he had drawn blood after besieging the courthouse, he decided to protect himself and his followers by raising a full-scale rebellion against white rule. The casualty toll of 18 whites killed and 31 wounded on the one hand, and on the other, 439 blacks killed, 600 flogged and 1,000 Negro houses burned in suppression by the military authorities, is in stark contrast therefore to the 8 killed and 171 wounded, 32 of them by gunshot, during the 1938 revolt. Moreover, not a single white person, planter, employer, or bureaucrat or member of the forces of law and order died at the hands of workers.

Nevertheless, the Morant Bay Rebellion, in spite of its heavy death toll, was a localized affair. It served to emphasize the fact that the purpose of a major social revolution, the creation of a society of free men by the Act of Emancipation three decades earlier, had been aborted. It represented, also, a failure at the political level to use the existing instruments of self-government to effect the concomitant political revolution which would have made it possible for the ex-slaves to participate in, and influence the reconstruction of, society and thus establish themselves as truly free and equal citizens. The immediate consequence of the Morant Bay Rebellion was the surrender of self-government and the reaffirmation of two Jamaican communities differentiated on the basis of race and colour, culture and occupation.

The upheaval, or more precisely, rebellion, of 1938, on the other hand, precipitated a social revolution, which, though not very costly in terms of loss of life, captured and gave form to ideas which had been leavening the society for a decade. "Anyone looking back on the past ten years will realize that we in this country have been more and more concentrating upon our own affairs. We have thought more of Jamaica, spoken more about Jamaica, breathed more of the atmosphere of Jamaica than ever we can recall before in this country. And it has been symptomatic of the existence of an increasing number of organizations in all classes of the community, and most markedly in the growth of opinion among the young men of this country, of the dawn of the feeling that this island should be their home and country."[9]

What the local Commission of Inquiry referred to in commendation as "the good temper" of the labouring classes of Jamaica served to limit the scope of violence in their protestations. This in itself served to prevent possible polarization of Jamaican society, which might well have been the case, had liberal and progressive Jamaicans been forced, in different circumstances, to choose between revolutionary violence and bloodshed, albeit in the cause of social justice, and the preservation of law, order and private property, at all costs. By serving notice, however, that they would no longer passively accept the existence and consequences of two Jamaicas, the labouring classes forced upon the ruling and middle classes the politics of choice and identity. "As I see it today there is one straight choice before Jamaica. Either make up our minds to go back to Crown Colony government and have nothing to do with our government at all; either be shepherded people, benevolently shepherded in the interests of everybody, with as its highest ideal the contentment of the country; or have your voice, and face the hard road of political organization, facing the hard road of discipline, developing your own capacities, your own powers and leadership and your own people to the stage where they are capable of administering their own affairs."[10]

4

LABOUR
LEADER
TRIUMPHANT

It has long been a matter of speculation whether the leader creates the situation or conditions of leadership or is created by circumstances and environment. Nor can the element of chance be ignored in determining leadership. A leader may be accepted because he is considered to have superior qualities of intelligence, courage, training or experience. This superiority need not be an established fact. All that matters is that followers believe this to be so. But there is one requirement for personal leadership that must be met, and that is acceptability to followers. The workers and peasants of Jamaica had clearly indicated that no one, other than Alexander Bustamante, would be acceptable as labour leader.

At the same time, whatever his personal qualities and appeal, the leader is required to undertake or perform certain functions for those he leads or represents. His "representativeness" therefore cannot be in question. For he is expected to find solutions to their problems and concerns. It is in this area of activity that the capacity of leadership can be tested severely or be seen at its creative best. But to be able to offer appropriate solutions, he must be able to appreciate the nature of the problems or concerns of his followers. Thus the qualities of leadership depend upon the conditions under which that leadership operates. Nevertheless, analytical insight enables some individuals to anticipate problems and issues, to bring them into view, to dramatize their urgency and then offer appropriate solutions. This functional characteristic has been found in the leaders of progressive reform movements in all countries and in all ages.

Alexander Bustamante had helped to dramatize the poverty and moral degradation of the majority of the population and labouring poor in Jamaica. The nature and extent of that degradation was eloquently articulated by his cousin Norman Manley: "The vast majority of our people were political zeros, with no voice, no right and no share in the affairs of the country. Born to obey its laws and to suffer its hardships and for the rest, to pass silently and unnoticed to their graves." The time had come when this silent majority refused to remain silent any longer and the political quietude had been shattered violently as riotous action broke the thraldom of despair. Alexander Bustamante was chosen to lead the fight for better things and better days. "The fight has just begun for more pay. We are going to organize the entire Jamaica labour into one union."

The formation of that union was eagerly awaited. Bustamante, after his release from jail, had talked further about his brand of trade unionism. "The first labour union which I intend organizing with the help of the different barristers and lawyers in making up the constitution, will be the longshoremen's labour union. It is going to be a union, the discipline of which will be almost that of an army, for without discipline we cannot succeed and with disorder we will fail." Some initial spadework had already been done in the formation of the trade union. At the height of the upheaval, when Kingston lay in a state of nearly complete anarchy and Bustamante and Grant were held in police custody, Ken Hill (brother of Frank Hill), a young journalist on the editorial staff of *The Daily Gleaner* and founder-secretary of the National Reform Association, had urged dockworkers to welcome Norman Manley's efforts at mediation and to form a labour union under Bustamante's leadership. Hill, himself, had been engaged earlier in organizing chauffeurs and drivers into a trade union. The next step was the setting up of a small unofficial committee — the Trades Union Committee — to help in the organization of the projected Bustamante-led union, as well as to coordinate the activities of all existing unions until a Central Advisory Council could be set up to which all unions could be federated. At the same time, Ken Hill and N.N. Nethersole, Solicitor and President of the National Reform Association and an associate of Norman Manley, began collecting names of prospective members, and as enthusiasm ran high a list of over 2,000 names was quickly compiled.

At another level of activity, Edna Manley and one Aggie Bernard, had organized a relief soup kitchen to feed workers during the five hectic days of the waterfront strike. Norman Manley appealed for donations to support the women's effort, and contributions poured in from citizens of all walks of life. It was the balance of these funds, about £100, along with the list of 2,000 prospective members, which was handed over by Manley on Bustamante's release to constitute the nucleus of the new trade union. The labour chieftain subsequently announced the formation of five trade unions with himself the head of each, in which would be enrolled maritime workers, transport labour, factory workers, municipal employees and general labour—the general labour union to be a catch-all for agricultural and other labourers who did not fit into any of the other four unions.

Bustamante's main concern at this time, however, was not organization. There was much to do and he was going at an incredibly hectic pace for a man of fifty-four years of age. There was the seemingly endless stream of disputes to be dealt with. Before one dispute could be settled, many more had arisen to demand his attention. For Bustamante, there was the personal challenge of adapting his rather carefree role of critic and agitator to meet his newly found responsibilities as labour leader and negotiator. The "enfant terrible" was now to be found attending conferences with the Governor, accompanied as an accredited labour leader by his team, including his chief lieutenant, St. William Grant, the Union's solicitor Ross Livingston, and the General Secretary, no less a person than Hugh Buchanan, who had engineered Bustamante's separation from the Jamaica Workers and Tradesmen Union (J.W.T.U.) in 1937. Bustamante did not demur when in the spirit of collaboration which followed his release Buchanan was suggested as a suitable General Secretary. Anyhow, Buchanan's term as General Secretary was to last for only a few months. On 20th July 1938, both he and Stennett Kerr Coombs, as co-editors of *Jamaica Labour*, were arrested for seditious libel. The offending article had been published earlier in the June disorders and was captioned "Police Terror in St. James. Innocent People Beaten and Shot. Jails Crowded." The article contained strong accusations: "St. James is under Martial Law. Government is determined to kill every working man or woman in the parish of St. James, Hanover, Trelawny and Westmoreland . . . who raise their voices in defence of labour. . . ." Although defended by Norman Manley, the two were convicted and sentenced in October 1938 to six months imprisonment. Bustamante promptly appointed J.A.G. Edwards as the new General Secretary and when Buchanan came out of prison, he found no place in the Bustamante Union.

If organization was not Bustamante's main preoccupation in the weeks following the upheaval, it was because he was more concerned to consolidate his position as "undisputed boss" of the trade union movement in Jamaica. There were already a number of independent trade unions in existence and new ones were beginning to make their appearance. Between July and September many of them were absorbed by voluntary resolve in some cases, or by challenge and take-over in other cases. Bustamante's concern was quite consistent with the notion prevailing at this time of a single unified labour movement to be led by himself, working in conjunction with a single unified political party to be led by Norman Manley. To ensure his position, he set out to dispose of his most important rival and former associate A.G.S. (Father) Coombs, President of the J.W.T.U. In June, beginning with nearby Spanish Town, Bustamante easily persuaded L.W. Rose, head of the thriving St. Catherine Division of the J.W.T.U., to switch to his union and carry the membership with him. Rose was rewarded with a Vice-Presidency in the Bustamante Union. J.W.T.U. branches in St. Thomas also announced their transfer of allegiance. In July, Bustamante decided that the time had come to take on Coombs in his stronghold, Montego Bay, where the J.W.T.U. was entrenched among banana workers and lightermen. The showdown came on 24th July. In early morning rallies, Coombs appeared to be holding his own, but as the day wore on, Bustamante's magnetism appeared to be carrying the day. Press headlines blared "Busta conquers MoBay" and "Busta scores at Montego Bay". The rupture between the two men was complete, although two near-successful attempts were made subsequently to reconcile them, first by Manley and Labour members of the West India Royal Commission in November 1938, and again by Norman Manley in February 1939. Coombs doggedly persisted with his organizing activities in the parish of St. James and by 1942 had sufficiently regrouped his forces to register the Jamaica Radical Workers Union with headquarters in Montego Bay. There he remained an uncompromising foe and a thorn in the flesh of Bustamante. The skirmish with Coombs, however, proved to be but the first of a chain of events which was to test the mettle of Bustamante's leadership.

A rash of unauthorized strikes broke out, spearheaded by waterfront workers, and an irritated Bustamante threatened to resign unless workers desisted from calling strikes whenever they felt so inclined. Perhaps he would have been less frustrated had he been able to appreciate then, as no doubt he soon did, that the strike was being used to serve its primary function as a medium of protest. As early as 1863, work stoppages had been used as the normal means of bringing to management's attention that a grievance existed. As such, they represented a failure of communication between the parties. The strike, instead of being the ultimate sanction to be used to enforce a settlement, preceded even the formulation of demands, to say nothing of collective bargaining.

Even as Bustamante struggled to cope, on the one hand, with the assertiveness of workers who were still basking in their powers of disruption and, on the other hand, with the intransigence of paternalistic employers, serious dissension broke out within the Bustamante Union. In mid-August, at a public meeting on Pier No. 1 of Kingston's Waterfront, St. William Grant denounced Bustamante's chief lieutenants and his own working colleagues for graft, treachery and malicious gossip designed to undermine his (Grant's) position. Tearfully, he complained, "Busta is surrounded by a group of thieves and rascals." Bustamante publicly praised the men impugned by Grant, apologized for the behaviour of his erstwhile companion in trouble and three days later expelled him from the Union. Grant was not to be banished that easily, however, and took his case to workers publicly at North Parade, his familiar stomping ground. He maintained that the union or unions should be known as the Bustamante-Grant Union. Bustamante countered that Grant wanted his name to appear on everything and that as part of his severance compensation, Grant would be kept on the payroll for three months and receive two-thirds of his normal pay. The crisis stemmed from anxiety on the part of St. William Grant, who boasted sixteen years of trade union experience behind him in the United States, that he would become one of the unsung heroes of the 1938 saga. The schism, it may be noted, coincided with announcements that money was being collected from grateful workers to purchase a new automobile, and an expensive American model at that, for "Busta the Chief". At a second mass rally at North Parade on Grant's behalf, some 2,000 workers demanded his reinstatement, and the next day a deputation escorted the colourful Garveyite to the union office, where he apologized to Bustamante.

The *Jamaica Labour*, for all practical purposes Bustamante's publication, complained that Grant was anti-union and interested only in a back-to-Africa movement. Bustamante, however, began to proceed more cautiously. Only three months before, he had been faced with a threatened split in his ranks when Garveyites took umbrage at disparaging remarks he reportedly had made about Marcus Garvey. In August, U.N.I.A. branches were proposing that Garvey be invited back to act on behalf of labour. St. William Grant had been a key figure in rallying U.N.I.A. adherents behind Bustamante both before and after the disorders. Having made his point by disciplining Grant, Bustamante could afford therefore to be conciliatory and he promptly announced that Grant would be given a new post as general organizer in the Union, but as such, he would not be an officer of the Union.

The era of personalism or of Bustamanteism in the sphere of labour-management relations had begun, but not without evoking some concern. The President of the Chauffeurs Union, a hold-out against joining the Bustamante Unions, warned that "when you name a union after any one man, it is a sure sign that somebody is going to be a dictator." Father Coombs, from his bailiwick at the Westerly end of the island, seized upon the issue. It could not be ignored. Ross Livingston, solicitor for the Bustamante Unions, volunteered to the public that he had urged the naming of the union(s) after Bustamante so as to prevent confusion in the minds of illiterate workers. Queried on the same point three months later by members of the West India Royal Commission, Bustamante explained that he had decided to bestow his name as other people were going around representing themselves as union officials and collecting money from workers.

By the end of August 1938, therefore, Bustamante had succeeded in consolidating his position within the Union and then could set about the task of recruiting staff and of organizing members. On 1st September 1938, Ken Hill was named Vice-President of the Transport Workers Union of the Bustamante group. Hill had encouraged omnibus and allied operators to merge under Bustamante's leadership.

Lest employers might have taken his internal squabbles as a sign of weakness, Bustamante warned that he would call a general strike if employer victimization of workers did not cease. It was a threat to which he reverted more than once as the weeks went by. There was the reluctant admission on the part of employers and the press that Bustamante might not be a passing phase after all. For one thing, no longer were employers contending with Manley and Bustamante, the two-some, but with Alexander Bustamante, established labour leader. Norman Manley, busily engaged preparing the ground-swell for the launching of the People's National Party (P.N.P.), took time to observe to the press that "Mr Bustamante is Jamaica's labour leader by the only test which matters and that is the support and confidence of labour." What then was Bustamante's philosophy or perception of his role as labour leader at this time? Before the upheaval began on 23rd May 1938, Bustamante had provided occasional glimpses as to how he might be categorized. In a long letter to the editor, published in *The Jamaica Standard* on 1st March 1938 on the issue of private versus public ownership of a radio broadcasting station for the island, Bustamante opted for private owner-ship and ended saying, "In conclusion, the writer being somewhat of a *revolutionist*, hopes that you will not debar this letter from your press. Of course he is not writing in ragged gait or smeared with blood of barricades, nor is he disguised in a morning coat, but promises pleasant manners and is a businessman." The Editor noted, "But it is strange to find a self-confessed revolutionary ready to support any obvious monopoly. Maybe it is because Mr. Bustamante is indeed a businessman."

In an attack on the same newspaper made in April from the platform of the Jamaica Social and Reconstruction League (successor to the Anti-Mortgage and Hire-Purchase League), Bustamante asserted, "I want the *Standard* to know I represent the lower and middle class people of Jamaica." But as he went on to attack the Governor Sir Edward Denham from the same platform, he continued, "I am not advocating a revolt. . . . I know you all would support me — but a military revolution would not do us any good." Only a week before the island-wide strikes and rioting began, Bustamante said in an address to the Federated Artisans Union, "I think there are too many unions here and too little unity, too many societies and too little socialism. . . . I am not a communist. I am not against capital as such. I believe the poor should get a square deal." In June, he told K.S.A.C. workers, "I am no communist, I am a radical socialist reformer and I am going to unite every form of labour in the island for the betterment of the workers."

Obviously, Alexander Bustamante was not one to worry about subtle differentiations or even distinctions between political ideologies or their conceptions. He was a "revolutionist" who could see that a military revolution would do no good; and a businessman who, in spite of being biased in favour of private enterprise, could still bemoan that there was not enough socialism. It was not that he was against capital, but for a square deal for labour. Perhaps it would be best to let Alexander Bustamante speak for himself, when after twenty-one years of highly successful public service and years of hindsight and retrospection he told the author in an interview in 1959 — "My thinking did not extend beyond the fact that my people needed a friend and I was their answer."

His first public elaboration of his conception of the role he should play as labour leader was given in response to goading by G. St. C. Scotter, columnist of *The Daily Gleaner* and a virulent anti-labour critic. In a letter entitled "Why I want power" published in *The Daily Gleaner* 31st August 1938, Bustamante replied to Scotter: "A news article appeared in *The*[Daily] *Gleaner* of Friday, August 26, under the signature of G. St. C. Scotter. He wrote inter alia: 'What is at the back of Bustamante's mind? What are his personal motives? Are they purely altruistic? Does he do what he does simply for the people alone? Are they pecuniary? Is any money he may be paid for his labours the motive of them? Is it personal power that most fatal of all temptations to the strong?'

"May I ask if Scotter is losing ground, becoming weak somewhere or the other? I am delighted that Mr. Scotter realizes that I have a mind.

I just wish I could think that of others. Up to now I may inform Mr. Scotter I have been living off my own capital, expending excessive energy, perhaps ruining the excellent health I possess to prevent workers of all classes being trampled upon, as they have been in the past, as if they were footmats belonging to no one, not even the British Government.

"Whatever labour could ever be able to pay me would never be sufficient for me to live as well as I used to before I took interest in labour organizations and as well as I am still living.

"Perhaps Scotter would like to know how I came to organize labour. When I started, in a conversation with Mr. N.W. Manley, I told him of my intention; that I felt I could give labour forty per cent of my time free. I soon found out that I was wrong.

"The Unions have developed into gigantic organizations admittedly through my personal influence, but instead of being able to give labour only that per cent of time I have mentioned, I am kept occupied every day until the very early hours of the morning. What has been the result? Not one minute to attend to my own business, not even time to have my meals, but can I withdraw? No. The love I have for labour prevents me so doing, and I do not believe in a half-finished job. . . . The paltry sum that labour could pay me could never compensate me for all the money I am losing now, and Mr. Scotter's suggestion regarding pecuniary motives is impertinent. In Jamaica even strangers who have lived here for some time feel that no one can do anything that involves suffering and loss without ulterior motives.

"Yes, I want power, sufficient power to be able to defend those weaker than I am, those less fortunate, and that's what I have today —— POWER. That hurts Scotter and his type.

"It has been stated that I want to be a dictator. Yes, I do want to dictate the policy of the Unions, in the interests of the people I represent and the only ones who are giving results today are the dictators. The other elements, the minority have had their dictators too long.

"Then why should labour not now have a voice?

"It does not matter what is my reason for organizing labour, not the business of your correspondent so long as labour is satisfied and is benefited by organization.

"Mr. Scotter seems to think that everybody can speak for the Unions at the same time. I am the person authorized to do that. Again that hurts, for when I speak apparently that hurts Mr. Scotter and others.

"The voice of labour must be heard and it shall be heard through me, whether Scotter and his frightened few like it or not. Oh, Mr. Scotter, the workers' eyes are opened to your kind of propaganda which will never succeed."

Whatever Alexander Bustamante may or may not have been clear about — there was one thing of which he was never in doubt, and this he continually made clear to all and sundry. He had power and personal authority which could be exercised at any time, on behalf of, as well as over, the workers and peasants of Jamaica. This awareness was matched by an equally strong instinct of self-preservation, which made him extremely cautious about joining in any venture or collaborating with any person or group if the effect would be to lessen his commanding height of power or adulation. It was for this reason that he remained lukewarm towards the Conciliation Board. It was this reason that he greeted with suspicion the launching of the People's National Party on 18th September 1938. Only twelve days earlier, Norman Manley had convened a meeting at his home so that Sir Stafford Cripps (later Chancellor of the Exchequer in the British Labour Party Government of 1945) who was holidaying in Jamaica could meet with some of the leaders of the burgeoning trade union movement. Bustamante attended along with a team of his union officers, and to ensure privacy and informality, Manley and Bustamante agreed to deny admission to newspaper reporters. William J. Makin, the Englishman who had come out to Jamaica to set up *The Jamaica Standard* and be its editor, found himself denied admission to Manley's home and seized upon the "secret" meeting to intensify his campaign against the P.N.P. Makin was alarmed at the prospect of Jamaica having only one political party. "Manley is wrong in imagining that Jamaica will unite in forming a single strong and solid political party." He called for someone to announce another party. "Whoever does so is advancing Jamaica towards real party politics." He professed, at the same time, to see in the meeting at Manley's home a sinister design to oust Bustamante as labour leader. In an editorial on "Who are Labour's Leaders", Makin contended that there were three groups bidding for leadership of Jamaican labour.[1] First, there was Norman Manley, labour mediator and acknowledged leader of the People's National Party. Next, there was another group that was labour oriented and led by Bustamante, who was already having to contend with the challenge to his leadership posed by St. William Grant. Third, there was within the P.N.P. a small group of radical "half-baked" intellectuals, all avowed communists, who were bent on establishing a dictatorship of their own and would use Manley and Bustamante to achieve their own purposes. The only certain casualty in the power plays would be Alexander

Bustamante. "Already the other groups are arguing that Bustamante's day is ended, that temperamentally he is unsuited for the rapidly advancing labour unification. Whether that be true or not, it is clear that Mr. Bustamante is doomed." Norman Manley gave short shrift to Makin's dramatization of events. Alexander Bustamante however did not. After all, it was *The Jamaica Standard* which had helped to make Bustamante's name familiar throughout Jamaica in the months immediately preceding the May uprising. Given the task of challenging the monopoly of the century-old and entrenched *The Daily Gleaner*, Makin sought to find a local *cause célèbre*. He decided that Alexander Bustamante and the cause of labour were news and gave them wide coverage even as the new daily quickly achieved the very respectable circulation of 18,000 copies daily.

Alexander Bustamante took his cue and proclaimed at a North Parade meeting: "There is a communistic group working behind the scenes of this P.N.P. being formed . . . What they aim to do is bring about the fall of myself and Mr. Manley in turn, and then ride to Legislative Council power on the shoulders of a Labour Party they hope to control." He then warned his followers against joining the P.N.P. until he could assure them that the Party had been purged of harmful conspirators. Nevertheless, Alexander Bustamante occupied a seat of prominence on the platform at the Ward Theatre on 18th September 1938, when Sir Stafford Cripps gave the inaugural address to launch the People's National Party.

The arrival in the island, on 1st November 1938, of the West India Royal Commission provided Bustamante with the next occasion to take stock of the events which had shaken Jamaica and to spell out some of the things he wanted for Jamaican labour. Appearing before the Royal Commission, at the head of a Bustamante Union delegation to elaborate upon the Union's memorandum, he demonstrated that he was no respecter of persons and was as irrepressible as ever. He accused the Governor and Government of Jamaica of being fascist for having preferred to use bayonets instead of investigating disputes. While he personally was not intimidated, he had lost respect for the Government: "Because I realize that I have more power in this country than Government has." His strictures extended: to the elected and nominated Members of the Legislative Council, the former for being "imbeciles", the latter for being "yes-men"; to middle-ranking Jamaican officials or bureaucrats, for "on the whole they cannot stand success . . . The moment our coloured Negroes reach a position of any authority they become brutes to their fellowmen"; and to the police, for their barbaric brutality. When he first returned to Jamaica, said Bustamante, he had advocated native officers for the police force and the throwing out of English and Irish Inspectors and Sergeant-Majors. But now, he had changed that view, especially after the way the police acted on the morning of 23rd May.

It may be noted that Bustamante's pronounced antipathy to the police did not stem from any mistreatment or harassment personally suffered at their hands, but from his emotional identification with the working classes for whom the police did epitomize the forces of oppression in Jamaican society. In the absence of collective bargaining machinery and procedures which would have enabled the orderly processing of grievances and the resolution of conflict through third-party intervention, workers were left no alternative but to protest through work stoppages or demonstrations. Similarly, as the Trade Union Law of 1919 did not make provision for peaceful picketing in trade disputes, it meant that protestations by workers whether in small or large numbers were liable to be treated as riotous or disorderly assemblies. Invariably, therefore, the police were drawn into labour disputes either to protect the employers' property rights or to disperse unruly workers and arrest their ringleaders. This, in many cases, deprived workers of their natural and rank-and-file leaders. In this way the forces of law and order were constantly arrayed against the underprivileged in the society. But as Bustamante pointed out, even in the face of extreme provocation Jamaican workers were characteristically peaceful; "Although nearly all possess[ed] machetes during the whole of the disturbances, there was not recorded a single instance of anyone being wounded by such an instrument."

When sympathetic members of the Royal Commission enlightened Bustamante that the Trade Union Law did not release the trade unions from liability for suits for damages arising out of strikes, nor legalize peaceful picketing, the labour leader responded in characteristic Bustamante style: "I will see that all unauthorized strikes are stopped, if that clause is omitted. But I intend to uphold unauthorized strikes until the law is amended." The Amendment came the same year.

In enunciating his union's social policy, Bustamante made two proposals which aroused the Commission's interest. He called for the establishment of a minimum wage of four shillings (one dollar) for all workers as well as the payment of a pension of ten shillings per week for eligible workers at the age of forty. Bustamante conceded that the application of a general minimum wage in an agricultural country such as Jamaica might present some difficulty, but then he felt that it was based on necessity and most of the industries could afford to pay. Furthermore, because of low wages and its baneful effects, workers attained maximum productive efficiency by forty years of age, hence the proposal that they be eligible for pension at this age. The remainder of Bustamante's proposals were along conventional lines: legislation to regulate the employment of girls under eighteen years; to require protection for workers using dangerous machinery; and to provide for Workmen's Compensation.

Queried as to how he would finance his social policy measures, Bustamante indicated possible sources of additional revenue: personal income tax; export taxes on bananas and citrus; and import duties on corn, canned pineapple, cheap imported shirts, all ready-made dresses, cement, sweetened condensed milk and rice. At the same time, these industries should be promoted locally under the umbrella of protection if need be.

While the Bustamante Union's social policy contained proposals that were bold and imaginative, given the political and economic realities in the island, there was nothing that savoured of the radical in political or ideological terms.

Genuine interest and sympathetic questioning by two members of the Royal Commission, Sir Walter Citrine, General Secretary of the British Trades Union Congress, and Morgan Jones, Labour M.P., led Bustamante to talk of the organizational progress of the Union, including its structure and government.

The Bustamante Unions had become effectively a single union, the Bustamante Industrial Trade Union. Each of the five constituent Unions, to which two more had been added, had become sections or divisions. There were about eighty branches throughout the island, each with a local secretary administratively in charge. There was an Executive or Managing Committee as well as a Subordinate Executive Committee, but the functional and coordinating relationships were not spelled out. While Bustamante seemed to imply that at each level the elective principle was at work in selection of officers, it was modified or qualified by his right to designate key officers. Who would run the Union if he became ill? A difficult question to answer, replied Bustamante. No, he was not dictator of the Union. When the Union first started he was its dictator, but only until they had elected officers — in that sense dictator meant initiator. Bustamante also suggested that the Union had about 50,000 supporters with about half of them being active members. Government statistics disclosed, however, that in November 1938 the Bustamante Industrial Trade Union had about 8,000 regular card-carrying members, with dockers (about 2,000 in number) and agricultural workers (4,000 in number), concer ated mainly in the sugar industry, constituting the two major groups in Bustamante's growing Union.

The inclusion of "Industrial" in the Union's name had little significance or relevance. It could hardly have significance in an agricultural economy where manufacturing activity was limited to processing of sugar-cane into sugar, rum and molasses. Yet the Bustamante Industrial Trade Union assumed a significance which transcended Jamaica. For while it reflected in some ways the striking personality of its charismatic leader, it also manifested other features and characteristics so divergent from the conventional forms of unions found in industrially advanced countries, that this writer, as a student of trade unionism, was led to speculate in the early 1950's that a new type of unionism might have made its appearance in the emergent nations or the so-called underdeveloped countries in the post-World War II era.[2] For one thing, traditional economic analysis had assumed that industrial capitalism was the challenge to which labour movements were responses. However, trade unionism, as a sustained movement, arose in Jamaica, not as a reaction to industrial capitalism which was as yet undeveloped, but, rather, as a protest against poverty which found its root in Jamaica's failure to develop industrially. In the industrially advanced countries, exemplified in British experience, trade unions began first among skilled workers, whose standards of living were threatened by the introduction of labour-saving machinery and by economic liberalism which suggested that prices of commodities or services, including labour, should be determined by the interaction of the competitive forces of the market. In Jamaica, the unique contribution of Alexander Bustamante, as we shall see, was that he welded into a permanent and enduring association, a body of agricultural workers, a category which to this day has remained essentially unorganized and unorganizable in the industrially advanced countries. Again, in the industrially advanced countries, trade unions were created as working-class institutions to be led by workingmen coming up from the ranks. Alexander Bustamante, when he was acclaimed labour leader, could not be described by any stretch of imagination as a manual worker. Bustamante and the other trade union leaders in Jamaica were called to the job to become professional leaders and spokesmen for, rather than representatives of, the working classes. Considerations already referred to of race, colour and social class, and of the quality of the labour force in terms of education, skill and social status, all form part of the explanation of the need for professional leaders.

The Bustamante Industrial Trade Union (B.I.T.U.), which incidentally was registered on 23rd January 1939, was in effect a blanket union

LABOUR LEADER IN THE SADDLE: *Labour leader Alexander Bustamante, an outstanding horseman in his youth, caught in an unusual pose at Findlay's Cottage, Gregory Park, on Sunday, 8th October 1939, just before he was presented with an address and souvenir by the members of the district's branch of the Bustamante Industrial Trade Unions. "Move-a-while" was the name of the labour leader's mount.*

embracing all categories of workers and cutting across occupational skills and industries. In this respect also, the B.I.T.U. served as the prototype of the trade union in the developing country. Its loose blanket-type structure accorded with the realities of Jamaica's agricultural and non-industrialized economy and the quality of the country's labour force, comprised as it was of illiterate and unskilled agricultural workers. In spite of this, however, the B.I.T.U. could achieve a measure of centralization because of the pivotal role played by its leader. Along with the blanket structure went another characteristic feature of trade unions in the underdeveloped countries, namely, a high incidence of non-paying membership. This reflected the subsistence income levels of its members, their devotion to the leader rather than to the union as an institution, and the lack of institutional discipline.

If the internal structure and administration of the B.I.T.U. revealed by the labour leader seemed unclear and disorganized, it must be remembered that the Alexander Bustamante who appeared before the West India Commission in November 1938 was still the egocentric and embattled warrior, attacking the bastions of colonial society, but without any specific alternative blueprint in mind, conscious of power even while grappling to harness it and make it serve institutional and operational ends.

But underlying Bustamante's unbridled egotism, there must have lurked a feeling of basic insecurity, for he continued to be wary and suspicious of potential rivals within and without his Union. In the constitution which was finally drawn up to satisfy his requirements, Alexander Bustamante was installed as President General of the Union for life. No doubt he had in mind his earlier and abortive experience as President of the Jamaica Workers and Tradesmen Union.

When he appeared before the West India Commission, Sir Walter Citrine and Morgan Jones were sufficiently alarmed at the prospect of internecine warfare in the fledgling labour movement that they attempted to effect an accommodation, if not, reconciliation, between Bustamante and his foremost rival, A.G.S. Coombs. They invited both men, along with Norman Manley as an interested party and witness, to meet with them on the eve of their departure and after an extended session at the Constant Spring Hotel which lasted until 2 o'clock in the morning, Bustamante and Coombs agreed that a working accommodation was possible and that they would meet again under Manley's chairmanship to work out the details.[3] Sir Walter Citrine and Morgan Jones then were given an emotional send-off by the two labour leaders, escorted in a procession which left the Kingston Race Course at 3 o'clock in the morning by thousands of workers who had remained there throughout the night.

But when Bustamante and Coombs did meet again, it was to make war, not peace, and it came earlier than the two sympathetic members of the Commission might have expected. In fact, even before they left, restive labourers had begun staging "jobless marches" and "demonstrations" for work in Kingston. The infection spread to the rural areas. Banana workers in Islington, St. Mary, where four workers had been shot dead by police early in June, stopped working. Other outports, along the north coast where Coombs' J.W.T.U. was active, were soon affected. Only two weeks after his peace talks with Coombs, Alexander Bustamante announced that there would be no union or association between himself and his rival. Meanwhile, labour unrest grew, and by 3rd January 1939 the Kingston waterfront was paralysed, and the Constant Spring Hotel closed down, in separate strike actions. Bustamante warned yet again of an island-wide strike but was reminded by the press that the Governor had the power to prevent a recurrence of May 1938. Bustamante then called for industrial peace but workers refused to heed the call. As tension mounted, the Governor announced that he was setting up an Arbitration Board to deal with the Waterfront and Constant Spring disputes and the news was hailed by Bustamante at the B.I.T.U's first Annual Conference on 6th January 1939. At the same time, however, he denounced the Conciliation Board of May 1938 whose members were "97 per cent capitalist", called for the establishment of a Labour Department and endorsed the suggestion of setting up labour camps as a last resort to prevent starvation. Clearly nettled by the new wave of unrest, Bustamante fulminated unauthorized strikes and warned, "If workers will not obey, the military will be used if need be to crush unauthorized strikes."

As the Government announced the names of the members of the Arbitration Board, Bustamante voiced strong objections to the three employer nominees selected by the Chamber of Commerce, because they were "affected with an infliction against labour". To meet his objections, the Government eventually replaced not only the three employer representatives but the entire membership of the Board.

Bustamante then turned his attention to the outports and, with most of his officers in tow, began a tour of the north coast which culminated in Montego Bay on 10th February where he was acclaimed by thousands of well-wishers. He was now ready for Coombs. The occasion came three days later when a worker employed by the United Fruit

Company and an ardent supporter of Coombs jostled St. William Grant, the B.I.T.U.'s activist organizer.

Bustamante and Grant demanded instant dismissal of the worker, but management declined to do so, acting on instruction from the Head Office in Kingston. In making this decision, the company was not unmindful of the threat by Coombs to close down the port of Montego Bay if his supporter was fired, and Coombs, rather than Bustamante, controlled the outport. Bustamante had gambled and lost but he could not afford to concede a victory to Coombs, for what was now at stake was the future of the B.I.T.U. in the entire country of Cornwall, embracing the four most Westerly parishes. His show of strength now had to involve workers from other parts of the island, and accordingly, Bustamante issued an ultimatum that if the offending worker was not dismissed by 6 o'clock that evening, he would call sympathy strikes throughout the island. The company, welcoming the opportunity for a showdown, refused to budge. A telegram was sent by Bustamante to Ken Hill, the only senior officer and member of the Executive remaining in Kingston, to issue the strike call to Kingston's longshoremen. There was, however, partial response from waterfront workers who only recently had been coerced to end an unauthorized stoppage.[4] Moreover, Bustamante's presence was not there.

Back in Montego Bay, Bustamante despatched telegrams to all his local secretaries throughout the island to begin, in effect, a general strike. This time, however, a worried postmistress decided to seek clearance from higher-ups in Kingston and received instructions emanating from the Governor himself, that the telegrams should not be forwarded.[5] Meanwhile, anticipating that shippers might divert ships to the outports, Bustamante raced by car along the north coast heading for Port Antonio. There, that very night, largely as a result of the influence of H.E. Allan, then elected Member of the Legislative Council for Portland, the strike was broken by employing strike breakers and giving them police protection. Demonstrating B.I.T.U. followers also were dispersed by police with fixed bayonets firing warning rifle volleys.

In Kingston the next day, Governor Sir Arthur Richards, a tough-minded colonial administrator, declared a State of Emergency, banned all meetings and marches and demanded of Bustamante an unconditional calling-off of the strike. There would be no negotiations until this was done. Tactics similar to those used in Port Antonio were employed to break the waterfront strike in Kingston. Ex-servicemen and out-of-town workers were brought in under police protection to work on the wharves.

The United Fruit Company and other shippers decided to seize the opportunity to break the trade union movement and initiated wholesale dismissal of labourers and clerical employees. The entire labour movement was in danger of collapsing. Caught in a quandary, Alexander Bustamante turned to his cousin Norman Manley. He suggested that Manley might go to England to publicize the plight of the trade union movement. Instead, Manley proposed entering into negotiations with Sir Arthur Richards, and an accommodation was reached before long. Under the terms worked out, the Governor would immediately lift the emergency once the strike was called off. Employers would be told, by the same token, to cease immediately the victimization and harassment of workers. On the other side, a Trade Union (Advisory) Council (T.U.C.), conceived of by Manley on the pattern of the British Trades Union Congress, would be established, "to rally all voluntary efforts on the part of persons willing to assist in the orderly and progressive development of the trade union movement, to prevent frivolous strikes, to unify policy, to eliminate strife amongst the workers' organizations and between labour and capital and to pool all the labour resources for the common good". Finally, the name of the Bustamante Union would be changed. Richards was insistent on this point. He knew of no other trade union which bore its founder's name. This last condition Alexander Bustamante, however, absolutely and resolutely refused to accept. Nevertheless, the general strike was called off by Bustamante only four days after Richards' declared State of Emergency. It in turn was lifted the following day. An exchange of letters between Manley and Richards setting out the terms of the settlement was made public. They contained no reference to the changing of the name of the B.I.T.U.

At a public meeting called by Norman Manley at the Kingston Race Course on 21st February, some 8,000 workers enthusiastically heard Manley outline the details of the settlement and then voiced approval of the names of members of the Trade Union (Advisory) Council as they were read out one by one by Alexander Bustamante. Inclusive of Norman Manley, legal adviser and counsel, the twelve-member T.U.C. included five trade union representatives. One of these, N.N. Nethersole, solicitor and president of several small craft-oriented trade unions independent of the B.I.T.U., became president of the T.U.C. The B.I.T.U. was accorded three representatives including Bustamante, the Union's solicitor and its general secretary. The non-unionists included two members of the May 1938 Conciliation Board, two officers of the Jamaica Progressive League who were well known supporters of the P.N.P., a medical practitioner and a housewife — rounding out the T.U.C. membership.

It seemed as though a new era was about to dawn for the trade union movement. At a meeting described as historic, held under the auspices of the P.N.P. at the Kingston Race Course on 25th February 1939, labour unity was proclaimed and Alexander Bustamante and his inveterate rival A.G.S. Coombs shook hands and pledged themselves "to fight together and as never before in the cause of labour". Coombs paid glowing tribute to Bustamante's work and spoke of the need to sink personal differences for the common good of all concerned. Alexander Bustamante was more reserved: "The reason why Mr. Coombs is here is not because I personally need him, but because it was necessary for all branches of labour to unite for the good of Jamaica." Norman Manley was reported as saying that no longer would individual unions negotiate for the settlement of major disputes or on any matter affecting the general welfare of workers. This trust had been transferred to the Council.

Another significant and reassuring development occurred a few weeks later when Government established a Labour Department to foster (among other things) the growth of trade unionism and collective bargaining as well as to provide conciliation services.

Most of the existing trade unions promptly sought affiliation with the T.U.C. No application was received from the B.I.T.U., nor was one forthcoming. In spite of his membership, Alexander Bustamante remained suspicious of the Council. His instinct of self-preservation was aroused. Institutional containment could hardly be an acceptable lot for the man of whom workers chanted "we will follow Bustamante 'till we die".

For the next year and a half, Alexander Bustamante went quietly about his business, in the process disengaging his union's membership from the P.N.P. This he did by intimating that the time had come for workers to choose between the B.I.T.U. and the P.N.P. The P.N.P. which by then had established over 500 branches throughout the island, began to lose worker support rapidly as groups dwindled to a third of their original numbers. However, there was no open schism between the Union and the Party. In fact, a reconciliation of sorts was effected when Bustamante and Manley jointly led the second Labour Day march in May 1940 from the B.I.T.U. office to Tivoli Gardens.

The outbreak of World War II and Britain's involvement were major factors contributing to the period of quiescence which set in from September 1939 to September 1940. Defence and Emergency Regulations in reducing the scope of civil liberties also limited the scope for normal trade union activities, and membership as well as revenues of the trade unions fell significantly.

Alexander Bustamante, however, was not a man for quiet times. Neither by temperament nor by inclination was he disposed to sit at his desk and become a trade union bureaucrat. By September 1940 workers had begun to chafe at wartime restrictions which upset the island's economy, disrupted shipping schedules and increased unemployment. As consumer prices rose, and workers began to feel the pinch, they demanded higher wages and on occasions, as tempers flared, could not be restrained from protesting in the now traditional Jamaican manner.

On the Kingston waterfront, workers began to talk of strike action and were addressed by Bustamante. On 8th September 1940 Governor Richards acted without warning to intern Bustamante, W.A. Williams, Vice-President in charge of the Maritime section of the B.I.T.U. and several others, mainly officers and supporters of the P.N.P.

The immediate cause of Bustamante's detention was remarks attributed to him as he addressed restive waterfront workers. "I have stood for peace from the first day I have been in public life, but my patience is exhausted. This time if need be there will be blood from the rampage to the grave." Sir Arthur Richards might have had good reasons to doubt Bustamante's leadership capabilities in a war emergency situation. But at the same time, Bustamante's assertion that he had stood for peace was not without merit. During the 1938 uprising he had stood staunchly against blind recourse to violence. He had threatened severe action against unauthorized strikes. In January 1939 he had intervened to save the life of a police constable who had shot dead an ex-convict even as Bustamante addressed a rally in Montego Bay.

If, however, in the tradition of colonial politics, Alexander Bustamante had to suffer imprisonment and martyrdom to become the authentic hero, Richards could not have chosen a better time to deprive him of his freedom.

Facing the strictures of a wartime economy, and the limited scope which it provided for Bustamante's aggressive and flamboyant style of leadership, the Bustamante Industrial Trade Union had become "run-down". Its membership had fallen substantially and dues-paying membership was but a fraction of the total membership. Bustamante was removed from the scene therefore at a time when his leadership abilities would have been severely put to the test. As it was, he was out of sight at Up Park Camp, but not forgotten.

With Bustamante's internment, Norman Manley came forward to

the rescue once more. He visited Bustamante and received from him a mandate to overlook the running of the B.I.T.U. On his first visit to Bustamante, Manley tried to console him by making light of his predicament. "Be of good cheer. You have achieved something great. The best thing for an agitator is martyrdom and the best place for an agitator in a time of war is prison."[7] Alexander Bustamante did not think it funny. Nevertheless, the caretaker arrangement could be mutually advantageous to both men. Manley had a political party which faced formidable opposition from vested interests. Bustamante had the B.I.T.U., a promising labour organization in spite of the rough going. The P.N.P. leaders decided to put aside party work and to spend their energies helping to keep the labour movement alive. Moving cautiously, so that Bustamante's colleagues would not feel that they were being taken over, Manley called upon the rich human resources of the P.N.P. and other trade union leaders to revitalize the B.I.T.U. The formidable array of talent included names which were to become familiar on the labour and political fronts in Jamaica — N.N. Nethersole, Frank Hill, Ken Hill (who had resigned as Vice-President of the B.I.T.U. after the debacle of the General Strike of February 1939), Richard Hart, Arthur Henry, Thossie Kelly, Osmond Dyce, Roy Woodham, Ken Sterling, Winston Grubb and Florizel Glasspole. H.M. Shirley, Vice-President, upon whom the administration of the Union formally devolved, also established liaison with the Trade Union Council. Worker solidarity received a new impetus when Frank Hill assumed editorship of the B.I.T.U. weekly, *The Jamaica Worker*, which was welded into an effective organ for disseminating news on union policy and action, as well as labour propaganda.

Early in January 1941, the B.I.T.U. served demands upon employers in the sugar industry for wage increases to meet the mounting cost of living. Restive workers were told, however, to await recommendations of the Minimum Wage Advisory Board set up by the Governor on 7th January 1941. Dissatisfaction spread and there were frequent stoppages of work during the month. Up to this point, Alexander Bustamante had been attempting to conduct the affairs of the Union from the internment camp, receiving and discussing union affairs with his visitors. Messages and instructions were conveyed by and through his private secretary and faithful confidante Gladys Longbridge, who also was Treasurer of the Union and a member of its Managing Executive Committee. Governor Richards decided that this was not desirable as Bustamante had had ample time in which to arrange for the administration of the Union during his absence.

As labour unrest grew during February, Norman Manley, working closely with B.I.T.U. Acting President H.M. Shirley (reporting regularly to Bustamante), took command of the situation, and enlisting the support of his associate and colleague N.N. Nethersole, President of the T.U.C., gave a dramatic demonstration of how a trade union could be directed and made effective even within the limits imposed by wartime restrictions. The high-powered organizers of the P.N.P. were made fulltime organizers of the B.I.T.U. and went into the parish of St. Thomas to organize the first of what was intended to be a series of strikes involving, in turn, the other main sugar-producing parishes of Clarendon, St. Catherine and Trelawny. Organizers in St. Thomas received carefully written instructions from Manley.[8] Ten centres were established and delegates selected by organizers were sworn in on the Bible by Manley to be loyal to the cause. Strike instructions were taken by delegates directly to workers at their homes, who were told not to walk in numbers greater than two's. Even as police and soldiers stood by for ten days, the Serge Island Estates was brought to a standstill in what was probably the first really organized strike in Jamaica's history. Even as Norman Manley was preparing to escalate the paralysis of the sugar industry and was swearing in sugar delegates for the parish of Clarendon, he received a late evening summons from Sir Arthur Richards to discuss the strike situation at King's House. Manley arrived an hour before midnight and by 2 o'clock the next morning had signed with Richards a secret agreement providing for immediate wage increases and cost-of-living escalator clause to govern future adjustments.[9] The larger sugar manufacturers would underwrite smaller producers and Government would bear half of any cash support needed. This agreement was subsequently translated into a formally negotiated Collective Agreement, the first such in Jamaica's history.

The Agreement constituted a landmark in collective bargaining. Over 35,000 field and 6,000 factory workers benefited directly. It set the pattern for all future largescale agreements in the country and served as the model in later years for collective agreements in other British West Indian colonies. The membership of the B.I.T.U. rallied and grew by leaps and bounds. Claim after claim was served on employers and negotiated successfully. When Bustamante resumed leadership of the B.I.T.U. in February 1942, total membership had risen to 20,612 (13,741 paying) as against 8,133 (5,200 paying) a year earlier. During this time, efforts were intensified by Manley, P.N.P. associates and the B.I.T.U.'s Executive to secure Bustamante's release from detention. Letters and petitions were forwarded to Sir Walter Citrine of the British T.U.C., to Members of the British Parliament, and to the Secretary of State for the Colonies. Manley himself had interviews and pleaded with the Under-Secretary of State for the Colonies (seen also by Nethersole as President of the Jamaica Trade Union Council) and Governor Richards, and as President of the P.N.P., had sent a petition to the Labour Committee of the British Labour Party so that questions were asked almost ceaselessly in the House of Commons about Bustamante's continuing detention. In Jamaica, a Council for Civil Liberties was formed to protest against unjust detentions, and largely as a result of their representations, Richards established an Advisory Committee.

On 8th February, Governor Sir Arthur Richards released Alexander Bustamante as abruptly as he had apprehended him seventeen months earlier. He was forbidden to speak "in public" or to more than forty-nine persons at any one time inside a building without official permission and he could not leave Kingston without notifying the police. Invited by the B.I.T.U.'s managing Executive Committee to attend a reception to celebrate his release, Bustamante not only declined, in a written reply, but charged that certain officers of the Union had conspired to extend the period of his detention and that further there was an "unholy combination of certain persons with political ambition whose objective is that of destroying me and then to assume control of the Union as a political machine and to serve their own big friends". Subsequently, he alleged that Acting President H.M. Shirley had been guilty of using the Union's car and expense account without authorization.

Summoning an emergency meeting of the P.N.P., Manley announced that the time had come to break with Alexander Bustamante and the decision was taken after an eight and a half hour debate and a fairly close vote. Manley then emphatically denied Bustamante's allegations and countered that Bustamante's attack on himself and the P.N.P. was the quid pro quo for the labour leader's release by Richards. Having had to reorganize the B.I.T.U., Manley also charged that in the first two years of its existence Bustamante had squandered the union funds for unaccountable reasons, hence his charges against Shirley, the scape-goat, were a cover-up. He accused Bustamante of continuing ingratitude and recounted all that had been done on his behalf by Manley himself, the P.N.P., the caretaker administration, and sympathizers at large. Manley, supported by Shirley, specifically charged that Bustamante had had his salary fixed in 1938 at £30 per week plus £10 per week for entertainment while Shirley, his Vice-President, received £3.10/- per week. Manley also asked Bustamante: "Is it true that the Union constitution provides that Bustamante shall be a standing committee of *one* with power to hire and fire all officers, including every member of the Managing Committee with the exception of Shirley who holds a position which is elected by Annual Assembly and to control all funds of the Union?"[10]

The latter question was answered by Bustamante with action rather than words. Within three weeks, he had fired a number of senior Union officials, including the Union's solicitor, Ross Livingston. A letter signed by Ross Livingston and published in the press broadened the issues being brought to accountability. He disclaimed any responsibility for the administration of the B.I.T.U.'s Assurance Fund covering sickness and death benefits. He explained that the assurance fund was supposedly being administered by Bustamante and himself as trustees. However, the Deed of Trust was non-existent, and the assurance fund was not being kept in a separate account, nor had it been registered under the Friendly Societies Act.

On the issue of his salary, Bustamante sought to make the distinction between the salary he was entitled to and what he had drawn: "I have never in my life in this Union drawn £2,000 in any one year. It is the Executive Managing Committee which must vote me . . . But even if they had given me £2,000 per annum that would only work out at less than a half-penny from each member per week; if they paid me £5,000 per annum it could not repay me for the loss of my own financial business which I have had to close down, much more for my health, the effort and energy I have expended, the night and day work which I have had to do." The peasants and workers of Jamaica, especially outside of Kingston, apparently shared their leader's sentiment that he could never be adequately compensated for his sacrifices. For from then on, Alexander Bustamante remained impervious to allegations made by union rivals and political opponents that he had derived financial advantage from the B.I.T.U. A ready answer given by workers was that he had helped them more than he had helped himself.

Alexander Bustamante's victory over Manley and Shirley was never in doubt. His reconstituted Executive Committee at a "support for Bustamante" meeting at the end of February issued a five-point denial of the charges made by Manley and pledged unswerving loyalty to Bustamante, the President General. Shirley attempted to launch his own union, the Jamaica Workers Union, to accommodate disaffected B.I.T.U. adherents. The new union was welcomed by Manley and T.U.C. associates in the Trade Union Council as a counterpoise to the B.I.T.U., but it never really moved off the launching pad and fizzled to death long before it was dissolved in November 1945. At a general meeting attended by delegates from all over the island at the Ward Theatre on 31st March 1942, Alexander Bustamante was reaffirmed as hero and saviour of the working classes. "Bustamante . . . is a good man, Bustamante never did wrong. We will follow Bustamante . . . 'till we die." At the same time that Alexander Bustamante was being raised up to a position of new invincibility, Norman Manley and Shirley were symbolically buried: "Shirley gone, Shirley gone, Shirley gone to a silent home. And forever with Manley . . . Amen, so let it be."

And what of the split between Manley, the P.N.P. and the T.U.C. on the one hand and Bustamante and the B.I.T.U. on the other hand? Had it been deliberately fomented by Richards? In his statement issued from Edelweiss Park, Headquarters of the P.N.P., Manley said, ". . . Last August I heard that people were suggesting to Bustamante that if he would agree to denounce the P.N.P. he would get out. I heard that and I spoke to Bustamante. I asked him, 'Is it true that people have said that?' — because I knew the little group that was going around saying Busta was detained because he was associated with the P.N.P. and Government did not like the P.N.P. I asked him if it was true and this is what he said — Government had taken him out of Detention Camp before a high officer and asked him to sign a paper promising to denounce the P.N.P. as a condition of his getting out. . . ." Manley's suspicion became a conviction when Bustamante remarked on his release that had he been in the Governor's shoes he would have done as he did. This was taken as evidence of "the understanding", as also the fact that Bustamante promptly despatched union representatives around the island telling B.I.T.U. branch officials "not to have anything to do with any political organization". There is no doubt that the P.N.P., as an avowedly socialist party, espousing public ownership, especially of public utilities, universal suffrage and self-government, as well as reconstruction of Jamaican society, was anathema to the Government and business community.

In declaring the P.N.P. a socialist organization at the Party's Annual Conference in September 1940, Manley had declared that socialism "does involve a demand for the complete change of the basic organization of the social and economic conditions under which we live. If it involves anything less than that then it is something less than socialism. . . . Socialism is not a matter of higher wages, of better living conditions for workers, though these things are important; but it involves the concept that all the means of production should in one form or the other come to be publicly owned and publicly controlled." He then attempted to allay the fears of adherents. "You are not being committed either to revolution or to godlessness."

On the other hand, there was no need for the Governor to have made a "deal" with Bustamante to "attack" the P.N.P., and Richards (now Lord Milverton) has denied in personal interviews given to Jamaican scholars as late as 1970, that there was any "deal" as a condition of Bustamante's release. The rupture would have taken place anyway. Shortly after his abortive general strike, Bustamante had refused to co-operate with the Trade Union Council and had begun to disengage B.I.T.U. supporters from the P.N.P. Manley would have known that it was only a question of waiting for the opportune time to make the break. It was just that Alexander Bustamante with his unerring instinct and quest for power took the initiative. The greater the success of Manley and his associates working in conjunction with Shirley and other union officers in revitalizing the B.I.T.U., the more Bustamante, prone to be suspicious, felt himself threatened as the "labour boss" of Jamaica. Moreover, Bustamante had his own grounds for suspicion.

When Bustamante rashly called the General Strike of February 1939 and brought the labour movement to the brink of disaster, the more radical left-wing group within the P.N.P. who saw the need for a political ideology for the labour movement consistent with the broader goal of social, economic and political reconstruction of Jamaican society concluded that Bustamante was not equipped for leadership beyond the more limited horizon of trade unions. It was for this reason that Ken Hill had resigned and parted, though amicably, from the B.I.T.U. in April 1939. If for no other reason than tactical advantage, it seemed to make sense to this group that the break with Bustamante should be made while he was in detention and they were active within the B.I.T.U. But Norman Manley, taking the position that "it is just one's duty, if you believe in the progressive movement, to see that the workers' labour movement is the first concern of the country" and recognizing Bustamante's unique role in the budding labour movement, decided that B.I.T.U. should be preserved intact, and in fact, he himself did much to keep Bustamante's name alive. At the same time, within the Trade Union Council which was functioning as the integrating agency for the entire trade union movement, there were members who kept pressing for revision of the constitution of the B.I.T.U. to make it consistent with accepted principles of democratic labour organization. While they saw nothing wrong with Bustamante being President General of the B.I.T.U. for as long as the members were prepared to elect him, they could not be resigned to his presidency for life, being enshrined as it had been, in the constitution of the Union.

To Alexander Bustamante who was being kept informed fully and regularly of developments both within and without the B.I.T.U. by confidante and Treasurer, Gladys Longbridge, it must have seemed suspiciously odd that some of the persons known to be clamouring for his release from detention should be pressing for a remodelling of the Union and its constitution before he was set free. Bustamante's enforced absence had made it possible also for the secondary leadership to acquire experience and develop a status and following of their own within the Union, so that H.M. Shirley, Vice-President and Acting President, could be considered as a feasible successor, in organizational terms, to Alexander Bustamante. The moment he was freed, therefore, Bustamante moved quickly and decisively to dismiss those secondary leaders in the Union who, both by their association with Manley and middle-class intellectuals within the P.N.P. and T.U.C. and their continuing activities within the B.I.T.U., might have forced him to adapt his highly personalized and egocentric style of leadership to the demands of a more rationally structured B.I.T.U.

Once more firmly in control of the B.I.T.U., Bustamante was soon hard at work, providing aggressive but sober leadership, and taking advantage of the solid base of achievement established by the "caretaker" administration. Then, in August 1942, after a tour of the country parishes, he announced at a public meeting that he intended to form a political party, the Jamaica Labour Party, of which he would be the unquestioned boss. "I will be the boss of my party. If any member goes to the Council and deceives me, he shall have a hot time: for I will be boss. I will direct you how to vote and for whom to vote." He promised that he would put into the (Legislative) Council many of the "common boys". Once a man is capable, he should be given every chance to achieve the greatest heights. The Labour or Workers Party was described as "a party with liberal policies and progressive outlook that will recognize the legitimate claims of both labour and capital for adequate representation". Bustamante avowed he would be satisfied to take 75 per cent of the elected seats in the Legislative Council. The aspiring politician also gave an indication of his party's election platform. The eight planks included:

1. Financial state aid for expectant mothers, a few months before and after childbirth;
2. Medical examination of all criminals before they are made to serve sentences;

3. Legal protection for all persons prosecuted by the police;
4. A more extensive land settlement scheme;
5. Old age pensions;
6. Eight-hour day for all workers;
7. Minimum Wage Law for all workers;
8. Workmen's Compensation Law.

It was not merely a coincidence that the first of Bustamante's eight planks concerned the welfare of women. Like Jamaica's earlier "Messiah" Alexander Bedward (the Prophet) and minor prophet Brother Sal of the Cross, Alexander (Moses) Bustamante aroused a very strong following among working-class women, who accorded him an undying devotion and a fanatical loyalty.

The programme and social philosophy outlined by Bustamante represented the transference of trade union goals into political action or "labourism", if you will. There was no stirring call for constitutional reform or for self-government. The fact of the matter is that Bustamante was little concerned at this stage with constitutional reform. Nevertheless, the debacle of the General Strike of 1939 had brought home to him the limitations of purely trade union power and action. Once, however, it became apparent that Manley and the more ardent nationalists would insist on úniversal adult suffrage, Alexander Bustamante sensed the possibility of achieving and exercising political power. Not much notice was taken by the press of Bustamante's declaration that he would form a political party, nor was it taken seriously other than by his followers.

The pro-Bustamante weekly *Labour and Capital* shrewdly observed that once universal suffrage was conceded, there could be no question but that Bustamante would sweep the field and leave the P.N.P. holding the bag. "In the country parishes the P.N.P. has small groups here and there, but there again Bustamante towers over them like Joseph amidst his brethen; in every nook and corner of Jamaica there is a branch of the B.I.T.U. There are men and women working in the fields, on the farms, in the factories and in every sphere of human activity willing to follow Bustamante's dictates to the last man; with this class or type of people Reason is at a tremendous discount, Logic and Treatise on Socialism 'A Plan for Today, etc.' matters nought; their fixed resolution is 'Busta lead and we will follow.'" It was a prophetic judgment, for the split between Manley and Bustamante had left the P.N.P. without much grass-roots support. Up to this point the P.N.P. was essentially a middle-class organization, and its very name presupposed a certain degree of sophistication on the part of the electorate. It is one of the ironies of history how the name Jamaica Labour Party came to be reserved for Alexander Bustamante. When Norman Manley announced during the height of the disorders in Kingston in May 1938, that he felt that the time was ripe for a Labour Party, one C. Beckford complained that a Jamaica Labour Party had already been launched at a public meeting in Kingston on 12th April 1937 and that contact had been made with the British Labour Party. O.T. Fairclough, founder and manager of *Public Opinion* who did the spadework in the launching of the People's National Party, decided to drop the use of Jamaica Labour Party in deference to Beckford's complaint to him also.[11] Eventually, after a historic debate which lasted for hours, it was decided by a narrow vote to call the party "national" rather than "labour" party.

Such worker support as Manley and the P.N.P. were left with came from relatively skilled workers in the public services who had been organized by Manley's associates into several small craft-oriented unions affiliated to the Trade Union Council. Even as the P.N.P. was reeling from Bustamante's onslaught — disengaging B.I.T.U. followers from the P.N.P. and demolishing its revitalized group structure — Sir Arthur Richards moved against the leaders of the T.U.C. as well as a number of P.N.P. supporters. On 3rd November 1942 Richard Hart, brothers Ken and Frank Hill, and Arthur Henry (who became celebrated as the four H's) were interned by Richards under Defence Regulations. Richard Hart, a solicitor, was President of the Jamaica Government Railway Employees Union. Ken Hill was President of the Government Auxiliary Workers Union and Secretary of the Postal and Telegraph Workers Union. Frank Hill was President of the Public Employees Union, while Arthur Henry, seaman and employee of the Government Railway, was Secretary of the Railway Union.

As a coherent and articulate left-wing group within the T.U.C. and P.N.P., the four H's and their colleagues had intensified organizational work among government workers for two reasons. Firstly, faced with a hostile and powerful blanket B.I.T.U., the only hope of the T.U.C's survival lay in shutting out the B.I.T.U. from government workers who could be influential beyond their numbers because of their strategic location in essential services. Secondly, the four H's decided that an imperialist war should not delay intensification of pressure for self-government, especially as industrial action could be used both to benefit workers and to embarrass the Colonial administration. Meanwhile, Sir Arthur Richards realizing not only the gravity of the war situation but of labour disruptions had, in April 1942, gazetted a Defence Projects and Essential Services (Trade Disputes) Order, imposing severe restrictions on strikes and lock-outs and requiring compulsory referral of disputes to, and conciliation by, the Labour Adviser. If conciliation failed, the Labour Adviser would so certify to the Governor who would appoint a tripartite industrial Tribunal to hold hearings and make a binding award.

On 23rd June 1942, the Jamaica Government Railway Workers Union (J.G.R.W.U.) representing over 1,000 employees of the Railway (already brought under essential service) under the leadership of Richard Hart, was registered under the Trade Union Law. It had, however, made representations on behalf of railway employees before being registered, and this had been one of the reasons which had prompted Richards to promulgate the Defence Project and Essential Services Order under War Emergency Power. In September the J.G.R.W.U. served demands on the Railway, which management refused to entertain. The dispute was referred to the Labour Adviser who refused to certify it on the grounds that the Union's administrative officers were not employees of the Railway. The Defence Order had stipulated that the Union's administrative affairs must be directed by officers who were themselves employees in the establishment or occupation represented. This was obviously out of keeping with the pattern of professional trade union leadership developed in Jamaica and the Railway Union promptly filed with the Supreme Court writs of mandamus and certiorari in which it sought to establish that Government was wrong in withholding certification of the dispute and in refusing recognition to the Union. Richards acted quickly, however, to invalidate the proceedings and on 22nd October, proclaimed the Authorized Associations (Government Departments) (Defence) Regulations which declared that a union in a Government Department which had non-employees among its members or officers should not be an authorized association. Succeeding orders likewise invalidated by 31st October the trade union status of the fledgling Public Works Employees Union and the Postal and Telegraph Workers Union. Finally came the interning of the four H's. Richards' high-handed actions proved, however, to be an aberration for on 20th November 1942 under direction from the British Government he revoked the Authorized Associations Regulations, and subordinate employees were restored the right to organize under leaders of their own choosing.

In his attempt to deny representational and bargaining rights to the T.U.C. affiliates under their professional leadership, Richards had shown that he was prepared not only to interfere with the internal structure and government of the unions, but also with the due processes of law. His high-handed action did much to foster a sense of Jamaican identity and nationalism. Middle-class Jamaicans and professionals of diverse social and political outlook joined in denouncing Richards' escalating encroachment on civil liberties. In December 1942, he was summoned to London for talks on constitutional changes, but he had already made his views known on this subject: "The great majority of the Jamaicans do not want self-government and do not think themselves capable of coping with (governmental) problems." By January 1943, however, a delegation of four Members of the Legislative Council (three elected and one nominated) and one Member at large, Norman Manley, had been chosen to go to London to represent Jamaica concerning the new constitution. Alexander Bustamante felt himself slighted at not being included in the delegation. He protested by telegram to Richards' stand-in that "all Elected Members combined don't represent even 5 per cent population nor views. If going to England to represent political, economical, will have public manifestation, cost what it cost. Manley represents lost, minute, negligible minority. Libel on Jamaica electives represent majority views country." The smell of politics was in the air. Alexander Bustamante was merely serving notice that he was not to be taken for granted. In July 1943 he formally launched the Jamaica Labour Party (J.L.P.). It was nothing more than a political label for the Bustamante Industrial Trade Union. The J.L.P., like the B.I.T.U., was Bustamante. The constitution, such as it was, gave to Bustamante the right to select and approve all candidates. The editor of a sympathetic weekly excused: "That at heart Bustamante has a great leaning to Dictators' principles none but a blatant fool or hypocrite would attempt to deny, but let us not forget that it is the people themselves who have helped to mould his disposition this way."

Bustamante's paternalism could also be justified: "We can see nothing fundamentally wrong if a people unable for the most part to do for themselves, delegate into the hands of a trusted leader of their choice the right of selecting their candidates for them."[12]

As far as workers were concerned there was no doubt as to Bustamante's moral authority. In Seaforth in the parish of St. Thomas, Norman Manley, who had successfully argued an appeal against conviction on behalf of forty-four sugar workers, was told nevertheless, that the next time he planned a P.N.P. meeting for Seaforth he must bring "Daddy" Bustamante, or receive a passport from him before attempting to penetrate the Apostolic Parish of St. Thomas, Parish of George William Gordon, Paul Bogle, Alexander Bedward and now a "Moses Bustamante" citadel.

On Monday, 20th November 1944, Sir John Huggins, Richards'

successor as Governor, proclaimed a new constitution for Jamaica and set 14th December as the date for the General Election. In the meanwhile, to avoid any possibility of being disqualified because of having been nominated as a candidate under a name not legally his own, Bustamante legally confirmed his name-change by deed poll.

The Constitutional Charter called for a two-tiered House of Assembly, an Executive Council, reserve or paramount power in the hands of the Governor, political equality of women and an initial five-year operative period for the Constitution. The Lower House or House of Representatives was to be comprised of at least twenty-four Members elected by universal adult suffrage. In fact, thirty-two constituencies were proclaimed for the General Election. The Upper House or Legislative Council boasted fifteen nominated Members. The Executive Council as "the principal instrument of Government" was to be comprised of ten Members, five of whom were destined to come from the Lower House. The five elected Members would also be Chairmen of the Committees of the Lower House — in effect, quasi-Ministers. The Governor, in the exercise of paramount power, could assent to Bills approved by the Executive Council but which may not have been passed by the Houses of the Legislature.

On the surface, the election appeared to be a straight contest between the P.N.P. and the Jamaica Democratic Party (J.D.P.), a businessmen's party formed in March 1943. The latter's platform of free enterprise was opposed to the P.N.P.'s espousal of socialism. There was little news of or reference to the campaign activities of the Jamaica Labour Party. This was understandable for the programme of the J.L.P. was in effect the programme of the B.I.T.U. Similarly, its organizational base was the network of the union officials located throughout the island. There was no need therefore for Bustamante to sell his platform. He derived his legitimacy from his personal charisma. He did, however, denounce the socialism of the P.N.P. as expropriatory and atheistic. In so doing he made no distinction between revolutionary communism and socialism. To the land-conscious peasant whose plot of land symbolized his status of independence and remove from slavery, it was frightening to be told that a socialist government might require him to divide and share the little he had. Bustamante also denounced self-government as "brown man" (middle-class) government, and a return to slavery. When the smoke had cleared away from the hustings, Alexander Bustamante and the J.L.P. had captured twenty-three of the twenty-nine seats contested and all but nine of the available seats. The P.N.P. had been all but annihilated, winning but four of the nineteen seats it had contested. Norman Manley failed to win his seat. The remaining five seats were held by Independents. Alexander Bustamante's party received 41 per cent of the popular vote, Independents 30 per cent, the P.N.P. 23 per cent and the J.D.P. 4 per cent.

The political victory of the B.I.T.U., for such it really was, ushered in the era of political unionism. Alexander Bustamante had added another dimension to the character of unionsim in the underdeveloped country. To the characteristic features of middle-class (non-manual) leadership, strongly oriented to the cult of the personality, blanket-type organizational structure with accompanying high incidence of non-payment of dues, was added direct involvement of unions in politics and fusion or inter-locking of union and party.[13]

This should not be taken to mean that trade unions in the industrially advanced countries did not involve themselves in politics. Far from that, the tradition of involvement in politics, and radical left-wing politics at that, is as old as unionism itself. The difference was that in the industrially advanced countries, because trade unions were working-class institutions created and led by workers themselves, trade unionists insisted on retaining their independence from the political parties to which they might be affiliated, so that they could be free to pursue whatever action they deemed necessary in furtherance or protection of their primary sectional interests. Thus the trade unions and political parties developed as parallel yet distinct movements. What is more, their respective purposes could be clearly differentiated. The political party is interested in capturing political office and this requires mass support. The trade union provides an easy way of mobilizing a large number of votes behind the party's platform. It is a means to an end, not an end in itself. In the event of conflict between union and party the party would expect the unions to sacrifice their interests to ensure a party victory.

The trade union on the other hand is basically interested in political parties for the sake of union objectives. It finds that certain economic objectives may be more readily achieved through legislation, especially where social or legal barriers make union action on the industrial front ineffective or difficult. But the readiness to support a political organization which promises to enact legislation favourable to labour does not deny the independent objectives which are to be pursued on the industrial front through collective bargaining. On the other hand, in the Jamaican situation, when Alexander Bustamante formed the government, there was no question but that trade union or labour objectives predominated. It was not a question of the Jamaica Labour Party politicizing the trade union movement and providing a programme and ideology appropriate for the working classes and their movement. On the contrary, the Jamaica Labour Party became the vehicle for expressing and translating into political programmes and into governmental policies a social and political philosophy of the B.I.T.U. which was essentially that of a traditionalist and conservative labour force.

The strength of the Bustamante Industrial Trade Union lay in the fact that it provided institutional security and focus for workers who were still affected by the remaining vestiges of the slave-manned plantation of the nineteenth century and the increasingly rationalized administration of the modern twentieth-century sugar estate. In spite of Emancipation, the discontinuance of the indentured workers system and the shift from status to contract, wage relationship remained relatively undifferentiated for the majority of Jamaican sugar workers until the 1930's. To the permanent estate workers, the landless proletariat and the indentured Indian, the estate was a complete community towards which his allegiance must be directed, with a hierarchy of authorities who exercised over him a control much more exhaustive than that of police or law courts and within which, so long as he obeyed its rules, he was secure.

The changes in the 1920's and 1930's endangered the stability of these relationships. Difficulties were cumulative: falling sugar prices; closing down of overseas opportunities; the spread of familiarity with new political ideals, a large part of which could be attributed to returning migrants; and steadily increasing population pressures. The unavailability of new agricultural land for peasant cultivation was another factor though limited in operation.

But the end result was that more and more of the working population were thrown outside the operation of the social system which had traditionally governed their relationships. The "disorderly" type of West Indian and Jamaican unionism started among these unskilled labourers displaced from the social system and left to roam as migrants or crowd into the cities. Among waterfront labourers and skilled urban workers, long adjusted to the "atomization" of city life, a more orderly type of unionism was observable. The early longshoremen's unions founded in 1918 and during the 1920's certainly were closer in approach and philosophy to unionsim in the advanced countries.

The changes which had led to the gradual disintegration of the estate and plantation community affected the workers in a number of ways.[14] Firstly, they affected his economic status, diminishing his income and regularity of employment. Secondly, they affected him emotionally, because the state of proletarianization into which he was thrown was an offence against the social ideals he had been accustomed to entertain — society appeared to have wronged him. Finally, the conceivable remedies as far as the worker was concerned — some form of social security — relief work — better social services — were matters for governmental action and were unwelcome to the existing government. Hence the worker was forced to contemplate political agitation and action.

Only the first problem would be the direct concern of trade unions, and the third might be entertained so far as it was necessary to provide the legal basis for industrial action but not for the kind of general social change which the Jamaican situation called for. The second problem, the emotional, would not properly be the formal concern of a conventional type union. This is where Bustamante made his contribution in providing a unionism which assumed this additional function. He used abrupt and forceful language to employers which workers understood and approved of. For on the sugar estate it had been as important for the worker to manifest respect, as for him to work efficiently. A strike might meet resistance from an employer not because wage concessions would cause him economic embarrassment, but because it involved lack of respect for workers to have to bargain for what they should, by traditional way of thinking, have sought by deference. Bustamante changed all this. The sugar worker could now make vocal his protest to his overseer in a way in which he never could before. "Busta" was there to defend him by shutting down the estate if necessary. It took nearly a decade for employers to get over the shock of Alexander Bustamante, for he was prepared to meet high-handed action with high-handed action.

The victory of the Jamaica Labour Party and the B.I.T.U., therefore, was not just a personal vindication of Alexander Bustamante. It was also the victory of black working-class Jamaicans. They were given a feeling of self-respect and self-assurance that could have come in no other way.

The mass support of the B.I.T.U. made it possible for the Jamaica Labour Party to emerge as a genuine conservative or Tory Party akin to the British Conservatives. The twenty-three winning J.L.P. candidates were a representative cross-section of Jamaican society. There were six active trade unionists, thus giving substance to Bustamante's boast that he would put the common man in the seats of government. Through the B.I.T.U. and the J.L.P. the working-class man could hope to be socially and politically mobile. The six businessmen elected could be said to represent the other element in the labour-capital partnership and reflected Bustamante's free enterprise orientation as a businessman. The remaining Members elected included four school masters, two farmers, two lawyers, two ministers of the gospel and one electro-dermatologist.

The 1944 election, therefore, reflected clearly the contradictions inhering in colonial Jamaican society. It saw the exploited, politically aroused and newly enfranchised black agro-proletariat, joining with the white plantocracy and employing classes which had traditionally exploited them, to give electoral support to Bustamante and the B.I.T.U./J.L.P. in preference to Norman Manley and the P.N.P. — which was seen as the party of the urbanized middle classes espousing radical change and threatening traditional values and the established order of things.

For the black masses it was a question of voting for the nominee of the man who was a trusted friend, who understood their needs, had been willing to stand-up for them and who could be expected to look after them and promote their welfare. For the white plantocracy and the propertied black and coloured middle classes, Bustamante the agitator and rabble-rouser was still to be preferred as the lesser of two evils, to Manley, the exponent of "expropriatory" socialism.

In espousing a political and social philosophy of conservatism the B.I.T.U./J.L.P. provided one departure from the model of political unionism which characteristically saw the association of radical ideology (usually Marxian) with trade unionism in ex-colonial and developing countries. This flavour was provided in Jamaica, nonetheless, by the T.U.C. unions, initially also urban-based, which came to constitute the rival union bloc providing the P.N.P. with its mass support. For given the election results, there could be no ambiguity as to what the future role of the T.U.C. should be. Given the antagonism of the white and economic elites and fragmentation of the middle classes on the issue of socialism, the only hope for the P.N.P. lay in fragmenting Bustamante's overwhelming support among the working classes. Thus was the basis laid for the emergence of the two-party political system in Jamaica.

5

TUTELAGE IN POLITICS AND NATION-BUILDING

"**M**any countries have had the misfortune to throw up unworthy leaders. Jamaica was fortunate in throwing up among its leaders one man, Sir Alexander, who gave confidence to the masses of the people of this country, who won their affection and love to the most extraordinary degree, and their loyalty, and who proved afterwards by the whole course of his life that he had accepted the responsibilities of that time, and grown in stature with them as the years passed. And in considering Sir Alexander's rightful claims to the growth of democracy in Jamaica, I think it is the first thing that ought to be said.

"And then there came the time, Mr. Speaker, when Sir Alexander made what history may come to record as his greatest contribution to democracy in Jamaica, and that was the formation and creation — for it really was an act of creation — of the Jamaica Labour Party, which had led to the establishment of the two-party system in Jamaica.

" . . . Mr. Speaker, I have spoken with complete sincerity about what happens to a country after trouble when it throws up leaders. In the case of Sir Alexander I record the fact that this man, who was, I think, originally by nature and temperament autocratic, had very strong and firm opinions of his own, and was able to face the fact that, having said 'let there be a party and there was a party', it had to become an organized body. . . ." Thus said Norman Manley in paying tribute to Sir Alexander Bustamante in the House of Representatives on 26th February 1968, consequent upon the latter's retirement from active politics.

The story of Alexander Bustamante after 1945 is indeed the story of Jamaica growing up, for when he came to power in December 1944 and ushered in the era of political unionism, "he incarnated the counter-vailing forces that inhered in a society manifesting all the contradictions of the Colonial connection."[1] What were these countervailing forces and contradictions? The adult population of Jamaica were voting for the first time under universal adult suffrage to choose the political leaders who would manage their affairs within a constitutional framework

94

that offered partial self-government. The extension of the franchise had been won because of the insistent advocacy of Norman Manley and the P.N.P., in spite of the fact that Manley had been warned by Governor Richards and others in his own party that the chances of victory for the P.N.P. at the polls might be diminished rather than enhanced by the extension of popular franchise. Norman Manley had been quite prepared to take that risk. For he was well aware that the ideas which lay at the basis of the nationalist movement — self-government, democracy, and social reconstruction of society — would not be accepted without a struggle. "It is not in the first instance a struggle against an external adversary; it is a struggle with ourselves, with our mental lethargy, with the inertias of our historical background."[2] Manley's persistence in his demand for universal adult suffrage reflected, therefore, his abiding faith in the capacity of the masses and people of Jamaica to ultimately take complete control of their own destiny and affairs. But although the proven friend of labour, Norman Manley was also the leader of a political party which derived its organizational support mainly from the urban middle classes — a party which espoused new and radical doctrines, which threatened traditional ideas and the traditional order of things.

Deprived of its grass-roots connection by the defection of Alexander Bustamante and the B.I.T.U., the P.N.P. could not establish its credibility with the masses as the organization to bridge the gap between the classes in Jamaican society. Alexander Bustamante, on the other hand, grasped how profound the cleavage was between the social classes in Jamaica and the distrust which the black working classes and peasants had for the condescending brown middle classes. The two Jamaicas lived in worlds apart, separated not alone by race and colour and associated economic status, but by differences that "involved widely different acceptances and rejections of values, that involved different interpretations of reality, that involved the use of identical words to express different concepts and understandings".[3]

Alexander Bustamante drew, then, on deep-seated fears and suspicions (which he also may have shared) when he alleged that a victory for the independence party would mean "brown man" (middle-class) government and continuing enslavement of the masses. The masses chose to accept the word of — and to vote for — the man who had led them on protest marches, had suffered imprisonment on their behalf, and had organized and led them to seek improvements in material well-being through a union which was in many respects recognizable and meaningful as a

95

working-class institution. For after his purge of the B.I.T.U. caretaker administration in 1942, Bustamante had embarked upon a phase of vigorous expansion and collective bargaining. By 3rd March 1943, membership had risen to 28,762 (15,498 paying), representing an increase of 8,150 over the previous year and, in total, about 88 per cent of the organized labour force. A year later, B.I.T.U. membership was reported to be 37,113 (23,868 paying), reflecting another annual increase of 8,350 new members. Membership was still rising rapidly when the General Election was fought in December 1944, for three months later the B.I.T.U. returned a membership of 46,538 (29,930 paying) and representing this time 85 per cent of the island's total trade union membership of 55,072.

Bustamante had continued also his policy of appointing as branch secretaries, chief delegates and organizers in the field men and women who were members of, or readily identifiable with, the lower middle and working classes. The promise of better wages and working conditions (rather than the promise of self-government) was in accord with the temper as well as expectations of the masses. Indeed they had demonstrated in 1938 that accommodation, and not overthrow of the existing political system, was what they wanted. The promise of self-government or middle-class government as Bustamante interpreted it, and with it the implication of the eventual withdrawal of the protective arm of a paternal British Monarch, was calculated then to evoke fear rather than challenge. Norman Manley could envision that it was only by building up the independence of spirit and self-reliance of the people that great efforts could be obtained out of them, and "that the people must consciously believe in themselves and their own destiny and must do so with pride and confidence and with the determination to win equality with the rest of mankind — an equality in terms of humanity which, irrespective of power and wealth, can be measured by the growing values of civilisation and culture".[4] The reality of the Jamaican experience, however, was that the masses ever since 1865, had come to view the British Crown as their protector against the plantocracy and the black and coloured middle classes. Thus, the call for self-government ran counter to the condition of psychological dependence prevailing not just among the masses, but in fact among all classes of society. "The Empire and British rule rests on a carefully nurtured sense of inferiority in the governed."[5]

Generations of Jamaicans had been taught about the rise, the fortunes and the greatness of a mother country presiding over an empire on which the sun never set. They had been taught a lot about great men and great events of other countries. In the history of their own homeland they could find nothing but a past of enslavement and shame. That past had attempted to destroy the influence of ancestral Africa which had given to the mass of the population their race and colour. Yet the reality of race and colour was something that was not allowed to enter into polite conversation. The conditioning of Jamaicans of all classes to the acceptance of external domination and the superiority of the rulers was as unrelenting as it was subtle. The pageantry which surrounded the arrival of Governors on the island, the resplendent tours with high ceremony through the country undertaken by ceremonially plumed and bedecked Governors, all were designed to impress the "natives" with the grandeur of the ruler from afar. The Jamaican community which welcomed the Governor was one "where white men were social aristocrats merely by token of their skin colour and where his [the Governor's] official position gave him an importance unrelated to any personal merit . . . [in] a local white society whose members were eager to welcome him as their ceremonial head and their most prominent social exhibit".[6]

In spite of the fact that he left for the first time when he was twenty-one and was overseas for most of twenty-nine years, Alexander Bustamante shared the strong attachment of the Jamaican working classes to the British Monarchy. Giving evidence before the West India Royal Commission in November 1938, he could proclaim, "I am very glad we are a colony of Great Britain." Admittedly this did not deter him from castigating the Colonial administration in Jamaica. On this same occasion, the editor of *The Jamaica Standard* was led to conclude, "Although Bustamante spent his youth in Spain, a period in Cuba, and a profitable period in the United States, in no other place than the British Empire could he find his place and survive. In other countries not a thousand miles from Jamaica, he would either have become a dictator following upon revolution or else a victim of early assassination. Bustamante senses this in himself. That is why although he declares himself republican he also declares his loyalty to the Empire and to the Throne. Such a contradiction in political beliefs is possible only within the British Empire." It is quite possible that Bustamante's travels and sojourns in Latin American republics may have served to deepen his respect for British political institutions and traditions. But at the same time no one could ever accuse Alexander Bustamante of suffering from an inferiority complex. This does not mean that he was not conscious of his own lack of formal education and of his limited political and administrative experience. But both these deficiencies, if they could be regarded as

97

such, were more than compensated for by his vast common sense, an incredible memory, the ability to learn from his opponents and a quick adaptability. When, however, it came to dealing with the agro-proletariat whom he represented, Alexander Bustamante was very much alive to the "colonial condition" or "dependence syndrome" of the Jamaican labourer and peasant. It was the source of both his strength and his political concern. For the overwhelming majority of his followers were illiterate, superstitious and deeply religious. They had learned to depend on others to make decisions for them and to respect the authority of those in command. Nor was the dependence psychology any less for those who had received a modicum of education, for the purpose of that education would have been to inculcate the values of submission to superiors and to God. Furthermore, the educational system was but one of a set of systems and institutions, administrative, social and familial, which, according to the weight of sociological opinion, tended to produce authoritarian personalities.

Alexander Bustamante's autocratic temperament fitted in, therefore, with the tradition of authoritarianism in a colonial society. His authoritarianism, however, was tempered by his deep compassion for the labouring classes and his commitment not only to improve their economic lot but to make their voice heard in the determination of public affairs. As he himself began his tutelage in politics and public administration, so Alexander Bustamante felt a corresponding responsibility towards the workers and peasants at large. Paternalism was the characteristic quality, therefore, of his early leadership at the political as well as the trade union level. In the House of Representatives, his colleagues were urged to speak their minds provided they were not too pointed in their criticisms of the Government, at least to the extent that, as Leader of the Majority Party, he had to identify himself with the Government. For this was an identity he was not always willing to accept.

In March 1946, the House of Representatives was engaged in discussion of a Ten-Year Plan for Jamaica which had been prepared by a committee of nine, including Bustamante and his four quasi-Ministers. The Plan was inspired by Whitehall to facilitate the allocation of Colonial Development and Welfare (C.D.&W.) grants to the colonies under the C.D.&W. Acts of 1940 and 1945. The grants, which were instituted on the recommendation of the West India (Moyne) Royal Commission, were intended to promote "the development of the resources of the colonies and the welfare of their peoples". The Ten-Year Plan followed on the heels of two reports which launched a debate — which is still continuing — as to the main strategies which Jamaica should adopt in order to accelerate economic development and growth and thus make possible higher living standards for all.

The Economic Policy Report, the work of an Economic Policy Committee appointed in 1943, confirmed that there was serious unemployment and underemployment and that agriculture was crude, unattractive and precarious for those engaged in it. The Committee were pessimistic about the prospects for industrialization and looked to improvements in agriculture and the tourist trade for such economic progress as could be made. The essential elements of an Economic Policy for Jamaica, therefore, were reorganization of the agriculture economy, withdrawal of surplus peasant population into secondary and tertiary industries and a limited programme of industrialization based on the colony's resources. The Report also acknowledged that in the development of an underdeveloped country, the state has an active part to play which may necessitate a radical overhaul of its administrative machinery; that heavy expenditure would have to be made to raise the educational status and physical efficiency of the mass of the population; and that reckless population increase would limit the effectiveness of any economic policy.

The second Report — that of the Agricultural Policy Committee — stressed agricultural extension and social welfare and saw little or no future for economic development through industrialization. Five years later, writing on "The Industrialization of the British West Indies", Professor Arthur Lewis was severely critical of the Economic Policy Committee's Report for posing an either-or choice between agriculture and industry as far as development strategy was concerned. The major obstacle as he saw it was the *laissez-faire* philosophy of British West Indian administration.

Back in March 1946, however, the P.N.P. parliamentary Opposition took the position that the Ten-Year Plan was not a developmental plan in the accepted sense, but rather a project for budget expansion along normal lines of certain unexpended funds accruing from Colonial Development and Welfare Schemes and other accepted budgetary expenditures. As such, the Ten-Year Plan had no stated goals and set no targets.

Bustamante as a member of the Ten-Year Plan Committee acknowledged that the Plan was far from perfect and insinuated that there were things that he would have liked to have had inserted. This did not prevent him, however, from claiming credit for whatever was praiseworthy in the Plan. As he saw it, there was room for constructive criticism, although "anybody can criticize but not anybody can criticize constructively and that goes for the members of my party and the members of any other party."[7] He was the benevolent schoolmaster, continually reprimanding his colleagues in the House of Representatives, and presumably schooling them in the intricacies of government and administration.

He complained, "These Members [i.e., J.L.P. Members of the House of Representatives who were questioning the bona fides of a Relief Works programme] seem to believe that they do not form a part of this government and that they have no duty whatever to make suggestions. They are here, they seem to think, to make themselves ridiculous; and those are the same members who generally tantalize me with telegrams to have something done in their parishes . . . and the only thing they ever have to suggest is that roads be worked, for they are essential." Faced, therefore, with complaints from Opposition M.H.R.'s that their constituencies were being penalized by Government, as well as importunings from his own party colleagues seeking a better deal for their constituencies, Bustamante adopted the posture of benevolent chieftain or patriarch sharing a concern for all Jamaica. "I make recommendations as I think best in the interest of the country and not just in one place." Yet there could be no doubt that for Alexander Bustamante "interest of the country" meant primarily the interests of the majority of the black labouring population. Politics for him, certainly at that time, could only mean the exercise of political power to give effect to working-class interests, interests which in the first instance were articulated through, and represented by, trade union activity. It could mean nothing else, for the only politics that he knew came from involvement in trade unionism and had carried him from the bargaining table into the inner circles of government. The placing of working-class interests at the centre of political activity thus became Bustamante's preoccupation. Nor was it necessary to speculate as to what these interests might be or how they might be distilled. Institutionally, they were embodied in, and given expression by, the Bustamante Industrial Trade Union which received the bulk of its support and strength from strongly traditionalist sugar and agricultural workers in the sugar and banana belts.

Alexander Bustamante's paternalism was consistent not only with the traditional expectations and emotional needs of the agro-proletariat he represented but also with his thoroughgoing conservatism in the economic and political spheres. For Alexander Bustamante was a labour leader in spite of being a businessman, and nowhere was his businessman's philosophy more evident than in his approach and attitudes to government and public administration. Undoubtedly influenced by nineteenth-century folklore of business management, he began on the premise that public bureaucracy meant waste and inefficiency. To the extent also that the upper and middle echelons of the Civil Service were drawn almost exclusively from the middle classes, which he regarded as the natural enemies of the working classes in Jamaica, Bustamante's preoccupations as a businessman were reinforced by his pronounced antipathy towards the middle classes. He remained convinced for a long time that he could not expect whole-hearted cooperation from middle-class bureaucrats and that they would attempt to sabotage his party's administration. In his maiden budget speech in 1945 his orientation and fears were made quite explicit. "Everybody in the Government Service now is an officer — no clerks again. This is a government of officers; a government of generals. . . .

"We have too many officers doing the work, more than it was intended to have. The Director of a Department wants a Deputy Director to do the work that he is entitled to do. Then he wants a principal clerk. If he has not got an administrative assistant it is a crime. Bustamante is a bad man: I know that many heads of Departments are against me. But what do I care? When they see me they must smile . . . Well, they said when Rome burns Nero plays and Rome is burning. That is one of the curses in the country. The unnecessary excessive expenditure in the Government Departments."

Incidentally, in attacking the Civil Service, Bustamante was taking on the most entrenched bastion of colonialism and British imperialism. Conditioned by education, training and social values to look to England, the mother country, and to give loyalty, allegiance and service to that most sacrosanct of persons, the British or Colonial Administrator, Jamaican civil servants could not have viewed but with misgiving and foreboding the prospect of even partial administrative oversight by elected representatives of the people as quasi-Ministers. It is no accident that so many of the former British colonies, including Jamaica, have found it very difficult to transform colonial bureaucratic administrations into dynamic and modern systems more appropriate to the needs of developing economies and emergent nations. For, while native anglophiles will concede that the British endowed race, colour and class discrimination along with the Empire, they are prompt to point out that the British colonies were also endowed with sound public administrations. Against this colonial administrative mythology Alexander Bustamante juxtaposed the equally dubious folklore of private enterprise: that business administration is always — presumptively — more efficient (however defined) than public administration. Nevertheless, Bustamante used his skepticism of the efficacy of bureaucracy to seize a psychological advantage for the newly elected and inexperienced political administrators, including himself. The bureaucrats, not the politicians, were usurpers and parasites. "Every office in this country — Government office — is overstaffed except this office which is over our heads." He knew then that his personal triumph, as well as the electoral victory of the B.I.T.U./J.L.P., would be viewed not just with foreboding, but with distaste. To predominantly middle-class civil servants, the triumph of the J.L.P. was seen as the triumph of illiteracy and ignorance over education and intelligence. For another thing, Alexander Bustamante came with the occupational background of business, by itself a sufficiently disreputable form of activity, to say nothing of the added disrepute of being a money-lender. For coloured and black Jamaicans of all classes, the first choice of career for income as well as status considerations lay with the liberal professions, or failing that, with the Civil Service. The private sector remained as the last resort for the "black sheep" of the family or those who could not make the grade otherwise. The business of engaging in trade for profit could be left, as Aristotle said, "to lesser mortals" — in this case to the latecomers to Jamaican society, such as the Chinese, Syrians, Lebanese and East Indians, as well as the Jews.

The central or organizing principle of governmental activity for Bustamante and his Ministers-in-embryo during the first five years in "office" (and to a slightly lesser extent during the second electoral term also) was proper (orthodox) financial and fiscal administration. Indeed it can be said that the major policy of Bustamante and the J.L.P. was to achieve fiscal respectability as a precondition for raising living standards. It was only as the confidence of foreign investors could be won, that badly needed foreign capital would be attracted.

At the same time, in his first budget speech, Bustamante showed great sensitivity to Opposition criticism, sustained for at least a decade, that his party had no coherent social and economic philosophy other than what flowed from his "business unionism", that is, a unionism which saw capital and labour jointly sharing the gains of economic activity, within the framework of a capitalistic economy and on a basis of joint determination through collective bargaining. "Time and time again the question was asked in the Honourable House: What is the policy of the Jamaica Labour Party?

"The policy of the Jamaica Labour Party is to work honestly, faithfully and sincerely to *bereft ourselves of the bankruptcy* we have taken over in the Jamaica Government, *so that we can get this country in a healthy financial position.*" This was necessary to create confidence of investors overseas. "We want them to invest so that they can make a fair percentage of profit upon their capital." Each time that he enunciated a specific policy objective — whether it was "to improve this country and to raise the standard of the people"; or "to make medical, educational and other conditions in this country better"; or "to get lands and to place in the hands of the people not just rock-stones"; or "to create industries in this country" — the Majority Party Leader repeated his essential and overriding priority "to put the island in a healthy financial position".[8] It would be a mistake, however, to conclude that Alexander Bustamante was completely carried away by the false parallel or analogy between financial responsibility of the businessman or firm and that of the state, although even here he could be excused for holding to an approach which had behind it the intellectual authority of classical and neo-classical economic theory, as well as the commonsense and everyday experience of countless men of affairs. The fact of the matter is that while Bustamante could not boast of formal schooling in economics, he could draw on common-sense experience. He was guided by pragmatism and realism which was made very evident in his approach to the problem of unemployment. "Now so as to get this country in a fair financial condition, so as to reduce unemployment. I use the word reduce unemployment for let no one deceive you that every man and woman in this country can have full work. It has never been done — it cannot be done — it will never be done even though every one wants it. Even as we sit here and say that we want full employment for every man we shall not see it in this House and our children will not see it. The most that we can do is to reduce unemployment considerably."[9] However, what really lay behind his preoccupation with sound (conventional) financial administration and fiscal solvency, and what reinforced his commitment to gradual and piecemeal social and economic progress, was his fundamental concern to prove to "well-thinking" people at home and abroad "that a Labour Government is capable of administering the Government, because it was once thought that Labour could only hold a pick and a shovel". The working classes and their leader, Alexander Bustamante, were on trial and Bustamante was determined that they should pass the test. "And then they will finally say: Did I not tell you that Labour couldn't run the Government? Did I not tell you that Labour has no brains? Did I not tell you that the people of this country had made a mistake in putting Labour in power? They will never say that though. We, the Majority Party, will take good care that this country is not placed into bankruptcy by those who would like to see the Constitution disappear."

Bustamante's gradualism or piecemeal welfarism during this period carried forward without interruption, therefore, the colonial policy of "tutelage" of subject or native peoples, with its promise that, hopefully, in the not too distant future, it would issue in a form of partnership which would recognize "a more nearly equal" relationship. At the same time, however, Bustamante was impelled by his own egocentrism as well as by the expectations of the psychologically dependent and worshipful black masses, seeking both dignity and a modicum of material comfort, to attack the colonial administration: "What this Labour Party shall endeavour to do, shall use every effort to do, is to reduce poverty in this country and the conditions and circumstances that cause such dire poverty, not alone in one parish but in every parish in the country, which is a reflection against democracy — a terrible reflection against the imperialistic system. It is true — democracy does not exist in Jamaica, has never existed, and I am a man as loyal as anybody to this country. I am not going to try and conceal my feelings or stifle my words. Much has been said about democracy, but if this was a democratic country, or if England was a democratic country, in truth and fact, the conditions that now exist in this country would never have existed. I am not of those who say 'Down with England,' but I say 'Down with poverty.' It may be said that I am a very temperamental person and that I am not a parliamentary person, but parliamentarians are a pack of hypocrites. If there was democracy in this country there could not have been the poverty which now exists in this country. We should not blame the past legislators alone. They were good and bad. It is a system that has been handed down to us from the time Queen Victoria helped to liberate our forefathers from slavery.

"A few live on the hills — they do not work but they live — while thousands work and starve. These are the conditions which have brought about this poverty. Sometimes I feel England should be ashamed to say she owns Jamaica. She should be ashamed at times to say she is fighting for democracy for other countries while we starve."[10]

His attack on the colonial administration projected an image of Bustamante as a radical critic and opponent of imperialism and colonialism, but his radicalism was manifest at the verbal and emotional levels only. As far as the black masses were concerned, however, Bustamante's assertion, as an off-white Jamaican, that he would become Governor of Jamaica, struck a much more responsive chord and gave more satisfaction than Norman Manley's politically much more radical call for constitutional advance which would give Jamaica an early start on the march towards self-government and political independence.

Bustamante's concern, however, was much more immediate. Labour had achieved political power unexpectedly and what was needed was time — time to develop expertise, to acquire confidence and, most important of all, to consolidate power. It made sense to him, therefore, to oppose self-government as an immediate or even short-run goal for Jamaica. In that insightful first budget speech in 1945 he stated clearly: "I oppose immediate self-government and I oppose more so those who are clamouring for self-government now." Of course, Alexander Bustamante, with whom almost all things were possible, as far as his followers were concerned, could hardly admit to the need for a period of tutelage, and so he explained the "why" in more polemical terms. "The reply is this. Most are atheists who do not believe in God." Furthermore, "Most are persons who believe or try to lead people to believe that if they get self-government they would be able to go to the man who had a property with ten cows, giving five to the self-governing sea-cow who is lazy and won't work."[11]

If the political strategies of Bustamante and the J.L.P. seemed crude and simplistic, and possibly even absurd, they were nevertheless effective. He was concerned in 1944 and after, not with creating a national consciousness, but with exploiting the potential of universal adult suffrage and acquiring political power. He had joined in battle with the P.N.P., but on what grounds was he going to fight them? On what issues were they most vulnerable? As the political arm of the B.I.T.U., the J.L.P. could claim to be a workers' party, promoting first the aims of organized workers and then, by extension, that of the working class at large. But the P.N.P. could also claim to be dedicated to the cause of labour and the working class.

As far as Norman Manley was concerned, the revolt of the labouring classes in 1938 had given birth to a single progressive movement with two arms — trade union and party — working in unison. That by 1942 the both arms were no longer swinging in unison did not alter the fact that there was a single progressive movement. Indeed in August 1945, Manley reaffirmed, "The time has come when the work for labour must be more closely harmonized with and coordinated with the work in the political field. It is not two progressive movements but one progressive movement, consisting of different classes of people and the foundation of its strength must be in the class at the bottom." The P.N.P. was committed then to the cause of the common man, a cause which included

105

his material, social and spiritual well-being. "It is perfectly true that the interests of all classes of people are bound together. But it is equally true that there is a common man in this country, whose interest must predominate above and beyond all other classes, because no man is democratic, no man is a sincere and honest democrat who does not accept the elementary principle that the object of civilization is to raise the standard of living and security of the masses of the people."[12] According to Manley, the best way to serve the cause of the masses, however, was to help them to help themselves, and to be masters of their own salvation. Essential to that salvation was the recognition that Jamaica had a destiny of its own, separate and distinct from that of any other country.

The people, however, must believe in themselves and their destiny and be able to develop a life of their own. This required that the common people as well as other classes in society must embark on the road to self-government — "a way of life" — which involved a national consciousness as well as cultural identity. In Manley's words, "Life is the growth and development of the common peoples, and real development of their own cultures, their own ways of thought, their methods of life, the impress they make upon the staff which they build as generations passed. That is the life of a country." By 1940, Manley and the P.N.P. had gone a step further and had concluded that fundamental changes in the economic and social structure of Jamaica would be necessary if all Jamaicans were to share meaningfully in the fruits of economic progress and be truly equal. These radical changes predicated the adoption of socialism as the ideology of the party. Having declared itself a radical left-wing party, the P.N.P. would have been obliged, if only on theoretical grounds, to make a special effort to attract labour support. For in left-wing systems of thought the working class, as the bearer of the dialectical forces of progress, has a key role in ushering in the new society.

As far as Manley and his P.N.P. associates were concerned, therefore, the labour movement was an integral part of the national progressive movement providing the operational link between the middle and the working classes. The intellectual and emotional link, on the other hand, would be provided by the common ideology of socialism. Because Manley and the P.N.P. could not be faulted in their commitment to serve the cause of labour, Bustamante, therefore, elected to fight the P.N.P. on the issue on which they were most vulnerable and one which they themselves had interjected, namely, ideology. Here again in characteristic fashion, Bustamante seized the initiative and showed himself a masterful tactician. Socialism was equated with communism, and communism meant tyranny and slavery. Besides, as the P.N.P. was also the party of the urban middle classes and was spearheading the self-government movement, a P.N.P. victory would mean tyranny and slavery by the middle classes, even as the protective arm of the British Crown was being withdrawn. By treating expropriation of property, especially of land, and godlessness as endemic evils of socialism/communism, Bustamante played upon the two most powerful influences operating in the consciousness of a traditionalist peasantry. In predicting dictatorship and loss of freedom he also drew upon the bitterest associations of the inglorious past. "God-lessness and atheism were unforgivable against a background of religiosity. The Jamaican countryside ... had been rehabilitated out of slavery partly with the help of Christian missionaries in the nineteenth century. Any creed that denied the existence of God would be unacceptable to a devout and Bible-minded people."[13]

When he equated socialism with communism and implied that a P.N.P. government in an independent Jamaica would result in dictator-ship, tyranny and godlessness, Alexander Bustamante obviously was seeking to make the most of a tactical advantage over his opponents, but what of the element of personal conviction? On the religious theme all that can be said is that throughout his entire public career Bustamante, by persuasion a Roman Catholic, showed a deep respect for the Church, as distinct from any particular denomination or sect, and acknowledged the importance of its role in providing spiritual and moral guidance for members of society.

On the ideology issue, however, Bustamante's assertion that P.N.P. and socialist rule would give rise to political dictatorship cannot be dismissed as being altogether political opportunism. Not that dictatorship *per se* would have been distasteful to Alexander Bustamante. For given his egocentrism and autocratic temperament such an eventuality could have been more readily envisaged under a Bustamante regime than a P.N.P. regime. The major constraint of course would have been the limited powers available to him under the 1944 Constitution. What Bustamante was decrying, therefore, was a dictatorship which would be exercised by a regime seemingly prepared to expropriate private property and establish public ownership of the means of production. But then, had Bustamante been given cause to believe that this was the real intention of the P.N.P. and the political route which the party intended to travel? After all, it must be remembered that Bustamante had been a member of the P.N.P. in 1938, and that as late as September 1940, in his dispute with the shipping companies over higher wages for Kingston's waterfront workers, he had been collaborating closely with Nethersole and his trade union opposites in the T.U.C.-affiliated unions who were prominent in the P.N.P. Indeed, Wills O. Isaacs, a leading member of the P.N.P., was with Bustamante on the public platform when he made the "blood-would-flow" speech which provided Governor Richards with the occasion to order his arrest and detention.

On the other hand, in fairness to Bustamante, it must be pointed out also that both before and after the May 1938 uprising, when he had been prepared to label himself (or to be labelled) a socialist or revolutionist, the P.N.P. had not declared itself a socialist party. It was over two years later, in September 1940 at the Party's Annual Conference, that Norman Manley made the declaration and spelled out what socialism would entail. While he reassured the party-faithfuls that they were not being committed to revolution or godlessness, Manley did insist, nevertheless, that socialism was not just a matter of higher wages and better living conditions for workers, but that "it involves the concept that all the means of production should in one form or other come to be publicly owned and publicly controlled." In defining socialism essentially in terms of public ownership of all the means of production, Norman Manley was putting forward the one definition consistent with the Marxian formulation of socialism, apologists for democratic socialism notwithstanding. Now, there is no *a priori* reason why socialism as a method of organizing economic activities (i.e., as an economic system) should not be compatible with democracy as a method of selecting political leaders and allowing for meaningful participation of the governed (i.e., as a system of government), or for that matter with any other political form of government. Admittedly (liberal) democracy and capitalism emerged historically, as concomitant and interrelated developments. But at the same time, there was the empirically valid and incontrovertible fact that all existing modern socialist regimes, beginning with the U.S.S.R., in which the means of production had been brought eventually under public ownership, had been established by violent revolution and had given rise to totalitarian dictatorships. However, these revolutionary regimes, identified with communism, were deemed by Manley to represent but one branch of socialism.

But was it reasonable to expect that a capitalistic economy, in which private ownership and private enterprise predominated, and in which economic and political power was shared with a capitalist class with an effective will to power and to resistance, could be transformed into a socialized economy within Manley's definition, without developing

108

and invoking a highly coercive power and apparatus? Now, Alexander Bustamante was not an avid reader and probably never read a serious work on politics in his entire life. He could hardly be expected, therefore, to appreciate the subtle differentiations between the variant forms of socialism. But on a purely "commonsense" approach, there need not be any inconsistency in equating the avowed socialism of the P.N.P. which, according to Norman Manley in September 1940, would involve public ownership and control not just of public utilities, but of all the means of production, with totalitarian communism. What is more, Manley went on to add that if socialism involved anything less than a demand for the complete change of the basic organization of the social and economic conditions under which Jamaicans lived, then it was something less than socialism. If, therefore, in 1944 as well as later, the P.N.P. became the victim of a "red smear" campaign and of Bustamante's political opportunism, Manley's own rhetoric must be taken into account as a contributory factor. But quite apart from considerations of electoral strategy, there can be no doubt that Alexander Bustamante's strong and abiding attachment to private enterprise and private initiative would have inclined him to be an uncompromising foe of communism. All things considered, however, it can be said that the stand taken by Bustamante against self-government and socialism did not stem as much from careful evaluation and deliberate rejection on his part of the changes which would ensue from a socialist regime, as from his appreciation that the surest route to power lay in exploiting the traditional values in Jamaican society.

In this lies the paradox and enigma of Alexander Bustamante. For given his tremendous personal hold and authority over the masses, he could have moulded and led them along the paths of modernization, human development and self-government much quicker than anyone else. But in so doing, he probably would have transformed or undermined the very bases of his authority and power. Alexander Bustamante allowed himself, therefore, to be moulded by the historical forces around him, without ever losing sight of his overriding objective of exercising and keeping political power. So long, therefore, as there were no compelling forces, Bustamante made no attempt to rationalize the structure or operation of his sprawling personal empire — the B.I.T.U./J.L.P. Moreover, springing directly as they did out of the emotional needs of workers at that time, the B.I.T.U./J.L.P. could afford to do as little systematic thinking and planning as a continuing organization need do.

Of course, one may ask whether Bustamanteism might not be seen and treated as a variant form of populism or agrarian radicalism which a number of countries at opposite and far reaches of the globe have undergone at particular stages of their social and economic development. There appears to be a natural urge, even compulsion, among social scientists, and academics in particular, to seek to establish universal principles and theoretical models into which social phenomena may be fitted for purposes of analysis and explanation, or to facilitate national and even international comparisons. Undoubtedly, such an approach may be useful in emphasizing the universality of certain human problems and challenges. A case in point was the delineation of the model of the "underdeveloped" countries in the post-World War II era by economists (for the most part trained in the industrially advanced countries) which saw the development and formulation of a substantial body of theory now characterized as developmental economics.

It soon became apparent, however, that the term "underdeveloped" (later changed to "developing") embraced countries at various and different stages of development or transformation of their economically backward economies, and that often vast differences in cultural and social heritage and values severely inhibited the uniform application of economic policies or technology, which may have been successful in other particular countries or regions.

Now stated in its simplest form, populism historically has been associated with political movements or political parties devoted primarily to the protection and advancement of agricultural interests. The desire for protection usually came to the fore when a rural class or classes felt threatened by the encroachment of urban interests upon some vital rural interest, whether it was absorption of the better lands by the wealthy, or the belief that the burden of taxation was lopsided, or that the monetary and credit systems were being manipulated to the disadvantage of rural interests.

Up to World War II, it was generally accepted that there were two main strands or brands of populism, one embodying the Russian experience of agrarian socialism or syndicalism, and revolutionary in temper, the other derived from the United States experience, and reformist in temper. In the United States the populist concern was not to reconstruct the economic system, but to put an end to exploitation of the masses and working people by financial interests and middle-men who were thought to be manipulating the monetary and credit systems to their own advantage. It may be noted also that agrarian radicalism emerged in both Russia and the United States in the nineteenth century even as both countries were being geared to embark on modernization and transformation of their economies within a framework of capitalism. In spite also of the very significant differences in the social, economic and political systems and structures obtaining in both countries, their respective populist movements seemingly shared a number of common elements and sentiments including: protest by the lower and working classes, particularly on the part of the rural classes; an attempt to reassert rural values (including religious values) in the face of rapid social and economic change and increasingly impersonalized market relationships; the tendency to idealize and glorify the simple rural way of life of a past golden era even as society was becoming more urbanized, complex and bewildering; a demand for more equitable sharing and distribution of income, and income earning opportunities, including ownership of land; an attempt to reduce intractable social and economic problems to manageable proportions by reducing them to a struggle between the innocent folk or the vast mass of working people — in town or country — and sinister powerful and vested interests, especially urban financial interests; and finally, the tendency for grievances of peasants and workers or the masses, generally, to be articulated and given an ideological flavour by intelligentsia or other elements who might not themselves be from the ranks of the masses.

The revolt of the Jamaican lower classes in 1938 and the emergence of political unionism, which was made possible by the crystallization of popular support behind Alexander Bustamante and the Bustamante Industrial Trade Union, can be treated as a variant of populism, however, only if populism is so broadly defined as to embrace all lower-class protest movements, rural as well as non-rural. To adopt such an approach, however, would be to deprive populism of the historical association which it has had with particular manifestations of agrarian radicalism. Nor would such a broad categorization take us any further in under-standing the depth and range of protest and reform movements which have arisen in the still considerable array of countries which can be regarded as having agrarian-based economies and are attempting to modernize their economies. Indeed, at a university-sponsored conference convened in London in 1967 specially for the purpose of discussing populism, scholars found it no easy task to reconcile the divisions of thought between those who conceived of populism as a strand within socialism and those who wished to extend the label to embrace many kinds of radicalism, including right-wing forms. Again, there were divisions between those who tended to identify populism as a peasant or rural phenomenon and

111

those who would extend it to embrace aspects of non-rural society. The end result was a definition which, according to one scholar, made populism sound like the "biggest growth industry — it led everywhere", and begged more questions than it answered.[14]

As far as the 1938 revolt of the lower-class Jamaican blacks and the ensuing rise of Bustamanteism are concerned, any semblances of populism must be regarded as purely incidental.

We have already noted that the Jamaican Emancipation of slaves and the creation of a society of legally free men gave rise to new wage and contractual relationships which remained undifferentiated in the minds of workers up to the 1930's. We have noted also that certain consequential adjustments in the operation and management of the sugar estate and plantation (piecemeal mechanization, some decasualization of the labour force, and the legal right of employers to disclaim responsibility for the welfare of superfluous hands, aged workers and dependents) threatened to endanger traditional expectations as more and more workers were thrown outside the system which had provided them with a measure of physical and emotional security.

But by no stretch of the imagination can it be said that the Jamaican economy had been launched on the road to industrialization or modernization. The structure of the plantation economy remained virtually intact. In many respects, Kingston, the capital city and centre of the island's trading and mercantile activity, was an extension of the plantation economy. Given the limited alternatives available to investment capital in Jamaica, the sharp clash of interests between commercial capitalism and industrial capitalism, so evident in the industrially advanced countries, did not arise in Jamaica. Nor could the black agro-proletariat in the rural towns or the urban proletariat in Kingston and environs, living in conditions of abject poverty on substandard wages and income, and the vast reservoir of the unemployed be said to be yearning for a more simple and traditional way of life, when the only past to which they could return was slavery.

Among the peasants, hunger for land was undoubtedly a factor contributing to social discontent, but it certainly was secondary to the demand for better wages and working conditions. The Jamaican upheaval was not, therefore, a manifestation of agrarian radicalism threatening to intensify the rural-urban dichotomy or to alter existing economic relationships. Rather it was a protest by the lower classes against poverty and the failure to industrialize and create new job opportunities.

Such was the depth of Alexander Bustamante's personal appeal that he was able to unite all segments of the labouring classes behind him, even where occupational differentiation provided room for conflict. Agrarian movements are often bracketed with labour movements in their various forms, but it is difficult to unite both movements, and they make an uneasy alliance or marriage. Thus in Jamaica, there has been continuing antagonism between small farmers, especially in cane, who for long remained ardent supporters of Bustamante and the J.L.P., and organized agricultural labourers traditionally represented by the B.I.T.U.[15] Faced with competition for labour from sugar estates and large plantations, as well as trade union pressures for higher wages and fringe benefits, small farmers have tended to regard trade unionism as being inimical to their interests. Of course, workers have not been unaware of the fact that, at best, the small farmers are able to offer intermittent employment only, and that even so, prompt payment of wages cannot always be guaranteed, given the precarious financial condition — or cash flow position — of many small farmers.

Nor could Alexander Bustamante be regarded as anti-capitalist. While he did fulminate against monopolies, especially when conceded by the state, he was a staunch supporter of free enterprise and a firm believer in orthodox financial administration, whether in the public sector or in the private and commercial banking sectors. He was anti-poverty, not anti-capitalist, as he took pains to make clear. Thus, while he realized that his main strength and support lay among farmers, peasants and workers in the rural areas, Alexander Bustamante — conservative businessman turned labour leader and politician — would not entertain any proposals for radical alteration or reconstruction of the Jamaican economy, even in the matter of redistribution of land to small settlers. There was no significant shift or expansion in the policy of acquisition and distribution of land to peasants which had been carried on by the Crown Colony administration. The fact is that Bustamante saw himself as representing all classes in Jamaica, but with special responsibilities towards the poor and deprived.

In view of what has been said, there would therefore be little point in regarding Bustamante as the leader of agrarian syndicalism or a populist movement in Jamaica.

The conversion of Alexander Bustamante to the cause of self-government and to modernization, including planned economic development and rational administration, had to await, therefore, the progressive development and compulsion of these ideas and forces in Jamaican society. The measure of compulsion was increasingly provided by the growing

113

strength and challenge of the combined P.N.P./T.U.C. Opposition. The role of the T.U.C. was critical, for at the same time that its leadership sought both to emulate and fragment Bustamante's popular grass-roots support, they carried out a highly successful programme of political education and ideological indoctrination of the masses. This was done effectively between 1945 and 1952, and the period must be regarded, therefore, as one of the most critical in Jamaica's modern history. For one thing, it witnessed an upsurge of violence, primarily at the political level up to 1947 and then predominantly at the trade union level up to 1951, unparalleled in the country's history. A decisive factor in this development was the ambiguity of the role of Alexander Bustamante who remained as President General and active leader of the B.I.T.U. at the same time that he was the Leader and elected Head of the Majority Party in a quasi-ministerial system.

In tackling the rather formidable assignment of breaking Bustamante's sway over the masses (organized and unorganized) the T.U.C. leaders enjoyed certain advantages as well as disadvantages. From its very inception, the Trades Union Council, the administrative umbrella for the non-Bustamante unions, had become the home of the left wing in Jamaican politics. The four H's (Hart, Henry, Frank and Ken Hill), as well as Nethersole and to a much lesser extent Florizel Glasspole, had from the very outset given an important place in their thinking to political action, not merely to meet the immediate needs of the Unions for legal protection and economic gains, but also to exert pressure for political advance through the P.N.P. and ultimately to recreate Jamaican society along socialist lines.

On the credit side, therefore, the T.U.C. leaders were motivated and sustained by an ideological fervour, which provided a will both to survive and to surmount. By training and temperament, also, the T.U.C. leaders attached considerable importance to formal organization and rational procedures for election and control of officers. They were, after all, mainly professionals, lawyers, journalists, accountants, small businessmen or white-collar employees. They were all very much aware of the nature of conventional labour organizations in Great Britain, as the choice of the name "T.U.C." implied. The calibre of membership also made possible a greater degree of rank and file participation. Finally, there was the common sharing of martyrdom (internment) with Bustamante by the four H's who had been interned in 1942 for four and a half months by Sir Arthur Richards. The T.U.C. was well equipped, therefore, to service the economic and political aspirations of rank and file. They had a com-

114

prehensive grasp of the political and social movements of the working classes and were in a sense the only ones equipped to bridge the gap between the inarticulate masses and the colonial administrators. In the context of the time, however, emotional needs assumed primacy and it was this factor which accounted for the meteoric rise of Alexander Bustamante. Thus, in terms of meeting the emotional needs of workers, the T.U.C. were at a decided disadvantage. The role of "Messiah" already had been pre-empted by Alexander Bustamante. The B.I.T.U./J.L.P had a tremendous head start, as the allegiance under the traditional estate system, which the planter/manager had exacted, and the obligation to provide employment, which went with this allegiance, had been transferred from the employer to Bustamante and the B.I.T.U. and, by virtue of Bustamante's personality, to the government of the J.L.P. as well. Not surprisingly, therefore, Bustamante assumed the portfolio of Minister of Communications which allowed him to determine the levels and allocation of public funds for public works and in the process to control the distribution of work and employment opportunities. The official side (i.e., non-elected colonial group) in the Executive Council could then be left to take whatever initiatives they wanted in other areas of policy and public administration. One immediate consequence of Bustamante's political unionism, therefore, was that political and trade union affiliation became the main criterion governing the employment of labour on governmental work projects as well as the recruitment of employees at the subordinate levels in the public services. This held true for both levels of government, central and municipal or parochial.

To the victor, then, went the spoils. Alexander Bustamante, as the head of the virtually fused B.I.T.U./J.L.P. and the Leader of the Majority Party constituting the elected side of Government, was uniquely placed to further the interests of the B.I.T.U. at the expense of the T.U.C.

This was reflected in the state of industrial relations during 1945. A record number of 145 labour disputes and 39 minor complaints were reported to the Labour Department. Of the 145 disputes reported, 97 resulted in strikes involving some 11,600 workers and a time loss of upwards 91,650 man-days. Over half of the strikes (53.3 per cent) occurred in agriculture, reflecting a testing by the B.I.T.U. of its new-found power as well as a drive for "closed-shop" agreements to exclude the T.U.C. As Bustamante later made plain in the Legislature in April 1946, "The Sugar Manufacturers have an obligation to see that unionists are first employed by them in the field and factory, because workers in the field and factory are members of the Bustamante Industrial Trade Union, skilled workers and unskilled." This approach brought results. Membership of the B.I.T.U. rose from 30,000 to 46,000 while that of the T.U.C. declined from 14,000 to less than 10,000 and five of its affiliates applied for cancellation of registration. Jamaica, however, had begun to reap some of the unfavourable consequences of the split in 1942 between Manley and the P.N.P. on the one hand, and Bustamante and the B.I.T.U. on the other. Labour solidarity had been destroyed and worker set against worker. In relatively small communities, plagued by mass unemployment, and in which even the fortunate few could not be assured of regularity of employment, the distribution of limited employment opportunities on the basis of party and trade union allegiance or affiliation was bound to lead to bitter animosity and violence.

The T.U.C. bloc, beleaguered on all sides, found itself, therefore, in a no-holds-barred struggle for survival. In the private sector employers who were suspicious of the T.U.C. Unions because of the ideological commitment of their leaders to socialism blatantly refused to accord recognition and bargaining rights and looked to a B.I.T.U. government to ensure that the going would not be easy for the T.U.C. In the public sector, the T.U.C. controlled the subordinate employees of Government in Kingston and St. Andrew, but demands for higher wages and improved working conditions ultimately meant negotiating with the Government of which Bustamante could be regarded as the titular head. Bustamante made his position clear concerning his rivals:"I am the only leader in this country and the only leader of a union that can protect the people." He was speaking in the House of Representatives in January 1946 before adopting a statement of his government's policy towards subordinate employees in the public services. It came as a result of a claim served by the Railway Employees Union — a T.U.C. affiliate — for higher wages, shorter working hours and other improvements. The Government's position was that "if the demands the Trades Union Council Unions are making were to be accepted by this Government it would mean bankruptcy for this Government."

Bustamante explained that the claims of one particular group of workers had to be weighed against the claims of other groups, as well as against the consequential burden on tax-payers at large. Government was not prepared to consider such requests until the financial position of the Railway had been re-examined in the light of an impending report. In regard to subordinate employees generally, the J.L.P. took the position that these employees had received substantial increases at frequent intervals in recent years, hence "the Government does not consider that any general increase in wage rates of Government staff is justified in present circumstances." The T.U.C., however, had not sought or claimed general wage increases for all subordinate employees of Government.

Bustamante and other ministers also accused that official returns filed with the Registrar of Trade Unions did not support the claims of the T.U.C. Unions that they represented the majority of subordinate employees in Government Departments. The enunication of Government policy concerning trade union representation held out no hope of the T.U.C. being granted exclusive or majority bargaining rights. "It is the policy of the Government to recognize Trade Unions as the representatives of their members in Government employment and to give to the Unions all reasonable facilities for negotiation with Government Departments, regarding the interest of their members.

"A difficulty, however, arises where two or more Unions represent the employees of one Department, where conflicting claims are made by those Unions as to their strength and where one of the Unions wishes to negotiate with the Department concerned on general questions of wages and conditions of service affecting all employees of the Department. In such circumstances the Government is not prepared to recognize one Union as the sole bargaining agent of all employees.

"To overcome the difficulty it has been suggested to the Unions that Departmental Unions should be set up in which the Unions would be represented according to their strength in each Department. This suggestion is in accordance with the recommendations of the Committe on Industrial Relations on which the Unions were represented. The Labour Adviser has been instructed to work out the practical proposals for the consideration of Government for the establishment of Departmental Councils and the Unions concerned have been invited to cooperate with him in the preparation of such a scheme."[16]

The Government's policy on trade union representation was greeted by the T.U.C. with a sense of foreboding and frustration. Ironically, within weeks, the first fruits of that policy were to bring a serious crisis in the life of Alexander Bustamante, who found himself indicted on a charge of manslaughter.

On 15th February 1946, some 280 nurses and general helpers at the Mental Hospital (Asylum) in Kingston went on strike demanding the removal of the Senior Medical Officer (S.M.O.), reputedly a sympathizer of Bustamante, and the redress of sundry grievances. The majority of these nurses and attendants were members of the T.U.C.-affiliated Government Hospital and Prisons Employees Union, headed by Florizel

Glasspole, accountant by profession, who had helped to organize shop assistants and clerks in 1936 and 1937, and was one of Manley's ablest lieutenants in the P.N.P. The T.U.C. recounted for the public's benefit the long history of unsatisfactory working conditions and frustrations at the institution and reminded that as far back as 1943 a review committee had found the S.M.O. and Matron responsible for employee tension and unrest and had recommended that they be retired. Government, however, demanded that workers return to work unconditionally before negotiations could even be considered, but the T.U.C. countered that Government had not adopted this attitude when Bustamante had called strikes on the waterfront and on sugar estates during the height of the war, and that the quickest formula was always found for resolving difficulties in favour of the B.I.T.U.

As a result of the strike, Kingston was overrun by escaped mental patients, some of them dangerous. The police, reportedly in sympathy with the strikers, did not act with alacrity to round up escapees. Bustamante, taking the position that the strike was against his government, advised the Governor by telegram, "With regard to the strike at Mental Hospital a large body of nurses belong to my union. You are to take an iron hand in this matter. No sympathy whatsoever must be shown." He thundered the denunciation, "This is not a strike, it is vandalism." Issuing an ultimatum to strikers, the Government brought in the military corps and orderlies to help man the institution. Bustamante visited the asylum on the first day of the strike and was hit by a stone thrown by an inmate — a fact corroborated by police evidence. He then returned to the waterfront and assembled thousands of dockers ostensibly to capture and return the inmates. In the process, of course, his followers anticipated clearing all T.U.C. and P.N.P. elements from the institution. One of the B.I.T.U. gangs searching for T.U.C. adherents accosted a citizen who was in no way connected with the dispute but was known to be a P.N.P. sympathizer. In self-defence, this man shot and killed one of the leaders of the mob, a B.I.T.U. delegate, and was in turn trampled into a bloody pulp by the rampaging crowd. The T.U.C. then retaliated by calling out on strike prison guards, firemen and railroad workers. Pitched battles ensued as rival groups manoeuvred and fought in the streets of Kingston. Three men were killed and scores wounded more or less seriously. As the police and military took over the prisons, N.N. Nethersole, President of the (Jamaican) T.U.C., cabled the Under-Secretary of State for the Colonies as well as the General Secretary of the (British) T.U.C. urging their intervention.

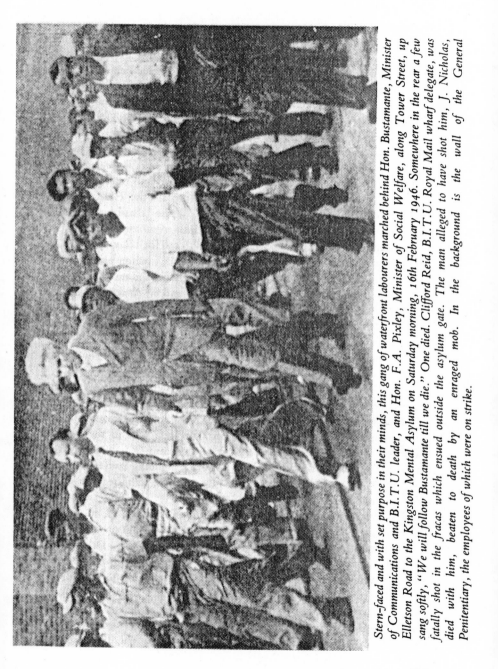

Stern-faced and with set purpose in their minds, this gang of waterfront labourers marched behind Hon. Bustamante, Minister of Communications and B.I.T.U. leader, and Hon. F.A. Pixley, Minister of Social Welfare, along Tower Street, up Elletson Road to the Kingston Mental Asylum on Saturday morning, 16th February 1946. Somewhere in the rear a few sang softly, "We will follow Bustamante till we die." One died. Clifford Reid, B.I.T.U. Royal Mail wharf delegate, was fatally shot in the fracas which ensued outside the asylum gate. The man alleged to have shot him, J. Nicholas, died with him, beaten to death by an enraged mob. In the background is the wall of the General Penitentiary, the employees of which were on strike.

119

Unhappily, the recapture of inmates did not write an end to the affair. A group of nuns offering their services were forced to withdraw on the grounds of strike-breaking. Improperly supervised, an inmate apparently started a fire which gutted the epileptic ward and fifteen helpless inmates were burned to death.

Manley warned that Bustamante was treading the perilous path of disorder. Three days after the strike had been called, the Government declared a State of Emergency under the Emergency Powers Law and labelled the actions of the strikers disgraceful and inhumane. Only police constables, special constables and persons with permits were permitted to carry firearms in public. As Government prepared to replace striking personnel, Nethersole hurried off to London to plead the T.U.C.'s cause before the British Government and people. In the Jamaican House of Representatives, a bitter debate full of recriminations ensued, with the J.L.P. Majority denying the Opposition P.N.P.'s call for a Royal Commission to investigate. Meanwhile, thirty-seven T.U.C. prison pickets were arrested and charged with unlawful assembly. Before the strike was over, the Mayor and Deputy Mayor of the Kingston and St. Andrew Corporation (K.S.A.C.) had resigned — the Mayor (a P.N.P. adherent) because of conflict of loyalty and interest, the Deputy Mayor because of frustration in the performance of his duties. A settlement of the dispute was reached in March and the State of Emergency was relaxed as strikers returned to work.

Early in April, after police investigations had been carried out, Alexander Bustamante, Minister of Communications, and Frank Pixley, Minister for Social Welfare, who had accompanied Bustamante on the march, were charged with manslaughter for their part in the "Black Saturday" rampage which had resulted in the death of J. Nicholas, the bystander, at the hands of the B.I.T.U. mob. Defending lawyers secured a change of venue and Bustamante and Pixley were acquitted upon trial in June 1946.

The strike had a number of salutary effects. First of all, it spurred Government to establish formal machinery for the resolution of disputes between the Government and its subordinate employees. During the year, Departmental or interim Committees were established in twelve Departments of Government to allow for joint representation of unions and employees. Secondly, the Government carried through the long overdue regrading of salaries of Government subordinate employees. The Minister of Finance, by way of introducing the measure, observed blandly that "certain recommendations were made at the instigation of the Minister of Communications (W.A. Bustamante) for improvements in the standard of wages of Government-employed labour and for improved increments to Government employees in the lowest grades."

Political violence, however, continued to mount as Jamaican society turned in against itself. P.N.P./T.U.C. supporters as well as the disenchanted and unemployed took to protest marches against Headquarters House — seat of the Legislature — the Labour Department (where the Kingston Employment Bureau was located), and the executive offices of the K.S.A.C., demonstrating against unemployment as well as discrimination and victimization in the selection of workers for employment on Government projects or in subordinate positions. In May 1947, the Bustamante Government introduced and passed in the Legislature a bill to prohibit marches within a prescribed distance of the three focal places referred to above, as well as other Government offices. This was to be but the first of a series of regulatory laws passed by the J.L.P. Majority, for, as the forces of opposition grew stronger in the urban corporate area, Bustamante became more and more preoccupied with the maintenance of law and order and with containment of political protest.

At the political level, also, skirmishes in the streets took on overtones of class warfare. In predominantly working-class areas, and especially in Bustamante's predominantly working-class constituency in Western Kingston, Jamaicans identified as middle class, and *ipso facto* P.N.P.-adherents by virtue of dress or complexion, attended political meetings at their own peril. Faced with disruption of meetings and molestation of supporters, actual or supposed, the P.N.P. retaliated by forming their own protective groups or strong-arm squads. Political violence reached its peak when, on 2nd October 1947, there was a clash between rival groups attending political meetings, which left a number of J.L.P./B.I.T.U. supporters dead and wounded in the streets in Trench Pen (now Trench Town). Days later, the J.L.P. Majority rushed through an amendment to the Gunpowder and Firearms Law to restrict the carrying and use of firearms. Opposition speakers chided Bustamante for not setting a better example as only days before he was reported to have brandished and discharged his revolver at the K.S.A.C. offices.

The Mental Hospital affair had brought into focus in a rather tragic way the ambiguity of the roles being played concurrently by Bustamante as head of the B.I.T.U. and elected head of the B.I.T.U.-based Government. But Alexander Bustamante continued undaunted. Only four months after, when his trial on the charge of manslaughter commenced in the north-coast town of Port Maria in the parish of St. Mary, B.I.T.U. dock workers went on a sympathy strike. The shipping companies issued a back-to-work ultimatum, threatening that non-B.I.T.U. port workers would be used to load and unload ships. Embarassed by the fact that ships were leaving Kingston with food supplies unloaded, a J.L.P.-sponsored motion was introduced and passed in the House of Representatives, calling upon the Governor in Executive Council to appoint a board with full powers to contact the Shipping Association and the B.I.T.U. and to advise the Executive Council on such settlement as it thinks fit. Again in March 1947, a deadlocked dispute over wages between the West Indies Sugar Company and the B.I.T.U. at Frome in Westmoreland was given a full-scale airing in the House of Representatives after a violent B.I.T.U. strike had failed to force a settlement. Bustamante denounced Robert Kirkwood — the Managing Director of the Company and a nominated Member of the Legislative Council — as well as the Governor Sir John Huggins "as a partner of this hideous moral crime that has been committed against our women". The "moral crime" referred to the allegation made both by Bustamante and L.G. Newland, General Secretary of the B.I.T.U., during the course of the debate, that the West Indies Sugar Company had retaliated by evicting families of workers who had refused to return to work until the wage dispute had been resolved. There could be no doubt, therefore, but that the political power of the B.I.T.U., exercised through the political arm, the J.L.P., would be used to protect and further the interests of the Union and its working-class following.

In the period of most intense political violence 1945–7, Jamaicans died, therefore, not in struggle against a colonial administration for political independence and freedom, but at each others hands in the forging of the two-party system. The emergence of the two-party system as distinct from its development, must be attributed then to the accident of personality conflict between Norman Manley and Alexander Busta- mante. Popular support began to crystallize behind these two outstanding and dominant leaders, and their continuing associations with different and competing parties and trade union affiliates institutionalized that rivalry. For the working classes in particular, party politics became co- extensive with everyday activity and existence itself. Trade union or party affiliation became embedded into the very consciousness and existence of the working man and peasant, for the simple reason that such affiliations governed the availability of economic and job opportunities.

Jamaica thus developed an "inverted" form of the "spoils system" — "inverted" in the sense that preferential hiring and discrimination in employment were limited to the subordinate categories in the public services. This found its fullest expression in municipal and parochial (local government at the parish level) politics. In 1947 local government elections were conducted for the first time on the basis of universal adult suffrage. The immediate consequence was the complete integration of municipal and parochial politics with national politics. In the corporate area of Kingston and St. Andrew, significant changes were made in the system of representation and governance of the K.S.A.C. Before 1947, the K.S.A.C. had been run by a Council comprised of eight Councillors elected to three-year terms, as well as Members of the House of Representatives, the Custos for each of the two parishes, all as ex-officio Councillors. The Councillors then elected Aldermen for one year terms. Finally, the Mayor and Deputy Mayor as the chief executive officers were elected annually by and from the Aldermen and Councillors. The reorganization of 1947 eliminated the Aldermen and provided for the direct election of Councillors on the basis of adult suffrage. The election was fought strictly on party lines with both J.L.P. and P.N.P. fielding full slates of candidates. The P.N.P. won seven seats to the J.L.P.'s six, but the J.L.P. nevertheless gained control of the Council by having five ex-officio voting Members (Members of the House of Representatives) to the P.N.P.'s one.

The result was that in November 1947, Alexander Bustamante was elected Mayor of the K.S.A.C. and began to wear yet another cap. L.G. Newland, M.H.R. and General Secretary of the B.I.T.U., was elected Deputy Mayor, and eventually Mayor for the succeeding term 1948–9. The same principle of political control was extended to parochial boards. Local government and politics became then the medium for dispensing political patronage and largesse as well as the training ground for budding national politicians. The impressive showing made by the P.N.P. in the K.S.A.C. elections reflected the growing strength of the T.U.C. among the urban proletariat. Significantly, Ken Hill, perhaps the most dynamic of the T.U.C. leaders and a very incisive and brilliant orator, was elected Councillor. Hugh Lawson Shearer, Bustamante's protégé and heir-apparent in the B.I.T.U., also made his political debut and likewise was elected a Councillor.

The events of 1947 must be regarded, therefore, as constituting a decisive turning point in the development of the two-party system. Outside of Parliament, the P.N.P./T.U.C. forces opposing Bustamante had shown that they would meet violence with violence.[17] As the political power of the J.L.P. was being used to further the interests of the B.I.T.U. through preferential hiring and job discrimination, the Opposition began to dramatize the situation by resorting to protest marches against the House of

Election of Councillors for the K.S.A.C. was held for the first time on the basis of adult suffrage in 1947. Standing from left to right: Mr. Newland, Deputy Mayor; Mr. W.A. Bustamante, Mayor of Kingston; Mr. Lewars, Town Clerk.

124

Representatives and the main employment agencies of central and local Government. The less traditionalist and correspondingly more alienated urban proletariat were responding favourably to the intense campaign — political, industrial and ideological — of the P.N.P./T.U.C. spearheaded by the T.U.C.

Jamaica thus developed a rather unconventional form of "mass participation" in politics, which saw the legislature and the administrative seats of public activity being made the focus of popular discontent. Mass rallies and protest marches constituted in themselves acts of politicizing which served to reinforce the bi-party system and partisanship associated with it. Of course, one consequence was that Jamaica developed a kind of "perverse" electoral accountability and responsibility system in which the political parties were judged and supported by working classes, not on the basis of the policies they had instituted or failed to institute in an attempt to solve the basic problems of the country — such as unemployment, subsistence levels of income for the masses, limited educational and employment opportunities, substandard housing, uneven distribution of income and so on — but on the basis of the necessity to maintain control (for the "in" party) or to gain control (for the "out" party) of the distribution of work on Government-controlled projects. Paradoxically, therefore, the fiercest political competition and violent partisanship came from those who suffered most from the inability of the two political parties to deal with chronic and structural unemployment.

The mass rally also became the accepted technique and medium of the political parties for communication with and carrying out political education of the masses. It not only accorded with the realities of a mass electorate and trade union membership characterized by relatively high rates of illiteracy and inability to communicate effectively other than in the "native dialect", but also relieved the political parties and the trade unions of the necessity to establish rationalized (branch) structures allowing for meaningful rank and file participation in the decision-making processes. On the other hand, this deficiency or lack of participation tended to be counteracted by the pervasiveness and intensity of politics in day-to-day life, to the extent that political and trade union affiliation governed the distribution of employment opportunities and other forms of patronage in every village, community or town.

At the political level, Bustamante reacted by embarking upon a policy of preservation of law and order at all costs. Between 1947 and 1948, the J.L.P. Majority pushed through laws to regulate marches against public offices, and the acquisition, carrying, and use of firearms.[18] This made

125

Bustamante vulnerable to the Opposition charge that he had used the techniques of protest marches, demonstrations and strikes in 1937 and 1938 to gain the devotion and loyalty of the masses and so become their leader, but that having acquired political power, he was now using it to deny these same avenues of protest to disaffected workers and rival unionists.

When Bustamante's strong penchant for law and order was joined to his equally strong commitment to private enterprise and to his obsession to achieve financial and fiscal respectability for his administration, his opponents were able to point out with considerable effect that the Jamaica Labour Party was not a "labour party" in the British, European or West Indian tradition (i.e., a socialist or social democratic party) but rather a Conservative or businessmen's party, manifesting a paternalistic concern for labour's welfare.

The interesting aspect of the situation is that while Alexander Busta-mante did not hesitate to use all the forces, political and industrial, at his command to frustrate or contain the forces of opposition in the streets and in the places of work, he showed a remarkable tolerance for, and sensitivity to, the criticisms of the P.N.P. rump Opposition in Parliament. Indeed the vigour of Parliamentary debate and the laying and observance of ground rules for the conduct of the people's affairs in the first five-year experimental period, when the Majority Party boasted twenty-two representatives to the Minority Party's five, must rank among the most creditable in Jamaica's legislative and political history. In his long, rambling maiden budget speech in 1945, the precursor of many such, some of which were to endure over four and five days, Bustamante was concerned to give guidance to an even more inexperienced Speaker of the House. "I am sorry I have to tire you so much as you are now in the Chair but I do hope and believe you will extend the same latitude to what is called the Opposition Party as you extend to us. That is the desire of my colleagues, that the same latitude you give us, you give others, that the same decision you come to in a particular matter regarding us, that you would come to that decision for the Opposition Party. All of us are here to express ourselves." That the Speaker did not always observe this injunction must not be held against Alexander Bustamante. He appealed also to the Opposition (Minority) Party. "Let us join together so that we can be one big family fighting for a cause, fighting for a broader constitution, fighting to get a ministerial system, not the system we have today, a system of Ministers in embryo fighting to have administrative rights." By 1947, therefore, Bustamante had begun to chafe at the constitutional limitations on executive powers of elected representatives. "That is why I have always complained of the unwieldy Constitution. That whilst we as the elect of the people bear the blame, and the burden of the blame, night and day others have a majority of the votes in the Executive Council. In other words we have a supposed Labour Government without authority — like going to the pond to fetch water without any container." Bustamante's position was, however, highly ambivalent. His strictures against the 1944 Constitution reflected more his sensitivity to criticism and the necessity of maintaining his legitimacy than any desire to accelerate the pace of constitutional advance. As Norman Manley observed as early as August 1945, "When it suits them, the Leader of the Majority comes in the House and says 'I am only half the Government — in fact I am not Government at all, don't blame me', and when it swings the other way they come in and claim the credit for everything; and you can't pin them with responsibility, because whenever you want to pin them . . . they say, and say with truth, that they are only half of the Executive Council."[19]

In July 1947, there was extended debate of a motion moved by one one of the independent (but pro-J.L.P.) M.H.R.'s that "this Honourable House of Representatives do humbly pray . . . to vest the necessary powers of enforcement in the position of Members of the Executive Council which it has seen fit to recognize as Ministers." This followed complaints by the "Ministers in embryo" that they were unable to enforce upon heads of Departments under their jurisdiction, matters of policy decided upon by the Executive Council. The P.N.P.'s parliamentray leader, Dr. Ivan Lloyd, in a very compelling speech pointed out that while Ministers did not have any individual responsibility whatever under the Constitution, nevertheless if "they use the powers in the Constitution as the Constitution stands today they can have enough and do have enough collective authority and power to see that their policies are carried out by heads of Departments. And it is here, Sir, that I was saying that Ministers have failed absolutely to use the powers invested in them under the Constitution, even though in a round-about way in order to enforce a decision arrived at in Executive Council." He therefore moved an amendment, which the Speaker declared to be a new substantive motion, "To increase the number of Ministers in Executive Council to nine by substituting in place of the Members of the Nominated House and the Finance Secretary and the Colonial Secretary four elected Members of the House of Representatives, and that the nine elected Members of the House of Representatives be given the constitutional powers of Ministers to enforce and maintain the policies of the

Executive in the Departments of Government."[20]

Although the amendment was ultimately defeated by the Majority Party, Alexander Bustamante initially spoke in support and made what was perhaps his most impassioned plea in his public career for constitutional advance. It showed also the extent to which he was being conditioned to accept self-government as a short-run rather than a long-run objective for Jamaica. He began by defending his administration: "But I say this, if we had full ministerial power as we should have in our country, we would have improved things more rapidly than it is being improved today." But at the same time, Jamaicans would have to overcome their inferiority and lack of confidence in their own ability to administer their affairs. "Then when the Normans invaded England, did the Englishmen say, 'Well we realize we are not quite civilized, so you, the Normans, can govern us '? No. They drew their swords against the Normans and after some time they drove the Normans back to France and they liberated themselves. The Englishmen had the weapon and the will to do it. But we in Jamaica have not the will to do it. We are accustomed too much to bowing down and looking upon the Englishman as somebody superior to us intellectually, socially and otherwise. We have been taught that by the Englishman. I was taught that too, but I went abroad and threw it off. The English should be made to know that Jamaicans are citizens and not subjects. We are not inferior. The word 'subject' makes us feel that we must look upon the Englishman as a superior being, a superhuman and superior. There is nobody in England superior to me with respect to His Majesty the King." He called for greater authority for Ministers. "I am saying this, now that we are ripe to have a constitution that will give us the proper authority in our country to administer the affairs of the people for the good of the people, particularly for the good of the majority." This might involve abolition of the Upper House (Legislative Council). "It should be annihilated. They are up there to prevent the progress of this country." Bustamante also recalled the struggles of Jamaica's earliest national heroes. "We must not allow the pain, the mental and physical pain of George William Gordon and Paul Bogle to go in vain. Those men fought in 1865. What did they gain? Nothing. They lost their lives. If we should take an example of them we would not think of our personal gain but the gain of posterity, and so we must fight — I am not suggesting military rebellion, but I am suggesting this, we must liberate ourselves at all cost." He issued a call to put freedom above party politics. "We must put it above politics. We must fight for it together. We can continue to fight each other, but let us join together and fight the British Government harder than we are fighting each other."[21]

The two rival party-union blocs continued their fight as Bustamante expected they would, only that from 1947 to 1951 violence was shifted from the political to the trade union or industrial scene, as the T.U.C. geared for the 1949 General Election. The first of the new wave of violent disputes flared in 1947 when the strongly pro-J.L.P. newspaper *The Daily Gleaner* refused to grant recognition and bargaining rights to the T.U.C. on behalf of its printing staff. Interestingly enough, printers employed by The Gleaner Company had been represented by the printers union, an affiliate of the T.U.C., earlier in 1944. The resulting strike lasted for six weeks and ended with recognition of the T.U.C. and an agreement to arbitrate the issue of wage increases.

Violence of a more spectacular nature featured in the Kingston Bus Service Strike in 1948. The T.U.C. on behalf of its affiliate the Tramway Transport and General Workers Union (T.T.G.W.U.) sought recognition in January 1948. The workers had been represented by a T.U.C. affiliate also in 1945. After a series of delaying tactics in which the management of the Jamaican-owned and -operated Jamaica Utilities Company Limited claimed it was too busy to discuss the claim with the Union, the T.U.C. issued the strike call. Bus drivers refused to return vehicles to the company's terminal and retained the ignition keys as well as the imprest or money allocated to conductors to make change. The Government promptly brought the service under the Public Utilities Protection Law. At a conference convened by the Governor at King's House, the Union agreed to return the buses to the depot provided the Governor would undertake to get the Company to agree to negotiations. The Company accepted the keys but refused to negotiate and set about re-establishing service. The T.T.G.W.U. retaliated with leaflets warning the public that buses were being driven by untrained personnel who were strike-breakers. The Company showed no inclination to meet the Union, and on 1st March a home-made bomb exploded in a bus carrying passengers. One person was seriously injured and eleven others required hospital treatment. The Government placed police on the vehicles to provide protection, ·but violence continued and buses were stoned and fired upon. One driver was shot and later died with the consequence that three striking employees were charged with murder.

Alexander Bustamante, as head of the elected Government, warned that sterner measures would be taken to stop terrorism. He accused communists and anarchists of fomenting violence. Further amendments were made to the Firearms Law, and regulations were published pro-hibiting the handing of packages into public passenger vehicles except with the approval of authorized persons. The Company and Union were eventually brought together through the efforts of a group of prominent citizens, but the T.U.C. effectively had lost the strike.

Taking stock of the situation the T.U.C. decided that a radical re-organization of its structure was necessary to make it more effective as a foil to the B.I.T.U. Fourteen registered small craft-oriented unions affiliated with the T.U.C. were merged into a blanket or general type union — the Trades Union Congress of Jamaica — to correspond more nearly to the B.I.T.U. The new organization represented a shift to more centralized direction. The overhead expenses of operating so many small unions, inter-locking personnel notwithstanding, had been a drain on the limited resources of all. The administrative rationalization dictated by political strategy, and carried out at the expense of a vibrant rank and file participation in the government of the smaller affiliates, nevertheless, enabled the T.U.C. to pay full-time officers and organizers. The revamped T.U.C. could then contemplate as a second phase, moving into the sugar industry to offer competition to the B.I.T.U. in "Bustamante territory". The T.U.C. after the 1944 election had decided to concentrate on breaking Bustamante's control over the working classes in Kingston on the assumption that disaffection of B.I.T.U. supporters in Kingston would influence to some extent the turn of events in rural areas. As indicated earlier, by 1947 the T.U.C. had succeeded to the point where Ken Hill could defeat a leading J.L.P. candidate in a key municipal election. Indeed, for the 1949 General Election, Bustamante felt obliged to abandon his predominantly working-class constituency in Western Kingston and run in a safe seat in the B.I.T.U. sugar stronghold in the parish of Clarendon. The Western Kingston constituency was won by Ken Hill.

When, however, the smoke had cleared from the election battlefield in December 1949, Alexander Bustamante (the Chief) was still head of the elected Government, although with a considerably reduced majority. J.L.P. won seventeen seats to the P.N.P.'s thirteen, with the two remaining seats going to independent candidates. The P.N.P. had emerged, however, with the overall popular vote of 43.5 per cent as against 42.7 per cent for the J.L.P. The P.N.P. established its appeal to, and hold upon, the parishes of the urban voters, winning five of the six seats in Kingston and St. Andrew. Interestingly enough, all of the M.H.R.'s of the P.N.P. elected in the Corporate Area, including Florizel Glasspole (re-elected), Ken Hill, Wills O. Isaacs, N.W. Manley and N.N. Nethersole, were experienced trade unionists with manifold trade union connections. Also elected on a P.N.P. ticket in the Montego Bay area was Bustamante's inveterate foe, A.G.S. (Father) Coombs, President of the Jamaica Radical Workers Union. Following the 1949 election, the House of Representatives contained nine active trade unionists, five associated with the P.N.P. bloc and four with the J.L.P. bloc.

At the end of the first five-year experimental period of limited self-government, the characteristic features of Jamaican politics had become clearly evident. In this development, Alexander Bustamante had emerged as the key figure. By initiating the era of political unionism, Bustamante had made the support of organized labour a *sine qua non* or yardstick for party legitimacy. The process had begun when, largely as a result of the force of his personality and temperament, he first split with Norman Manley and the P.N.P. in 1942, and then in 1943, went on to launch the Jamaica Labour Party (the B.I.T.U. relabelled) to contest the General Election to be held under universal adult suffrage in 1944. Bustamante had left the P.N.P. in the anomalous position of declaring for socialism, historically the political ideology of the working classes, without having any organic link with the working classes, especially at the trade union level. For the P.N.P. to come out of the political wilderness and become a viable alternative to the J.L.P., it had of necessity to help develop, as well as ally itself to, a trade union wing which would provide a direct line with the working classes as well as mass support.

As a powerful and popular leader, Alexander Bustamante had chosen to be a political maverick, and in so doing forced the upper and middle classes to give recognition to the legitimate claims and grievances of the working classes, which constituted the overwhelming majority of the Jamaican population and society. For by no means all or even many of the middle classes, even within the P.N.P., shared Norman Manley's commit-ment to the cause of the common man or his abiding faith in the capacity of all Jamaicans, whatever their colour and class, to take control of the determination of their country's affairs.

In exploiting to the full his personal charisma and sway over the masses, Alexander Bustamante also gave expression to, and made manifest, the strength of the tradition of messianism in Jamaican society. His powerful egocentrism made it easy for him to embark on a career of "personalism", or Bustamanteism if you will, but here again, it is fair to say that Alexander Bustamante was "called" upon to fill a role and provide a type of leadership which has proven to be a characteristic feature of the politics in the developing countries, especially those emerging from colonialism. The enormous popularity of Bustamante and the apparent success of his highly personalized style quickly forced upon P.N.P. supporters recognition of the tactical need to raise likewise the status of their own leader, Norman Manley, to heroic proportions. The potential was there and the cost of not doing so for the P.N.P. was great. "Failure on the part of any leader to understand and exploit the force and necessity of this dimension ('dynamic of the leader's personality and of his personal characteristics in the environment of power') is a certain guarantee of failure to make a political impact. Those to whom charisma does not come naturally must find ways and means of developing the divine gift of political grace so as to ensure credibility and legitimacy. Manley possessed undoubted personal authority rooted in his achievement as a brilliant and consistently successful advocate as well as in a popular legend about his intellectual power."[22]

It is, then, to the institutionalized rivalry of these two leaders and the deep and abiding emotions and sentiments of loyalty and affection, as well as of political acceptance or rejection, which they aroused in their followers and supporters that Jamaica owes the initial development of bi-partism.

This emerging pattern was further reinforced by the commitment of the two men and their respective party colleagues to British parliamentary constitutionalism or the Westminster model, if you will. As Manley himself said in 1940, "However much we differ from the people of Britain in other ways, all our ideas about politics came from Britain."

It would be a mistake, however, to attribute the emergence of the Jamaican two-party system, even primarily, to compulsive emulation of the political forms and practices of the mother country. Admittedly, as far as Bustamante was concerned, the consciousness of being on trial, not only in the eyes of the British but also before the judgment bar of upper- and middle-class Jamaicans, was an important consideration. But there were other factors arising from the dynamics of political struggle within and without the legislature. Within the legislature, the tiny P.N.P. Minority was conscious of the fact that its survival as a parliamentary and political force lay in curbing the overwhelming dominance of the power-conscious and autocratic Majority Party Leader and was therefore led to insist on and struggle for the observance of British parliamentary practices and Westminster norms. At the same time, it was important for the P.N.P. that the experimental 1944 Constitution, limited as it was, be shown to be well within the political capabilities of elected representatives, so that the advance to self-government could be made as quickly as possible.

On the other side, the Westminster model was not without its compensation for Alexander Bustamante. If he could not rule as a republican president on the Latin American model, his absolute hegemony over, and exaction of absolute loyalty from, his parliamentary colleagues could still be reconciled with a parliamentary model and system which ultimately would make the Chief Minister or Premier or Prime Minister much more than the first among equals.

Without the legislature, the polarization of support between two contending political giants and the parties and affiliated unions associated with them was to make selection of government essentially a matter of choice between the two leaders, and it was only a matter of time before the two-party system would be elevated to a matter of principle by both of them.

On the one hand, then, there stood paradoxically a conservative labour-based party led by Alexander Bustamante: a man physically striking, flamboyant, egocentric and earthy, with a deep emotional attachment to the working classes and an equally intuitive and profound grasp of the psychology of the Jamaican working man and peasant; a man with an unerring instinct for, and single-minded pursuit of, power, amply supported by a demagogic ability to arouse his working-class listeners to fever pitch whenever he cared to; a man of easy affability and great personal charm, who seemed to grow upon those around him who were prepared to accept his leadership without question, and was able to inspire them to undying devotion and loyalty; a man of decision and action who could be ruthless in dealing with those he regarded as real or potential political enemies, but at the same time who never bore them lingering rancour or malice or personal animosity — for Alexander Bustamante time and again declared that he would never be so foolish as to put ammunition in the hands of those who might use it against him politically. A man of personal courage, yet prudent, displaying a youthful vigour which belied his years, Alexander Bustamante was sixty-five years of age when he began his second term of office. Here was a man, then, who knew his strength and revelled in it, who had the power and authority to mould those whom he led, but preferred to be moulded by the forces around him. Bustamante began and remained an enigma and this is why it can be said with sincerity, "He incarnated the countervailing forces that inhered in a society manifesting all the contradictions of the colonial connection."[23]

On the other hand, paradoxically also, was the P.N.P., a radical party in the context of colonial Jamaica, spearheading a nationalist movement, led by Norman Manley, a man whose training and achievements should have predisposed him to lead a conservative party. For Norman Manley excellence of achievement was the norm. An outstanding high school athlete, Rhodes scholar, decorated World War I veteran, prize man of Gray's Inn, first class honours in his Bar Finals, mathematician and brilliant legendary at the Bar and the first Jamaican to appear before the Judicial Committee of the Privy Council, the highest British Colonial or Dominion law tribunal. A man who placed his skills of advocacy at the disposal of the downtrodden workers in 1938, and who, in spite of the fact that he held over one hundred retainers representing nearly all of big business in Jamaica, when he entered politics, never appeared thereafter for a firm or employer in a litigation which involved worker interests. He never ceased to be a friend and counsel to organized labour; a man who had a vision of a new Jamaican nation that would be self-sustaining and re-habilitated from the ravages of colonial servitude; a man whose high standards of public utterance enabled him to articulate some of the most noble and inspiring sentiments about his country and people and his aspirations for both; finally, a man of great personal integrity who re-mained incorruptible and unimpeachable until his death in 1969. Each of these two leaders had a contribution to make which was uniquely his own, and so they complemented each other in laying the foundations for a new and modern Jamaica. They did it within a framework of rivalry and competition which involved strategies of conflict and accommodation. Some of the consequences of the strategy of accommodation were to become more evident during Alexander Bustamante's second term in office, in which he and his party graduated from the initial phase of imposed as well as self-imposed political tutelage. For even as the Opposition became stronger, and a formidable opposition it was between 1949 and 1955, so Alexander Bustamante and his party colleagues became more self-assured and less shrill and suspicious of conspiracies.

The 1949 General Election revealed clearly also the demarcation of Jamaican politics in terms of the urban-rural dichotomy. Bustamante and the J.L.P./B.I.T.U. remained entrenched in the rural areas among the traditionalist and illiterate agro-proletariat. The P.N.P./T.U.C. derived support mainly from the middle classes and the urban proletariat and increasingly among the urbanized rural (town) proletariat. The measure of success achieved by the T.U.C. in weakening the allegiance of the urban proletariat could best be seen on the Kingston waterfront. The port workers, originally the militant vanguard of the B.I.T.U., were induced to turn to rival organizations. In 1949 the Independent Port Workers Union and the United Port Workers Union (aligned with the T.U.C.) were both registered. The T.U.C., very conscious that it had brought the P.N.P. within reach of political power, could turn its full attention to the main bastion of Bustamante — the sugar estates. The influence of the T.U.C. and its left-wing leadership, especially of the four H's, was very much in the ascendance in the P.N.P. and even before the General Election in December 1949 there had been a straw-in-the-wind to indicate that the P.N.P. as a party and the T.U.C. as its union affiliate might have different conceptions as to what socialism should mean or entail in the Jamaican context. The occasion was the withdrawal of the British T.U.C. from the World Federation of Trade Unions (W.F.T.U.) on the grounds that the latter body had come under communist domination. The British T.U.C. then invited the Jamaican T.U.C. (which was at the time receiving some assistance from the W.F.T.U.) to withdraw from that body and seek affiliation with the newly constituted and rival International Confederation of Free Trade Unions (I.C.F.T.U.). The leaders of the T.U.C. of Jamaica, notably the four H's, were wary about disaffiliating, but the P.N.P. Executive, because of its close relationship with the British T.U.C., called upon the T.U.C. of Jamaica to withdraw from the W.F.T.U. Under great pressure, the four H's yielded, but having withdrawn from the W.F.T.U. decided to assert their independence and refused to affiliate with the I.C.F.T.U.

The test of strength found the right-wing elements in both the Party and the Union determined to counteract and confine the growing influence of the T.U.C.'s left wing within the P.N.P. However, the immediate challenge after the General Election was the B.I.T.U., and the P.N.P. and T.U.C. endeavoured to close ranks. Kenneth Sterling, the P.N.P.'s all-island supervisor, was seconded to the T.U.C. to help in organizational drives, particularly in the sugar belt.

The pattern of violent representational disputes thus resumed, with the T.U.C. introducing a novel feature into Jamaican trade union experiences — the professional picket. In February 1950, the T.U.C. demanded recognition from the management of the Myrtle Bank Hotel in Kingston as bargaining agents for the hotel employees, who up to that time had been represented by the B.I.T.U. The T.U.C. requested the Labour Adviser to conduct a membership poll, but he advised that he had no statutory powers to conduct a poll and could do so only if the management as well as the B.I.T.U. agreed. The Hotel management adopted familiar delaying tactics while the B.I.T.U. refused to agree to a poll. The T.U.C. then called out the Hotel employees on strike. The Myrtle Bank Hotel was at the time fully occupied by visitors who had arrived for the official opening of the University College of the West Indies. The Hotel, which was situated along the waterfront, was invaded literally by land and sea and overrun by strikers and professional pickets. The Riot Act was read and excited crowds as well as superfluous pickets were dispersed by tear-gas. The B.I.T.U. then expressed willingness to participate in an open poll based on a simple majority, provided that the Hotel's laundry workers, represented by the B.I.T.U., were included in the poll with the Hotel employees, mainly supporters of the T.U.C. The T.U.C., on the other hand, demanded a secret ballot, two-thirds majority and separation of the laundry and hotel workers. The strike was settled by an agreement to arbitrate and N.W. Manley presented the T.U.C.'s case. The arbitrator decided on a secret poll and simple majority, and that laundry workers were to be polled separately. The results of the poll conducted by the Labour Department yielded bargaining rights to the T.U.C. for hotel workers and confirmed continuing B.I.T.U. representation on behalf of the laundry employees.

The Myrtle Bank Hotel dispute established the procedure of non-statutory poll-taking in representational disputes.

Concerned that representational disputes would adversely affect labour relations in the post-election realignments, the Labour Adviser recommended, and the Government agreed to, the appointment of a Board of Enquiry into representational disputes and to recommend suitable machinery for handling such disputes. For the T.U.C. had embarked on a vigorous campaign not just to enlarge its support, but to wrest member-ship from the B.I.T.U. in a frontal attack. The T.U.C. began, therefore, to serve claims on employers who had previously negotiated with the B.I.T.U., using the strike weapon wherever it could, to establish that it had the preponderance of membership. Fresh from its triumph in the Myrtle Bank Hotel dispute, the T.U.C. went on to obtain bargaining rights for workers employed by Reynolds Jamaica Mines Limited in the newly established high-wage bauxite extractive industry. The collective agreement negotiated in this case proved to be the first written compre-hensive labour contract to be established on the North American pattern. It provided for an elaborate grievance procedure, including a no-strike clause until disputes had been taken through the grievance procedure to the final stage of arbitration.

In October 1950, the Board enquiring into representational disputes submitted its report and outlined the procedures which the Labour Adviser should follow in the taking of secret polls. It recommended that the procedures be given statutory force, but this recommendation was not acted upon by the B.I.T.U./J.L.P. government. By this time, however, the Labour Department had already established *ad hoc* guidelines for the taking of polls, and fifteen representational polls were taken during 1950. Alexander Bustamante and his colleagues, using the Legislature as their forum, continued to debate disputes involving the T.U.C. and to decry the tactics being used by that body. Within months, however, the T.U.C. had carried the challenge to the B.I.T.U. in the sugar industry and the result was the celebrated Worthy Park Estate strike which, fortunately, also saw trade union violence and rivalry pass its worst point.

On 24th November 1950, the T.U.C. issued a call to strike after expiry of a 48-hour ultimatum to the company. The Sugar Manufacturers Association, the employer representative body for the entire industry, claimed that its collective agreement with the B.I.T.U. would be in force until the end of the year and there could be no poll, therefore, unless the B.I.T.U. consented. The Labour Adviser, lacking statutory prerogative, took the same position, while Bustamante held that the sugar industry should be taken as a unit rather than as separate estates. Police reinforcements were hurried to the Worthy Park Estate in Lluidas Vale. As B.I.T.U. supporters armed with machetes poised to cross the picket lines, the T.U.C. hurried truck-loads of picket reserves from outside areas, and the estate took on the appearance of a battlefield. In the last week of December, young citrus plants were wantonly destroyed and cane-fields set afire. The Riot Act was read early in January 1951 and police, using tear-gas on T.U.C. picket lines, carried strike-breakers through the lines. Bustamante's car was stoned and he returned shots from his revolver. The strike was called off as a result of continued efforts of Church leaders, prominent citizens and the Labour Department. After agreement was reached to take a poll at that estate, the T.U.C. claimed representational rights at several others. The B.I.T.U., hitherto the undisputed boss in the sugar industry, agreed to negotiate jointly with the T.U.C. for the 1951 crop and also that the Labour Department should take polls at sixteen of twenty-three sugar estates where the T.U.C. claimed majority rights. The T.U.C. gained majority rights on only two of the sixteen estates polled.

While it is true that the T.U.C. had "chopped its way" into the sugar industry, Alexander Bustamante's decision to accord joint-bargaining rights to the T.U.C. was a generous one. Bustamante also acted at the political level to put an end to the practice, employed up to then chiefly by the T.U.C., of employing professional pickets to defend picket lines. An amendment to the Trade Union Law, eventually passed in 1952, made

137

it "an offence for any person to intimidate or annoy another person with a view to compelling him to act or refrain from acting within his rights; and for any person to picket other than an employer or employee of the firm with which a trade dispute is contemplated or has occurred". While the measure may have been introduced in a partisan spirit, it must be regarded as a landmark in the growth of the trade union movement towards maturity, for it took the violence out of the representational disputes which were to remain a characteristic feature of Jamaica's political unionism.

A second significant Bill, brought forward by the Bustamante government and also passed in 1952, introduced compulsory arbitration for settlement of disputes in essential services such as water, health and hospital, transport, postal and telegraph. The law prohibited strikes in such services unless a dispute had been first reported to the Governor in Executive Council and he had failed to refer it within a specified time period. The law thus guaranteed the uninterrupted flow of essential services while at the same time it removed from the T.U.C., which had organized most of these employees, a lever which had been used in the past to embarrass the Government.

The period 1951–2 thus marked an important stage in the development of Alexander Bustamante's career, for from then on, a certain "mellowing" became evident as he began to assume the role of elder statesman. He had travelled a long way since achieving power as a popular, charismatic leader in 1945. At that time his political programme, such as he did articulate, reflected mainly trade union or sectional concern. But his mandate had been based not on what he promised to do or not to do, but on the trust or confidence reposed in him by the masses. He had been a rebel, accustomed to denounce the Colonial administration and to pursue a policy of opposition and obstruction. It was not easy for him to reverse that role. Far from that, the constitutional limitations enabled him to maintain his accustomed posture and divest himself and his party of responsibility for even those measures undertaken at his instigation. Because the five elected Ministers could be stymied by the remaining five nominated Members and the Governor could overrule in exercising his reserve and paramount powers, Bustamante could continue to criticize the Government as though it were an "alien" institution.

The situation was compounded by the ambiguity of his role at one and the same time as Life-President of the B.I.T.U., head of the J.L.P. and Leader of the parliamentary Majority. Faced with highly effective and sustained criticism on the part of the P.N.P. parliamentary Minority, influential far beyond their scant number, Alexander Bustamante soon began to chafe at the constitutional limitations. For he was sensitive not only to criticisms but to the fact that the working classes were on trial. Yet at the same time he was not willing to press for self-government immediately, firstly because he was afraid that the P.N.P., the independence party, which was much better equipped in terms of human resources and skills, might come to power, and secondly because — in spite of his repeated boasts in the Legislature that "I claim nobody in this country, not even the Governor himself, knows anything more about the science of government than I do, and I claim to see further than many of them on the official side of Government" (August 1946), or again, "I personally think without any egotism that I know as much about the science of government as any of the geniuses that have been sent from abroad to govern us" (July 1947) — he was very much conscious of the fact that he and his party were greenhorns in government and administration. As L.G. Newland, General Secretary of the B.I.T.U. since 1942, stated on the eve of the 1949 General Election, "As a result of the elections in 1944 there was a great deal of apprehension in many quarters of this island as to what could become of the future of the country. The vast majority of us elected in 1944 were greenhorns to be representing the people in the House and there were only two or three other Members who had actually served in the older House. We have nothing to be ashamed of."[24]

The forces of opposition and bi-partism may well have been the main beneficiaries of the limited constitutional powers available to Bustamante as head of elected government during the first five-year experimental phase. For, from the very onset, Alexander Bustamante showed that he grasped that politics was concerned fundamentally with winning and exercising power. Thus he did not hesitate to use all the means of power available to him to contain his rivals. When, however, the forces of opposition grew in strength and refused to be frustrated or held at bay, Bustamante was quite prepared to concede a new structure of accommodation and a revised set of rules of the game. In 1947 when P.N.P./T.U.C. combatants routed combined B.I.T.U./J.L.P. forces in the battle for the streets of Kingston, Bustamante realized that continuing political violence would be too costly. The irony, of course, is that violence should have been a factor in sustaining the position of a leader of such overwhelming popularity as Alexander Bustamante. But apparently, his working-class supporters could not be denied the urge now that they were in power, so to speak, to give vent to the hostility they had long entertained towards the middle classes who were their social and economic betters.

Violence persisted much longer at the trade union level because the attempt of the rival union bloc to establish itself as a creditable claimant for workers' allegiance posed a much more serious threat politically to the B.I.T.U./J.L.P. Both sides realized that a party without worker support could not hope to win political office. Here too, Alexander Bustamante used all the means legitimately available to him to protect the B.I.T.U./J.L.P. When, however, trade union violence threatened to set the working class at war with itself, again a new structure of accommodation had to be worked out and this was done during 1951–2. Acting at the political level, Bustamante took the initiative to curb what he thought to be the "excesses" of the rival union bloc. The amendment to the Trade Union Law and the introduction of compulsory arbitration of disputes in essential services were designed to serve this end, but they were also consistent with Bustamante's preoccupation with law and order.

The same degree of inevitability or compulsion of circumstances underlay Bustamante's conversion to the idea of self-government. For although by 1949 Alexander Bustamante had become reconciled to the desirability of self-government, its timing could not be treated independently of his overriding concern to preserve his party in power. Early in 1949, he could still threaten the opposition P.N.P. "The Majority Party has no intention or desire to ask or demand of the Imperial Government that we should have complete self-government now. . . . Two reasons for that, why we do not ask it. A, there is the financial implication. . . . Secondly, sir, we are not proving to the Imperial Government that we are fit and proper persons to govern ourselves."[25]

To the extent that the P.N.P. was the self-government party, Bustamante's hostility to the P.N.P. was translated into hostility to self-government. "I desire to repeat a few things which I said — that we are not fit yet for complete self-government. It is a financial impossibility and there is not enough respect for law and order in this country for complete self-government. Furthermore it is the consensus of opinion among certain elements that follow the P.N.P. that if the party got into power whatever it did the great lawyer (N.W.Manley) would defend them and so even the honour of our women not alone in houses but even on the waysides would not be respected."[26]

In anticipation of the General Election of 1949, Bustamante persisted with the smear of communism and atheism and the consequences for Jamaica of a P.N.P. victory. "Do not deceive yourselves that communism is not rife in this country and that it is not out to destroy constituted authority, for it is felt today that there is only one way that certain people can rule and take charge of this country and that is by rebellion. . . . I call upon the churches of all denominations . . . to put their shoulders to the wheel to destroy communism for it will destroy them tomorrow if they do not destroy it today."

The General Election of 1949 brought victory and a second term of office for the J.L.P. but it also brought new challenges and situations which forced Alexander Bustamante to seek new directions for himself and the Jamaica Labour Party. He was faced with a formidable parliamentary Opposition led by his cousin Norman Manley which began to score the J.L.P. for its lukewarm support of self-government, as well as for its lack of planning and formulation of policies which would help to promote economic growth and development and accelerate the creation of job opportunities. For the P.N.P. attached great importance to planning — that is to say, the formulation, as much as possible in quantitative form, of comprehensive plans and policies in order to achieve certain economic objectives — as an essential feature of socialism in action. While in opposition between 1944 and 1955, the P.N.P. produced annual statements of policy as guidelines to planning a wide range of programmes that would lead to economic prosperity. In March 1950, Norman Manley successfully moved a private Member's motion in the House of Representatives that a Select Committee on Unemployment be set up to consider measures for immediate relief of the unemployed. He introduced his motion by saying that "nowhere in the world can free enterprise and the unrestricted operation of ordinary economic development deal with what is one of the greatest problems confronting all peoples everywhere, which is the problem of unemployment." The motion received Bustamante's support, for as he said, he could not conceive that anyone would bring such a motion for propanganda's sake. Three months later the Committee under the chairmanship of Sir Harold Allan, Minister of Finance (who had also moved for the setting up of the Unemployment Commission in 1935), laid before the House a unanimous interim Report. Meeting as a Committee of the whole House with a quorum of eleven members, the Committee had invited the public to send in memoranda. The Minister of Finance indicated that the recommendations which the House was asked to accept included:

1. Provision of £1 million over the next twelve months to enable the operation of island-wide development works during that period;
2. Representations to the British Government for a loan of £2 million at one per cent per annum interest for a period of fifty years to finance

large-scale development projects;
3. Introduction of (a) Purchase Tax on special and luxury items (b) Capital Gains Tax (c) Surtax on companies' profits;
4. Expedition of schemes already approved under the Ten-Year Plan;
5. Creation of a State Bank;
6. Investment in Jamaica of 50 per cent of the total amount of the Savings Bank.

Opposition Members drew the ire of Bustamante when they emphasized that the key to the whole Report was Paragraph 8 which read: "Unless there is a radical alteration of Government policy no proposals can be more than temporary expedients. The problem demands a planned economic policy with Government accepting responsibility for the initiation and development of that policy. Such measures as the creation of a Land and Agricultural Corporation and a State Bank are fundamental elements in such a policy and unless the examination of these and other basic matters is undertaken immediately, the interim proposals, if implemented, will do no more than relieve for the time being a small portion of the widespread distress, and in short while the natural increase in unemployment will overtake the result achieved."

Suspecting that this paragraph reflected the authority of the P.N.P. Members who participated in preparation of the Report, Bustamante reacted strongly to what he discerned to be an attempt by the Opposition to gain political advantage. "There is the word 'planned'. I have heard so much planning here, that I wonder if those who are speaking really mean it. It is a direct attack upon the government, and those who are not socialists or communists will realize themselves . . . We all know that paragraph was intended to be of propaganda value to the Opposition."[27] The P.N.P. however continued to make Paragraph 8 and especially the desirability of setting up an Agricultural Development Corporation the centre of controversy over months of debate. In September 1950 the Government sought approval of the House for a supplementary provision of £100,000 in the 1950–1 estimates to provide additional funds to special works to relieve unemployment in the country parishes and in the Corporate Area. The P.N.P.'s finance critic, N.N. Nethersole, however, proposed an amending rider which the Government could hardly accept: ". . . But regards the provision as entirely inadequate contribution to the relief of unemployment and deplores the lukewarm acceptance of those proposals in the Unemployment Committee's Interim Report not actually rejected by Government; repudiates the Government's rejection of Paragraph 8 of the Committee Report which calls for a radical alteration of Government's policy. . . ." Alexander Bustamante offered a spirited rejoinder in a speech which lasted for over two and a half days, which fell short, however, of his record established in June 1949 of a budget speech which extended over five days.

Less than a year later, however, in June 1951 the Jamaica Labour Party announced a proposal to create an Agricultural Development Corporation. Then in February 1952 came the decision to create a companion — Industrial Development Corporation (established in June 1952). Norman Manley welcomed both decisions which represented, as he saw it, the triumph of the spirit of socialism. "These proposals are far-reaching. They involve acceptance of the basic socialist approach that Government must forsake its role of confining its activity to the preservation of law and order, and to the maintenance of social services, and boldly go into the fields of practical enterprise. . . ." Manley saw the creation of both bodies as "key instruments for effective planning and functioning". It was an admission "that private enterprise has failed, for if it has not failed, you want no further corporation". Manley drew a further significant conclusion: "Nothing but the pressure of extreme events could have brought this Government to accept those proposals which it had steadily declared to be impracticable and contrary to their own philosophy."[28]

Alexander Bustamante would not have shared his cousin Norman's ideological assessment of these developments. What the proposals did reflect, undeniably, was the growing convergence of the two political parties and the maturity of bi-partism or the two-party system. As Manley himself observed later in an article written in 1967, "The parties must not differ so widely in their ideas of government and society as to compel one to seek to eradicate totally and destroy the other as an essential condition of the achievement of its own aims."[29] There may be some truth to the quip that socialist parties are necessary to formulate plans and policies but that conservative parties are elected to implement them.

By 1949, the Jamaica Labour Party had begun to move less cautiously towards the enactment of more positive legislation, positive in the sense of having favourable long-run consequences for social and economic development. In 1949, the Government enacted the Manufacture of Buttons (Encouragement) Law, which was followed by a more general incentive law, the Pioneer Industry (Encouragement) Law, designed to encourage the establishment and development of new industries. Other incentives and concessions, such as Customs Tariff Amendments, to induce the imports of machinery and materials; special incentive legislation for cement and textiles; tariff protection and quota restrictions had all been provided on an *ad hoc* basis and in response to overtures from vested interests. The Pioneer Industry Law of 1949 provided that, where any industry was declared a pioneer industry, any person who proposed to establish a factory under this aegis would enjoy relief or exemption from certain taxes. There had never been the slightest doubt in Bustamante's mind but that Jamaica would have to attract and rely on the inflow of foreign capital and investment to generate development and create job opportunities. Interestingly enough, by 1949 the P.N.P. had come around to much the same view as Bustamante. The earlier position of the P.N.P. had been that overseas capital was necessary but that "it should be solicited in the form of government to government loans and reallocated through the State Bank to be created for investment in both public and private sectors."[30] However, faced with the realities of increasing rather than decreasing unemployment in a society where both parties and their union allies were continually escalating promises and consequently the expectation of the masses — including the thousands of unemployed — that better things lay just around the corner, the P.N.P. shifted to a policy of attracting direct investment of private foreign capital on the basis of defined developmental and employment priorities and criteria. Alexander Bustamante saw no reason to change his position, and in February 1953 he could still say, "As long as we are not socialists and continue to invite investors here, we must endeavour to ensure them a fair profit, otherwise things are bad today, it will be worse tomorrow and much worse the other day."

In 1949 the Government also had received the Report of a Commission which it had appointed to enquire into the Public Service. The Commissioner, Eric Mills, C.B.E., an Englishman, recommended in the main:

1. Division of the Civil Service into administrative and clerical classes;
2. The absorption of the war bonus into substantive salaries;
3. Establishment of a cost-of-living index for application to weekly- and daily-paid employees only;
4. Regrading of existing posts.

The Report was given a hostile reception by Bustamante who moved that it be referred to a Select Committee of the whole House for detailed consideration. He objected to the emphasis on the upper ranks of the Civil Service and insisted that any regrading "must start from the lowest level and administer to them the highest percentage increase, which has not been the case of Mr. Mills' Report". The proposed division of the civil service into two basic classes aroused his ire. "As far as the creation of what I term a different class of civil servants, it will never have any approval. It will just breed or create more disunity amongst the civil servants or amongst us . . ."[31]

When, however, the Report of the Select Committee came before the House for implementation in August 1950, the new structure was approved, subject to two amendments moved by Alexander Bustamante: "That the administrative grade should be recruited from two sources (*a*) selection from among candidates of promise in clerical grades and (*b*) selection from candidates within the service of such educational standards as may be prescribed." Where the Commission had recommended that "wages be increased" Bustamante pointed out quite properly that this was the prerogative of Government and the House and should read "consideration be given to increasing their wages". Government also turned its attention to Temporary and Unestablished Clerks employed by the public service.

The contour of a modernized career civil service was completed when the J.L.P. government established in the latter part of 1950 the office of a Public Service Commissioner and a Public Service Board.

The results of the General Election in December 1949 had served notice on Alexander Bustamante and the J.L.P. that the P.N.P. was on the ascendancy and had developed a momentum which could take that party into power. For although forced by the necessity of survival to adapt political and trade union strategies to the realities of Bustamante-ism, the P.N.P. (and the T.U.C. as well) remained true to its conception of an "organization party" based on rational structures and procedures. It was, after all, a party led by a man who, by education and professional training, was pre-eminently a rationalist, had a penchant for hard work and painstaking detail and, above all, believed passionately in the efficacy of organization effort. Undaunted by the crushing defeat suffered at the polls in 1945, the P.N.P. and T.U.C. had doggedly set about the task of rebuilding and consolidating their shattered organizational bases. Admittedly, to counter the immense personal appeal of Bustamante, the "Chief", Norman Manley had had to lend himself to the cult of the personality and assume the mantle of "Father of the Nation" and "Man of Destiny". But as Nettleford has reminded, "Even then the growing personality cult seemed grossly out of character with the man to whom the cult of personality was secretly embarrassing if not reprehensible but who could not escape this gruelling imperative of nation-building politics."[32]

Faced with the consummate artistry and powerful intellectual thrust of Manley and the members of his first team or "shadow cabinet", Alexander Bustamante had to rely increasingly on his colleagues in the House, not only to sustain the burden of criticism, but to break out of the mould of creeping gradualism and lack-lustre government into which the J.L.P. had been cast by Bustamante's preoccupation with, and narrow conception of, proper financial management. A philosophy of pragmatism is not likely to be inspirational. This was brought out clearly in Bustamante's utterances on unemployment during 1950: "But it is our duty now to try and set a record of preventing the rising unemployment, to reduce it, to do things others have not done before. But let us face one fact. It is a matter of finance." Needled by the Opposition on a subsequent occasion he observed, "What I said was, and what I say now is the same as I said a few years ago, that it is not the duty of any government to provide work for each and every person that needs work. It is the duty of every country to relieve employment materially as it is within the possibility of finance."

Even in a matter so dear to him as Old Age Pensions, which he made the subject of investigations by a Government committee in 1945, Bustamante considered the financial constraint as being so severe that he conceded in debate in June 1950, that the Government could not contemplate even the most hesitant start within a couple of years. Perhaps the most salutary jolt ever administered to Bustamante's economic and fiscal conservatism was the Report of the Mission of the International Bank for Reconstruction and Development (World Bank) which at the invitation of the Government visited Jamaica in 1952 to report on the economic development of the island. Where the Mission took its departure from previous reports was that to attain the objectives they thought feasible, they proposed expenditures on a scale never before comtemplated by Jamaican governments. Commenting in the House on the Report which for a period became the economic bible of Jamaica, Alexander Bustamante observed, "I have nothing more to say except that we of the Government accept the principles of the World Bank Report, but that there is no money from general revenue to do that. Posterity must pay." That last admission coming from Alexander Bustamante was quite a concession.

In turn, therefore, Bustamante was forced by the growing strength and popularity of the P.N.P. as a coherently organized party and by the waning popularity of the J.L.P. outside of the strongly traditionalist rural parishes, to reorganize the party along more rational lines and so bring it more closely to the "structured" model of the P.N.P. This process

146

began in 1951 when the J.L.P. was given a formal constitution, which regularized machinery and procedures for the orderly election of officers of the Executive and other party officials. Furthermore, in a society which was being made conscious of the need for, as well as benefits of, education and training, Bustamante had to challenge the image of the P.N.P. as the party with a monopoly of the brains or intelligence of the country. He had of necessity, therefore, to begin drawing more liberally on the educated professional groups which traditionally had tended to gravitate towards the P.N.P.

The task of bringing in new blood and regenerating the J.L.P. was made much easier, however, for Alexander Bustamante than for Norman Manley and the P.N.P. For Bustamante remained undisputed boss of the J.L.P. without even the slightest suggestion of challenge to his leadership, which in any event was reinforced by his absolute and even tighter control — popularly received at that — of the Bustamante Industrial Trade Union.

T.U.C. notwithstanding, the B.I.T.U. remained a remarkably stable labour organization in terms of leadership as well as membership support. In 1945 the B.I.T.U. reported a membership of 46,538, with 29,930 paying. It rose to 59,722 (35,734 paying) in 1949 and to 64,859 (33,429 paying) in 1951. The paying membership remained consistently higher than for the rival T.U.C. and its successor in 1952, the National Workers Union, ranging from 50 per cent higher in the earlier years to over 70 per cent in later years. This reflected that enduring commitment and loyalty of workers to Alexander Bustamante, especially in the sugar belt. The growth of membership of the T.U.C., from 4,050 in 1949 to 23,312 (8,764 paying) in the 1950's, probably slowed the growth, if anything, of the B.I.T.U.; for an expanding labour force and development of sectors other than agriculture made it possible for the major union blocs to continue increasing their overall membership in absolute terms.

To the extent that Bustamante's complete overlordship of the J.L.P. made it relatively easy for him to bring in new blood at the higher reaches, it gave to the J.L.P. a flexibility and adaptability which could not be matched by the more bureaucratically administered P.N.P. in which newcomers had to contend with the "old guard" effectively in control of the party "machine". The narrowing of historical differences between the J.L.P. and the P.N.P. and the trend towards convergence was quickened considerably when the process of converting Bustamante to the cause, as distinct from the idea, of self-government was completed between 1950–3 and by an unexpected showdown between the left and right

147

wings in the P.N.P. which culminated in the purge of the T.U.C. left wing from the party in 1952.

The election of Norman Manley, the apostle of self-government, to the House of Representative in 1949 served to make this objective a central concern of Parliament and the country at large. Beginning in 1950, Manley and the P.N.P. waged an unremitting campaign to prod Bustamante and the J.L.P. into acceptance of a timetable of more rapid constitutional advance. In July 1950, Manley invited the House "to accept as a basic principle for constitutional reform today in Jamaica, that Jamaica is fit for complete self-government in local affairs". Bustamante later rejoined, "There are times when we must endeavour to walk before we climb." In July 1951, Manley unleashed a severe attack against, and indictment of, the Jamaica Labour Party for retarding Jamaica's progress toward self-government. He pointed out that Jamaica had fallen behind other British Colonies in constitutional reform in spite of the fact that Jamaica and Ceylon had been the only two Colonies to get constitutional advance during World War II. Reminding that the Majority Party had run an electoral campaign in 1944 in which the slogan had been "self-government is slavery" and that it would lead to brown-man (middle-class) rule, Manley assailed the J.L.P.: "It is a notorious fact that there is not one single person in this House in the Labour Party who ever lifted a little finger in the constitutional struggle in this House." He also disclosed that in 1950 when the House met in Committee there had been substantial agreement about the constitutional advances that were desirable and possible in Jamaica. "I have never known an occasion when there was an appearance of greater agreement between both parties on an issue which should transcend party politics. What happened after that? Under the orders of the Leader of the Majority Party the Members came here and told us, he told us that it would require a document signed by us as Leader of the People's National Party declaring that if any constitutional advances be regarded by the Secretary of State for the Colonies as requiring new elections to be held we do not want that advance." Still another year later, when the House was debating a J.L.P. proposal to increase the number as well as powers of Ministers, Manley declared that "the proposals for constitutional changes do not accord with the Jamaican desire and claim for self-government, and that further changes providing for full self-government in local affairs be introduced forthwith." In a major review of constitutional advance since 1944 he asserted, "I repeat there is only one test of a people's fitness for self-government and that is your ability to make effective demands." Three weeks later

Manley successfully moved "that this House declares itself in favour of self-government for Jamaica and appoints a Committee of seven Members of the House forthwith to prepare a constitution providing for self-government to be submitted for approval to the Secretary of State for the Colonies, at the earliest possible date." Alexander Bustamante rose to defend himself and his party: "It has been said that we on this side have not supported self-government for Jamaica. This is incorrect.

"One of the revised planks of the Jamaica Labour Party is to work incessantly and consistently for the freedom that is ours by right and this is what it says: To work towards self-government in Jamaica with a view to achieving Federation in the British Caribbean area and Dominion Status within the framework of the British Commonwealth of Nations."[33] Bustamante was quoting from the revised 1951 Constitution of the Jamaica Labour Party, and at Manley's request he walked across the floor of the House to hand him a copy. A year later (always it seems in July) Bustamante could assure Florizel Glasspole in the House: "I am determined to have self-government. You can look in my face and see that it is not fiction — not a fantastic idea — but it is something that is deep down in my heart."[34] If Glasspole needed further reassurance it was forthcoming: "I want self-government and during my lifetime. Not a few years to come but soon because my friend of Eastern Kingston has challenged my right to remain here for ever." Alexander Bustamante had travelled a long and hard emotional road. In May 1933, he became Chief Minister with the inauguration of the ministerial system, giving to the Jamaican elected Members in the Executive Council the power to initiate policy and to be responsible for departments set up under their ministeries.

The schism between the T.U.C. and the P.N.P. in 1952 had far-reaching repercussion and implication both for the P.N.P. and Bustamante and the B.I.T.U./J.L.P. For Manley and the P.N.P. it brought the parting of ways of comrades who had borne the heat of the day, had struggled for fourteen years to build the T.U.C. and P.N.P. into powerful organizations. The strain on the leadership in the P.N.P., as indicated earlier, began in 1949 on the issue of the withdrawal of the T.U.C. from the W.F.T.U. By 1951, however, the T.U.C. was at its peak of strength and popularity. Ken Hill, by hard fighting and rhetorical brilliance which had earned him the nickname "The Whip", had broken Bustamante's hold on the working classes in Kingston and was at this time Mayor of the Kingston and St. Andrew Corporation. Ten of the twenty-one members of the P.N.P. Executive were members of the T.U.C. There

was the possibility that the left wing of the party, by virtue of the control
of the trade union, could assume a preponderance of influence in the
P.N.P. The right wing of the T.U.C. as well as of the P.N.P. became
alarmed. Norman Manley's role historically as President of the Party
had been to remain in the centre mediating between right and left and
keeping friction within bounds. But on 26th November 1951, Thossie
Kelly and Walter McPherson, supporters of Florizel Glasspole, the leader
of the right wing in the T.U.C., and paid organizers and Executive members of the T.U.C., held a meeting at Sprostons (bauxite construction
company) in the parish of Manchester, announcing the formation of a new
union — the National Labour Congress. They resigned from the T.U.C.
and Ken Hill as President of the T.U.C. urged their expulsion from the
P.N.P. — as their action was in contravention of the Party policy of support
of the T.U.C. The right wing of the P.N.P. then alleged that there was
an attempt on the part of the left to seize control of the P.N.P. machinery
and rose to the defence of the secessionists. A P.N.P. committee was
appointed to investigate Kelly and McPherson who produced a famous
or infamous "document" alleged to have been used in T.U.C. training
classes from 1948, and which purportedly contained communist teachings.
The Committee — comprised of N.W. Manley; N.N. Nethersole
(Chairman), First Vice-President of the P.N.P.; V.L. Arnett, Secretary;
and E.B. Baker, Executive Member — felt obliged to investigate also
the countercharges of the right wing for, if as alleged, the left wing was
accepting the discipline of another party, presumably the Communist
Party, this also constituted an infringement of the Party's constitution.
The Committee found that through study course documents, prepared
and issued with the knowledge and approval of the four H's, Arthur
Henry, one of the four, had been teaching that only a communist party
means the workers any good and that workers would have to leave
the P.N.P. and form a communist party "at some stage of the movement
for freedom prior to which the working class may be part of a general
national party like the P.N.P." Moreover, the four H's and others had
formed a secret organization (caucus) within the P.N.P. to which they
were bound by discipline and which was working to disrupt the P.N.P.
 The leading members of the T.U.C. were given the choice of resigning
or expulsion. The investigating Committee's recommendation was
upheld first by the General Council and then by the Party Conference
to which the left appealed. There was widespread sympathy for the
left wing and Manley himself tried to avoid the split. The left wing,
however, seemingly miscalculated their strength at the Annual Conference,

for when Ken Hill made his defence, he lapsed into a bitter and abusive denunciation of the right wing which did the cause of the left little good. Having resigned from the P.N.P., the four H's took with them the T.U.C. to launch a new political party — the National Labour Party — with Ken Hill as President. After a few gasps of breath the N.L.P. faded into oblivion.

The purge of the left wing may well have seemed a vindication of Alexander Bustamante's charges made as early as 1938 and maintained throughout as an effective smear against the P.N.P. that the party contained communist elements and that a victory for the P.N.P. could give rise to political dictatorship. Bustamante's consolation, if any, would have been short-lived, however, for having lost its labour wing for a second time, the P.N.P. immediately launched a successor trade union — the National Workers Union (N.W.U.) — to fill the gap. The N.W.U. was registered under the Trade Union Law on 17th October 1952. It immediately applied for and was granted affiliation with the I.C.F.T.U. N.N. Nethersole assumed the presidency and Florizel Glasspole became General Secretary. Thossie Kelly in due course filled the position of Vice-President, eventually becoming President in 1955 when N.N. Nethersole became Minister of Finance in the first P.N.P. government.

In addition to having Nethersole, Glasspole and Kelly, all professional unionists in the Jamaican tradition, the N.W.U. was fortunate in attracting the services of Michael N. Manley, son of the party leader. Young Manley, a university graduate (B.Sc. Econ., London School of Economics) and journalist by profession, was given, as Sugar Supervisor, the formidable assignment of "cutting in" on Bustamante in the sugar belt. He displayed considerable organizational ability and flair in his campaign among sugar workers and enjoyed outstanding success. Michael Manley had a grasp of the social factors which had made Alexander Bustamante almost sacred among sugar workers and geared his strategy accordingly. No attempt was made to attack the "Grand Old Man of Labour" personally, nor to attack anything he had done. There was an enormous amount of things to attack otherwise. After all, the B.I.T.U. had been representing sugar workers for at least fifteen years. The structure of the B.I.T.U. was not operationally rationalized and many of the arrangements and interpretations applied to work agreements were personal arrangements between branch secretaries or delegates and management. It was therefore easy to find cases where claims of individual workers or groups of workers for some adjustment had not been pressed vigorously, and the N.W.U. was able in many cases to recover arrears of wages for

151

such workers, who then felt more adequately represented.

The N.W.U. also refrained from talking politics too early in the game and built up, to rival the B.I.T.U., a sugar organization which produced tangible results. As to how much advantage the son derived from his father's name, it is difficult to say. What he did benefit from was a striking physical appearance as well as personality which readily lent itself to the cult of the personality. In this respect the N.W.U. reflected an element of charismatic leadership, reminiscent of the B.I.T.U. and of Bustamante's earlier ascendancy.

The growth of the N.W.U. was spectacular. Its first task was to take over former T.U.C. strongholds and in this it was largely successful. A crucial factor for the N.W.U. was the take-over of the high-earnings bauxite workers after a strike for recognition, which lasted for twelve days and ended with a poll being taken by the Labour Department to establish the status of the N.W.U. The dissension in the T.U.C. and the appearance of the N.W.U. led to a scramble for membership and power in the trade union movement, and the Labour Adviser was obliged to enunciate a new set of criteria and guidelines for taking of polls in representational disputes which would preserve the principle that workers should be free to choose their representatives, without dishonouring collective agreements that had been entered into recently in good faith. Ironically, the T.U.C. had made the N.W.U.'s task of taking over its membership relatively easy. No other organization in Jamaica's history had (or has) done more to politicize workers. The four H's as well as secondary T.U.C. leaders and "helpers", such as Bancroft Edwards, Osmond Dyce, Roy Woodham, Winston Grubb, Leslie Alexander and Frank Gordon, had carried out intensive political education and had given workers an ideological orientation which left them committed to the P.N.P. as a socialist party. This loyalty to the Party overcame loyalty to the T.U.C., and the N.W.U. was able to make rapid strides. Thus the two-party, two-union bloc alliance survived its first serious threat. When the N.W.U. filed its first annual return with the Registrar of Trade Unions, it reported a membership of 5,025 with 1,842 paying as at 31st March 1953. By 1955, the year of the next General Election, N.W.U. membership had risen to 24,361 but with only 8,961 paying. In comparison with the B.I.T.U., which at that time had a membership of 64,164 (45,876 paying), the N.W.U. was decidedly the more political of the two organizations in the sense that the N.W.U. was carrying a very large proportion of members who were not supporting the union with financial dues, but could be expected to deliver electoral votes to the P.N.P. Undoubtedly the N.W.U. made a significant contribution to the victory of the P.N.P. in 1955. The P.N.P. captured 18 seats and 51 per cent of the popular vote while the J.L.P. gained 14 seats and 39 per cent of the votes cast.

The People's National Party, through dogged persistence and organizational effort at the grass-roots, had managed not only to survive but to become a credible and popular alternative to the Jamaica Labour Party. At the trade union level, the four H's and the T.U.C. left wing had succeeded in establishing a labour beach-head for the P.N.P. by truly impressive organization work and the will to fight back, even violently, when pushed to the limit. By 1955 the bogey of socialism apparently had been laid to rest as far as the P.N.P. was concerned. Not only had the fears of influential segments been allayed by the purge of the Party's left wing in 1952, but Bustamante and the J.L.P. had been deprived of a well-proven and effective electoral strategy. This, however, may not have been fully appreciated by Bustamante and the J.L.P. Four days before the General Election, in response to invitations issued to both parties by *The Daily Gleaner,* Mrs. Rose Leon, Chairman of the J.L.P. Executive, published a carefully prepared letter in which she posed the issue for the electorate in rather stark terms. "We desire above everything else to preserve our Christian democratic way of life, desire to maintain and foster a climate in which we can live peacefully together without hate, rigid controls and policing. But none of these desires could be maintained in an atmosphere where socialism and communism have their tentacles implanted. You have to decide the issue. You have to make the decision for or against socio-communism." On the eve of the election, D.C. Tavares, solicitor and Secretary of the J.L.P., who along with Mrs. Leon had been largely responsible for the J.L.P.'s reorganization and new constitution in 1951, wrote on the economic dangers of the P.N.P.'s policies and victory and pointed out that there is no such thing as little socialism. The J.L.P. was depicted as a capitalist party. "As you know the main bulwark of our policy is a firm adherence to the great principle of private enterprise, for we believe that it is thus alone that the latent talent and initiative of our people can be unleashed and sustained."

Alexander Bustamante, in an elaborate advertisement entitled "Final Appeal", placed in *The Daily Gleaner* also on 11th January, made an impassioned plea to save the country from a socialist government and drew upon the traditional Bustamante appeal: "If my own interest, my own safety and my regard for my freedom were the first thought

153

in my life I would never had faced bayonets in 1938 with open chest. I would never have placed myself in a position to have been sent to prison and placed on the bare concrete, even without clothing. For that was what was done to me in the Central Police Station. I would never have been sent to detention camp for seventeen months. In all my life I have always felt the greatest thing that one could do is to sacrifice one's self for others and one's country." He cried foul also that Manley should have been telling the people that he (Bustamante) had returned to Jamaica in modest financial circumstances in 1934, but was now a wealthy man, largely as a result of his involvement in union and public affairs.

But during the Election campaign the P.N.P. struck a responsive chord among the masses with the promise of developing an educational system which would bring quality education at all levels within the reach of working-class Jamaicans. What is more, the P.N.P. promised honest government and administration and an end to political corruption. On this score the J.L.P. was particularly vulnerable. As early as 1947 there had been dissension within the J.L.P. and resignations took place of Labour M.H.R.'s, who in defending themselves in the House implied that members of the J.L.P. had been prompted by pecuniary advantage to bring forward legislative measures favourable to business interests, such as the removal of the Excess Profits Tax instituted during World War II and the awarding of public utility and monopoly franchises.

Subsequently, two J.L.P. Ministers of Government were convicted and imprisoned for graft and corruption. Nor did Alexander Bustamante by his boastful declarations of personal wealth help to dispel the taint of corruption which his party had acquired. Concerned to sustain the legendary aspects of his life and career — such as the story which he himself had initiated "that he had made a fortune speculating on the New York Stock Exchange" — Bustamante boasted in the House of Representatives in 1946 of his bank account: "You would drop dead if you saw my Bank account. I have £75,000. No mistake about it. I have money. I have £75,000." At the same time he played on the admiration of the masses for someone who could come out ahead in the game: "I went abroad and I acquired my wealth. They say I stole it but if I stole it, I was wise to get away with it."

The fact is, then, that by 1955 Alexander Bustamante's halo as "Saviour" and benevolent "Chieftain" had begun to grow dim, certainly for the younger age groups. The continuing drift of the younger people, as well as the displaced agro-proletariat, from the rural areas to metropolitan Kingston and the bigger towns was serving to enlarge the concentrations

154

of relatively more sophisticated, urbanized voters, who were not always amused by Bustamante's flamboyant behaviour or "antics", as increasingly they came to be regarded.

In a sense, therefore, the dichotomy in Jamaican politics between town and country, between the Corporate Area and the rest of Jamaica, became also a dichotomy of older and more traditionalist generations versus younger and less traditionalist generations.

After ten years in office, therefore, Alexander Bustamante was to have his first experience in the political wilderness as Leader of the Opposition. The first decade of political unionism had come to an end. By placing the interest of workers at "the centre of the political cosmos", Alexander Bustamante had brought the working class into the mainstream of Jamaican political life. As the leader, effectively of a workers' party, he was given a unique opportunity, had he been so inclined, to pursue a "political economy" which might have made it possible, through either restructuring of the economy or refashioning of the instruments of economic control, for the working class to have been brought also into the mainstream of economic activity. But he was inhibited by his own conservative social and economic philosophy (as well as that of the working class) from using political power as the primary instrument for achieving social and economic justice. Instead, he continued to rely on collective bargaining as the primary institutional means for achieving distributive justice and used the political agency to redress specific inadequacies of collective bargaining.

The legislative record of the B.I.T.U./J.L.P. for the decade 1945–55 is, therefore, a rather modest one. Progressively, proclamations were issued under the Minimum Wage Law to establish or raise minimum rates of pay or levels of wages for workers in trades or industries which were partially unionized or difficult to unionize or in which collective bargaining was likely to be ineffective. These included alcoholic and non-alcoholic beverages; bakery, biscuit and catering trades; dry goods; printing; hotels; laundry and dry cleaning; and retail petrol. Regulations were also passed regulating opening and closing hours of shops for the benefit of shop assistants or store clerks in Kingston and other towns. Modest improvements were made in the salaries and fringe benefits of civil servants and subordinate employees of government and of quasi-governmental bodies, on the basis of periodic reviews and regradings.

An enabling Holiday-with-Pay Law was introduced in 1947. Amendments were made to the rudimentary Workmen's Compensation Act in 1952 and 1954 to effect modest improvements in benefits and extend the scope of the Law's coverage. A Sugar Industry Labour Welfare Fund was established under the Sugar Reserve Funds Law of 1948 and a Board appointed to administer its schemes for community and social development.

In 1954 Superannuation and Pension Funds were initiated for Kingston portworkers and sugar workers respectively. The Apprenticeship Law of 1881 was repealed and replaced by a new enabling law, but the nine-teenth-century Masters and Servants Law remained on the statute books.

Low-income housing schemes in Kingston as well as rural areas were pursued, but on so limited a scale as to be token gestures. The destruction of some 50,000 houses during the 1951 hurricane and the creation of an Emergency Relief Fund did lead to some heightening of building activity. Land settlement schemes for farmers as well as ex-servicemen were extended. Longer-term measures designed to lay down an administrative structure which would facilitate modernization and economic development included, as indicated earlier, reorganization of the Civil Service and creation of the Agricultural and Industrial Development-ment Corporations — all between 1951 and 1952 — as also the invitation to the World Bank to send a Mission to report on the island's economic development.

At the industrial level, the Bustamante Industrial Trade Union continued its thrust for economic betterment of workers, operating on the principle that workers were entitled to a fair wage and the employer to a fair rate of return. At the same time, as has been seen, the B.I.T.U. also functioned as an employment agency to the extent that its political arm — the J.L.P. — accorded preferential hiring and employment on government projects to supporters of the Union and the Party. Incidentally, successive change-overs of the two parties in office have served to refine rather than discard this rewarding feature of party politics.

There were of course the psychological gains accruing to workers and the working classes generally from Bustamanteism and political unionism. Alexander Bustamante embodied the yearning and quest of the masses for salvation, dignity, assertion and even exaltation. He never lost sight of his role as the invincible Chief. It was reflected in his irreverent approach in the Legislature, his long rambling speeches in which he interspersed personal references intended to sustain the legend of Bustamante. In debates, particularly during the early years of his first term of office, the House and the public at large were told of his experiences as traffic inspector in Panama and as a police inspector in Havana; that he was a graduate dietician with ten and a half years' experience in one of the largest hospitals in New York; that he came from a great engineering family and a great medical family, "and so I have the instinct for engineering."

There were references to travels in Spain where he owned a castle, as well as studies which had helped to develop his extraordinary powers. "No man in this country knows anything more about auto suggestion than I do, for I hold three diplomas through Spanish, Italian and Portuguese commercial correspondence. . . . By these courses I have taken in Spanish, Italian and Portuguese, I am taught to visualise a man's character 10,000 miles away through his letter."[35] He was businessman and financier, but had been prepared to make sacrifices. "I was elected on the sacrifice I made for this country." Always he was drawing comparisons between himself and the Governor as the symbol of imperial authority. "I must attack because any time a reflection is thrown against Government, it is thrown against me and no man from the Governor down knows more about Government than I do." To the extent that he had achieved all these things without formal university education, lack of education should not be the measure of man's ability. Bustamante displayed a marked antipathy not only to civil servants but to teachers whom he felt were naturally inclined to be pro-P.N.P. and anti-labour. If Alexander Bustamante epitomized the lingering uncertainties and resentments of the working classes, he also gave concrete expression to their hopes and aspirations. Isaac W.A. Barrant, Secretary of the St. Thomas Branch of the B.I.T.U. and an illiterate man, was appointed Minister of Agriculture by Bustamante when Barrant was re-elected in 1949 as one of the M.H.R.'s for St. Thomas. Barrant went on to earn the respect and affection of his countrymen from all walks of life.

The defeat of his party was not taken by Bustamante as his defeat personally. Alexander Bustamante believed too much in himself to accept the notion of defeat. In conceding loss of the election he was as irrepressible and egotistic as ever: "With no egotism, without any boast whatever, I am positively confident that what my Government has done for the last ten years no other Government will be able to do within thirty years. And what I have done for the working class of this country, no other man or other group of persons will be able to equal it, perhaps, within one hundred years." As one of his most ardent working-class supporters and a Minister of State said, "Only God can do more than Bustamante has done."[36]

A few days later, he telegraphed good wishes to Norman Manley. "You have won a close race and now have the opportunity you have longed for. I have always taken defeat without bitterness, and triumph without boasting. We shall be an honest opposition. Good luck."

Bustamante could also take comfort from tributes paid by analysts in overseas papers such as the British *Times*. "A spell-binding demagogue with a propensity for clowning in public, Mr. Bustamante did not deceive those who worked in close association with him. They know his principal characteristics to be a commonsense-shrewdness and fair-mindedness that seldom erred. He cooperated loyally with successive Governors and under his long leadership Jamaica has seen great economic development, a marked betterment of working conditions and steadily consolidated political advances."

For his supporters, especially in the rural area, there also was a measure of consolation in defeat, as Alexander Bustamante was rewarded with a Knighthood and became Sir Alexander. It was seen as another first scored against his cousin Norman Manley. There were others of course who saw this as the crowning of his career and a recognition that the Bustamante era had come to an end. But Alexander Bustamante refused to be dismissed that easily and that early from public life.

Alexander Bustamante receiving his knighthood on 8th June 1955.

6

FROM DEFEAT
TO TRIUMPH
1955–1962

After chiding the electors of Jamaica in true paternal fashion for their ingratitude in denying his party a third straight term in office after he had done so much for them, Alexander Bustamante quickly shrugged off his disappointment and assumed the role of Leader of the Opposition with good humour and vigour. And a challenging situation it proved to be.

After ten years in the wilderness of Opposition, during which time Manley and his colleagues had kept electoral hopes and morale alive by formulating plans and policies to deal with the more pressing social and economic ills of Jamaica, the new P.N.P. administration moved with assurance and despatch to give firm and purposeful direction to the country's affairs. Consistent with the P.N.P.'s espousal of socialism and his own penchant for organization effort, Norman Manley as Chief Minister immediately saw to the establishment of a Central Planning Unit and a Ministry of Planning and Development over which he assumed control, relinquishing the portfolio of Minister of Agriculture which he had taken during his first year in office. Planning and rational administration were to be the mainsprings of action in mobilizing, harnessing and exploiting the natural, human and financial resources of the country. In quickening the pace and the rate of economic development and economic growth, agriculture, education and the promotion of industry were accorded high priority by the P.N.P.

Public revenues and expenditures were expanded rapidly and assumed new orders of magnitude as successive budgets were geared to reflect and accommodate the new government's wide-ranging legislative programmes. In the first ten years of the J.L.P.'s administration, budget allocations and expenditure on education had risen from J$1.8 million to J$2.4 million and that on agriculture from J$792,000 to J$1.2 million. By the end of the P.N.P.'s first five-year term, the expenditure on education had climbed to J$8.4 million, while that for agriculture had risen from J$1.4 million (1955–6) to J$2.4 million. Whereas total public expenditures had risen from J$20.6 million in 1950–1 to J$34.2 million in 1954–5,

Sir Alexander Bustamante, now Leader of the Opposition in the Jamaica House of Representatives, on a private visit to Pope Pius XII in Rome, 31st August 1957.

161

during the next five years the total rose from J$37.2 million in 1955–6 to J$73.8 million in 1959–60. Of course it must be noted that the rapid expansion of the fledgling bauxite industry and the renegotiation by 1958 of increased royalties and taxation by Norman Manley, gave the P.N.P. administration a revenue base which the J.L.P. had lacked. Nevertheless, it is clear that Norman Manley (as also N.N. Nethersole, his close associate and Minister of Finance) under the influence of Keynesian economics, had been emancipated from the constraints of orthodox fiscal policy and public finance. In April 1956, Manley explained in the House, "A good budget for the small man is a budget which assumes buoyant and expanding revenues and proposes to spend them to the limit."

The P.N.P. Government introduced measures relating to tax and land reform, the establishment or reorganization of administrative, financial, and other developmental institutions, all designed to promote change and growth. In 1955, for instance, came the Facilities for Titles Law and the Land Bonds Law. The former made it possible for farmers to obtain land titles without the expense and delay of applying for registered titles. The latter allowed for the Government to pay compensation by way of land bonds for compulsory acquisition of land. In 1956, the Land Value Taxation Law stipulated that for taxation valuation, the unimproved value of land be substituted for valuation, based upon the composite value of land and all the work the owner/occupier had done on it. Also introduced at the same time was a new Local Government Reform Bill, to be followed by the Town Planning Act in 1957. Other significant legislation in 1956 included the Industrial Incentives Law, the International Business Companies Law and the Export (Encouragement) Law, all designed to provide additional incentives to foreign investors and to supplement, therefore, the general Incentives Pioneer Industry Law which had been introduced by the J.L.P. administration in 1949. Another very welcome innovation was the publication by the Central Planning Unit, beginning in 1958, of an Economic Survey of Jamaica which reported on, as well as evaluated, the overall and sectoral performance of the economy for the preceding year.

The P.N.P. Government also gave Jamaica its version of a ten-year development plan for the island. The "National Plan for Jamaica 1957–1967" proved to be a much more sophisticated and comprehensive document than the 1947 Ten-Year Plan, but did not reflect any radical departure from the basic policies followed by the J.L.P. If anything, the commitment to embark on a programme of "industrialization by invitation" was made quite explicit. "The Government essentially has a selling job to perform and in addition has to create the basic conditions and offer the necessary incentives which will persuade the investors to leave their own countries and invest abroad."[1]

What the National Plan did highlight, unwittingly, was the dilemma faced by the planners, not alone in Jamaica but in many developing countries, of reconciling the inherent conflict between economic growth and employment. Faced with chronic and endemic unemployment further aggravated by a rapid rate of population growth, the economy had to be set on a course which would make possible a "take off" into sustained growth and thus allow for increases in real income for those gainfully employed, as well as the creation of job and employment opportunities for the unemployed and new entrants into the labour market. In the absence of measures and policies designed to tackle the problem of reducing births, an elected government could not but follow measures aimed at increasing employment and reducing social tension. Given the state and structure of the Jamaican economy, this was likely to mean short-run policies and measures which were not likely to make a contribution to the long-run improvement of the economy and the attainment of a more highly developed economy. The framers of the National Plan sought refuge in an ingenious but uneasy compromise. It amounted to espousal of a dual system for the agricultural sector of the economy, where productive efficiency was to be encouraged for export crops, but work-spreading an acceptable objective in production for the home market.

One difficulty with this approach is that in seeking to effect transformation and modernization of an economy, it is quite unrealistic to assume that one can differentiate between the modern and traditional modes of production in each sector and to adapt the level of technology accordingly. As one analyst observed shortly after the 1957 National Plan was released, "The entire section in which policies dealing with employment and industrialization are discussed seems confused and contradictory. This is largely because the Government wants to provide the maximum number of jobs possible in the short-run. The approach which is advocated seems unlikely to result in Jamaica's long-run development, or in raising living standards. Indeed, its basic philosophy seems to be 'Keep Jamaica poor, but spread the poverty around.'"[2] Nevertheless, whatever constraints, economic, political or social, within which Manley and his colleagues chose or were forced to govern, the P.N.P. administration began work impressively and gave early promise of superior expertise.

As Leader of the Opposition, Alexander Bustamante refused to be awed or stampeded by the administrative vitality of his successors in office and took matters very much in his stride. Indeed, he continued to demonstrate that in the realm of politics he was without peer in Jamaica as a tactician or political strategist.

Whereas the P.N.P. Opposition between 1945 and 1955 had maintained that the J.L.P. lacked a coherent social and political philosophy and had been content to "muddle through", borrowing ideas and policies here and there from P.N.P. policy statements, Alexander Bustamante in Opposition took the line that the P.N.P. administration was merely "reaping the fruits of trees planted by the J.L.P." He could point to the establishment of the bauxite industry in 1952 with its revenue-earning potential, and the creation of the Agricultural and Industrial Development Corporations as major instruments to give effect to an economic policy which had, as a major plank, the encouragement of industry as well as the offering of incentives under an enabling or general incentives law to attract foreign investment.

Bustamante grasped quite readily, then, that acceptance of a parliamentary system based on "ins" and "outs" or Government and Loyal Opposition required also acceptance of the necessity of role reversal. It was not long, therefore, before the J.L.P. Opposition speakers were to be heard hurling against P.N.P. Ministers much the same denunciations and taunts which the latter had made, often with great effect, against the previous J.L.P. administrations. The first important occasion came in May 1956 when the P.N.P. Government proclaimed a State of Emergency which enabled Manley to use soldiers to unload goods urgently needed in the island and to put an end, effectively, to a strike which had shut down the Kingston waterfront. The three Unions, B.I.T.U., T.U.C. and N.W.U, and the Shipping Association, representing wharf owners, after months of negotiation under the auspices of the Joint Industrial Council (J.I.C.) for the waterfront, had failed to achieve a settlement of union wage claims. In accordance with the J.I.C. labour relations protocol, the parties therefore agreed to refer the dispute to arbitration, and a panel of three arbitrators was actually agreed upon. Two of the arbitrators, however, declined to serve and a good deal of bickering then arose between the Unions, employers and the Ministry of Labour concerning the membership of the Arbitration Tribunal. Finally, Florizel Glasspole, Minister of Labour and, until his elevation, a senior officer of the N.W.U., proposed that the Chief Justice be requested to provide the services of a High Court Judge to serve as Chairman of the Tribunal. The B.I.T.U. and T.U.C.

insisted, however, that they must know the name of the Judge likely to serve as Chairman before they could agree to his appointment. Glasspole rejoined that the Chief Justice alone had the power to assign Judges for specific duties. The Unions in the meantime resorted to strike action, and after four days when it appeared that ships would leave without unloading badly needed cargo, including flour and codfish, a consignment of stamps, a large quantity of currency and free food for children, the Government proclaimed a State of Emergency. Manley argued in the House of Representatives that the circumstances justified the use of the armed forces to unload cargoes which were necessary for the essential supply of the community to be preserved and that soldiers, because of their temporary and limited intervention, could not be regarded as strike-breakers.

The J.L.P. frontline Opposition spokesmen, including Bustamante, Donald Sangster, Hugh Shearer and Edwin Allen, argued that "the events and circumstances leading up to the proclamation were insufficient in law and in fact to support the issue of the proclamation and that the acts of the Government since the issue of the proclamation were illegal and unconstitutional — as the requirements of the law and constitution in relation to action in a State of Emergency have not been fulfilled."[3] While Manley used the weight of his professional authority to brush aside the legal arguments of Sangster, labour leaders Bustamante and Shearer were not so easily bridled and insisted on having a field day. "We consider it [the State of Emergency] totally unnecessary. We consider it an over-exercise of authority and a demonstration of tyrannical action," thundered Shearer. Moreover, the shippers were being provided with free labour to unload cargo. Bustamante alleged collusion between government and the employers and pointed to an earlier but similar situation.

"When I was a Member of the past Government, strikes occurred at the waterfront in Kingston and I remember on one occasion it continued for a long time not just four days. I can remember on one ocassion butter was badly needed, I didn't call the armed forces out because I am interested in the working classes and that cannot be denied. . . ." What he had done was to draw on his authority as Jamaica's labour boss. "I went down to the stevedores on the wharf and I told them that I wanted butter or whatever it was to be unloaded and at once they had the goods unloaded."

Clearly the P.N.P. administration regarded the waterfront strike as having political overtones, and they were in a position to know. The P.N.P. and its trade union affiliate, the T.U.C., had used similar leverage against Bustamante and the J.L.P./B.I.T.U. between 1945 and 1952. Alexander Bustamante was not one to miss his opportunity and two days before the enforced ending of the strike, he published a notice in *The Daily Gleaner* which read: "Portworkers: soldiers have been brought by the so-called Socialist Government to do your work — to unload ships. Neither the soldiers nor the police are your enemies. Be orderly and stand firm. Be grim, with a relentless determination to suffer under tyranny, starve, make up your mind to die from starvation rather than surrender to injustice either by your Government or your employers. Unless you do this, not alone will you suffer but your children and those to come. Be not afraid, you are men, prove your manhood to those who would like to destroy you. I have suffered — why can't you for a righteous cause?" A foreign observer might have been led to believe that Jamaica was on the eve of a civil war or grave industrial conflagration. Alexander Bustamante, however, was seeking in his inimitable and flamboyant way, merely to reinforce his position as the champion and real-life martyr of the working classes. It did not matter either that Manley and his colleagues were unmoved by the dramatics and used their majority in the House to approve the action of the Governor in Council in proclaiming the State of Emergency and the steps taken to ensure the maintenance of essential supplies.

On the other hand, there had been no stronger proponent of law and order than Alexander Bustamante during his party's two terms in office, and he had never hesitated to use his majority to take action or pass legislation when he felt that his government, or for that matter, the public interest was being threatened or that his political opponents needed to be contained. What mattered, however, was that if the J.L.P. hoped to supplant the P.N.P. and regain power, it had to preserve its image as the party of the small man, and the best way to ensure this was to preserve the hegemony of the Bustamante Industrial Trade Union, the enduring symbol of the "mental revolution" or the "Bustamante revolution" as the "Chief" unabashedly called it in the House of Representatives in April 1960.

The election of Hugh Shearer, next in line and heir apparent in the B.I.T.U., provided Bustamante with highly effective support. Shearer could be relied upon (as he did effectively between 1955 and 1961 but more so between 1955 and 1958) to embarass the P.N.P./N.W.U. alliance by moving resolutions that legislation be enacted to provide severance pay for workers with long service who might be retrenched or dismissed, or to provide holidays with pay for all domestic employees and all employees in trades covered by Minimum Wage proclamations. At the same time other labour-oriented measures, such as the regrading of government subordinate staff, could be criticized as being inadequate. P.N.P. Ministers and Florizel Glasspole in particular, responded with indignation that the P.N.P. apparently was expected to do in two and half years (and in fact was doing more) than the J.L.P. had done in these areas during ten years in office. Tactical considerations, reinforced by his unquestionable commitment to the cause of the common men, also saw Shearer seconding and supporting measures brought in by the P.N.P. Government, such as the establishment of the Pensions Authority in December 1958 and the inauguration eventually in 1961 of the Sugar Workers Pension Fund, or amendments to the Workmen's Compensation Law, the Holidays with Pay Law, and the Trades Disputes (Arbitration and Enquiry) Law.

Alexander Bustamante, never failing to rise and speak in support of such measures as a good trade unionist, continued to quip: "We boil the soup and you are going to drink." He was also quick to take the sting out of P.N.P. criticism by his very candour and forthrightness. A case in point was his objections to the severity of the penalties stipulated in the Pension Authority Law for failure on the part of applicants to furnish particulars required of them. When Norman Manley observed that "if you go through the laws passed when the Honourable Member for Southern Clarendon was Chief Minister, you will find they have very drastic penalties much worse than these." Bustamante retorted, "There is no reason to multiply bad law. I have grown older and do better now."

Alexander Bustamante's mellowing did not mean, however, the abandonment of any of the basic tenets of his economic or political conservatism. He could still say in 1957, "Conducting Government's business, Sir, is the same thing as conducting one's own property — never to credit more than you can afford to pay. Otherwise all the creditors turn against you." He also expressed his continuing aversion to economic planning. "I hate the word long-term" (i.e., connotation of planning). But then it must be remembered that he was seventy-three years of age at this time.

As he grew older, Bustamante saw himself increasingly as the elder statesman belonging to all Jamaica. "All classes of people today are suffering from the high cost of living, but no one suffers more than what is called the middle class. I belong to no class. I belong to all classes." Still, the characterization of his role as the elder statesman had to take

167

second place to the image of Bustamante, the legendary and swashbuckling hero and the man who had made it from rags to riches. "*But* I plead for the poor of the poor, for I came from the gutter of poverty and I once knew what hunger was and what nakedness was."[4] Even his moments of levity were carefully chosen and designed to be in keeping with the image he wished to emphasize. Thus on one occasion he sought the permission of the Speaker of the House to expose his "weapons", having first of all explained that "I was reading in the press this morning something which terrified me — that Ministers of Government challenged Members on this side to battle outside, so I thought of coming here today well armed. I ask any Minister to take a medical test, because when I deliver a left and a right they would die, and I would be tried for murder." He then laid on the table before him a long walking stick, a rolled umbrella and a revolver holster, all of which were hurriedly removed by the Deputy Clerk of the House. Undaunted, Bustamante continued, "My cousin (N.W. Manley) was a soldier and he knows the meaning of weapons. Mr. Speaker, when I came in here I looked a very innocent man and you could not have conceived that I was well armed. I am very glad Mr. Speaker has saved me from very serious trouble."[5]

What Bustamante's mellowing did mean was that he was prepared as Leader of the Opposition, not only to carry the main thrust of opposition debate with good humour and respect for the rules of the game, but to function a little more than he had done in the past, as a member of a team, along with frontliners Sangster, Shearer, Allen and Leon, upon whom he relied for more pointed and thoughtful criticisms of the Majority Party's policies and measures. In the process, his lieutenants began to gain in stature as accomplished parliamentarians in their own right.

The other main strategy of Bustamante and his colleagues, apart from trying to show the continuity of the P.N.P. administration in building on the foundation laid by the J.L.P. ("picking the fruits of the trees planted by the J.L.P.") was to dull the image of the P.N.P. as the radical party or party of change in Jamaican politics. Thus in April 1957 Edwin Allen sought to question the credibility of the P.N.P. by asking, "1. Does the Chief Minister propose to keep the election promise of his party to nationalize transport, broadcasting, electricity and telephone services?

"2. If the answer to question (1) is in the affirmative, will the Chief Minister say when he proposes to nationalize these services?"

In his written reply, Norman Manley asserted that nowhere in the P.N.P.'s election pamphlet "Plan for Progress" had it been stated that the Party would nationalize transport, broadcasting, electricity and telephone services. Nevertheless, in December 1958 the P.N.P. Government introduced legislation to set up the Jamaica Broadcasting Corporation as a state-owned and statutory corporation. Donald Sangster gave a boost to the convergence of the parties thesis, when he needled, during debate, that "the present Government of Jamaica proclaimed it is not a socialist Government following the true socialist system, but I repeat, there is no government which is a greater worshipper at the shrine of private enterprise than the present Government when it suits them."[6]

But the event which served both to add a new dimension to Alexander Bustamante's political career and to revive his hopes of an electoral comeback in Jamaica in the 1959 General Election was the launching of the West Indies Federation during March and April 1958.

BUSTAMANTE AND THE WEST INDIES FEDERATION

In anticipation of the formal inauguration of the West Indies Federation in April 1958, Federal Elections were scheduled in the unit territories for 25th March to determine the composition of the first West Indian Government. Most of the leading protagonists of Federation, especially in the larger of the islands, Jamaica, Trinidad and Barbados, campaigned under the banner of the newly formed West Indies Federal Labour Party (W.I.F.L.P.), led by Norman Manley. Opposing the Federal Labour Party was another grouping of the parties then in opposition in Jamaica and Trinidad along with the ruling party in St. Vincent.

The Federal Election, conducted under local election laws, produced a number of stunning upsets. The ruling People's National Movement in Trinidad, led by Dr. Eric Williams, and the P.N.P., spearheaded by Manley, suffered crushing defeats. Using the theme "If you vote for Manley, he is going to sell you out to the small islands", Bustamante and the J.L.P. played upon the fear that Jamaica might have to subsidize the smaller and remote Eastern Caribbean Islands in the Federation and mobilized the majority of rural voters in Jamaica to capture twelve (to the P.N.P.'s five) of the federal seats. The J.L.P. secured 54 per cent and the P.N.P. 46 per cent of a poll which involved only 53 per cent of the listed voters. The turn-out was lower than any general poll in Jamaica up to that time (and since) and showed the extent to which the Jamaican populace were either apathetic to, or suspicious of, Federation. The election results also served to confirm the fears which had been expressed by Norman Manley only two months before at a mass rally on 15th January 1958, when he announced that he considered it his plain duty to stay in Jamaica rather than seek to become the first Prime Minister of the West Indies, so that he could "fight to the finish" a dangerous anti-Federation movement being launched by the J.L.P.

It had been widely assumed, within and without the West Indies, that Manley, acknowledged as the most outstanding of the West Indian leaders, would stand and secure election to the Federal Parliament and thus become Prime Minister. Manley's decision to stay at home came as a disappointment not only to the Eastern Caribbean but also to Busta-mante who had thought that it would be easier for him to win the General Election in Jamaica in 1959 with the P.N.P. leader off the scene in Trinidad, the seat of the Federation. The Federal Election also highlighted the extent to which the Federation had been conceived, planned and executed from above, without much grass-roots involvement or participation, certainly as far as Jamaica was concerned.[7] As was the case with all previous attempts at West Indies Federations, the initiative was taken by the British Colonial office in the interest primarily of achieving greater administrative efficiency.[8] Federation thus remained the special concern and preoccupation of the West Indian middle classes, into which most of the leading politicians, intellectuals and trade union leaders fell. Thus, while the West Indian trade union movements under the auspices of the Caribbean Labour Congress (excluding Bustamante and the B.I.T.U.) provided much of the local thrust for Federation, their professional and often middle-class leaders found no occasion, or saw no necessity, to make the Federation an issue even of educational concern for the rank and file members, although Federation was supposed to be the vehicle for overcoming insularity and parochialism and achieving a West Indian identity and nationhood.

The West Indies Federal Labour Party with twenty-two of forty-five seats, nevertheless, emerged as the Majority Party eligible to form the Government but with a wafer-thin majority. Its parliamentary group represented eight islands altogether, but more than two-thirds of the M.P.'s came from Barbados and the Leeward and Windward islands. With Norman Manley and Dr. Eric Williams non-starters, the Prime Ministership fell to the lot of Sir Grantley Adams, Premier of Barbados. On the other hand, the parliamentary strength of the Opposition Party, which was formally constituted as the Democratic Labour Party (D.L.P.) only after the election, consisted entirely of successful candidates from three islands: Jamaica (twelve), Trinidad (six) and St. Vincent (two). Sir Alexander Bustamante, who from the begining had had no intention or desire to seek federal election or office, became leader of the D.L.P. so that his rivalry with Norman Manley was carried over into the wider West Indian arena. Bustamante made a determined effort to consolidate the opposition groups within the D.L.P., but the attempt was doomed to failure. "Both the W.I.F.L.P. and the D.L.P. were contrived in expediency — both lacking distinct foundations in doctrine, traditional themes and standards around which leaders of territorial Federal Parties, so diverse in pattern and status, could rally. The fact of each alliance being headed by the founders of the two Jamaican Parties for twenty years at 'war' with each other, also contributed to the weakness of both Federal Parties."[9]

Unhappily, lack of cohesiveness was not the only disability suffered by the D.L.P. The barriers to effective communication, physical as well as interpersonal, were even more formidable. Quite apart from the great distance separating Trinidad and Jamaica, there was the fact that Bustamante had had no inclination to, and had not succeeded in, establishing close personal ties with any of the Eastern Caribbean leaders, either at the trade union level or at the political level.

At the trade union level, the starting-point of Bustamante's insularity and isolationism was the entrenchment of his leadership and control of the B.I.T.U. through a constitutional life presidency. This provision not only ran counter to the traditional theory of union democracy fervently upheld in the Anglo-Saxon world, but seemed to smack of labour leadership in the unstable and "so-foreign" Latin American or "banana" republics. Bustamante's reservations about facing up to annual or even periodical leadership contests were made explicit in 1945 in a dissenting Minority Report which he attached, as a member of the Industrial Relations Committee, to the Final Report submitted by that Committee to Government in March 1945. Appointed by the Governor in April 1943, the Committee had submitted an Interim Report in October 1943 which Bustamante had signed without reservation. But then the Interim Report had contained no recommendations relating to the structure or government of trade unions in Jamaica. The Final Report, on the other hand, recommended that the Trade Union Law be amended to provide, among other things, for (1) Government right to audit trade union accounts, (2) limitation of the use of trade union funds along the lines of legislation in England and (3) election of officers and the Executive Committee of every trade union at a properly convened meeting of members. Florizel Glasspole, the other leading trade union member of the Committee, objected to the legal imposition of Government audit of trade union accounts, while Bustamante took exception to the proposal relating to leadership elections.

"I have good reason for coming to the conclusion that if this recommendation is adopted, hostile political agencies who have in the past made and still continue to make strenuous efforts to infiltrate the Bustamante Industrial Trade Union, with a view to dominating the masses, will use every means in their power to influence unsuspecting workers in the union elections so as to further their political aims and objectives. It is conceivable that difficult and embarassing situations might arise if undesirable persons who are surreptitiously affiliated with hostile political parties are elected to certain important posts in the Union by means of underground coercion by such hostile political organisations."[10]

The undemocratic structure of his union and Bustamante's sensitivity to rebuff served, then, to keep the B.I.T.U. out of, and at the same time defensively aloof from, West Indian and regional labour bodies and affiliations such as the Caribbean Labour Congress or international federations such as the World Federation of Trade Unions and its successor in the Western Hemisphere, the International Confederation of Free Trade Unions. What is more, the membership first of the T.U.C. of Jamaica, then of the N.W.U. in these bodies, meant that objections to B.I.T.U. membership or affiliation could be maintained from within.

At the political level, Bustamante had found also that his Jamaican mass appeal was not exportable. At public meetings in Barbados and Trinidad, but especially in Barbados, with its more literate and sophisticated audiences accustomed to audience-interjections and witty platform repartees, Bustamante was severely heckled. This was a situation to which he was not accustomed. In Jamaica, a listener or dissident who attempted to heckle him, certainly in a pro-Bustamante crowd, would do so in peril of his life. Neither could Bustamante mesmerize audiences in the Eastern Caribbean by substituting antics or clowning for serious discourse. This was, however, an expected feature of his political appearances in Jamaica. This writer can recall, as a teenager, seeing Alexander Bustamante demonstrate to an enthralled audience in Kingston how Manley and the P.N.P. candidates would writhe from his political whiplash, as if beaten with cow-itch (a vine which produces severe itching and irritation on contact with the human body) and then proceed, with mock contortions, to take off his shirt, all the while "scratching" the supposedly affected areas. The performances kept his supporters in "stitches" of laughter.

While Bustamante had no occasion, and even less of an inclination, to display histrionics of this sort in the Eastern Caribbean, the general inclination, nevertheless, was to regard him as a bit of a buffoon and an egocentric. Not only that, he tended to suffer by comparison with his illustrious cousin Norman, who was widely acclaimed for his legal eminence and intellectual brilliance. It was to be expected therefore that Grantley Adams, fellow Oxonian and Barrister-at-Law, and Dr. Eric Williams, Oxford don and scholar-turned-politician, would find it easier to develop close personal ties and relationships with "fellow traveller" Manley than with the conservative and egocentric Bustamante.

More important than any of these considerations, however, was the fact that Bustamante had never been an ardent supporter of West Indian Federation. Indeed at the 1947 Montego Bay Conference summoned by Arthur Creech Jones, Secretary of State in the British Labour Government, to enable West Indian governments to discuss the establishment of Federation, Bustamante had reacted negatively to a Caribbean Labour Congress resolution demanding "a Federation providing for responsible government equivalent to Dominion Status" and concomitantly internal self-government for the units, by declaring against "a federation of paupers, foisted by Britain to escape her ancient responsibilities". This did not deter the same Bustamante by the end of the Conference from lending support to conference resolutions and declaring in a more kindly mood, "Everyone realizes that there are obstacles in the way of our final goal, but that we should be big enough to blast away the obstacles."

The Jamaican Legislature went on to endorse the results of the Montego Bay Conference and at a follow-up conference in 1953, Bustamante was unequivocal in his support of Federation. Jamaican readers of *The Daily Gleaner* were given an insight as to the kind of briefing being given by the Chief Minister to L.L. Simmonds, Minister of Education and leader of the Jamaica delegation. "I am going to telegraph Simmonds that he must not be influenced by any person or persons who think that he has such good influence as to destroy the spirit of Federation. . . . Whether one or two leaders do not want it, there will be Federation because Jamaica is backing it wholeheartedly, not I alone but the great majority of this country, of all classes including investors."[11]

Later, in December of the same year, Bustamante succeeded in making an enormous impression upon the Eastern Caribbean leaders (with the exception of Adams) whom he was meeting for the first time en bloc at a Regional Economic Council meeting in Barbados. On this occasion, Bustamante was in a cooperative and expansive mood. He was still on the crest of this swell, so to speak, when seven months later, he said in the Jamaica House of Representatives, "I agree with my friend, the Head of the Minority Party, that we should federate. We must federate and we hope one day to have British Guiana and British Honduras with us." Federation, then, had captured the imagination of the West Indian leaders and intelligentsia, and Bustamante did not wish to be left behind or to seem "unprogressive". Moreover, up to this point, nothing had been said to suggest that Jamaica's economic interests might or would be endangered by Federation. For there could never have been any doubt but that Bustamante would adhere to a Jamaica-first policy.

In 1955, the J.L.P. suffered its first defeat at the polls, and it fell therefore to Norman Manley, one of the earliest and strongest exponents of Federation, to lead the Jamaican delegation to the Constitutional Conference convened in London in 1956, which was expected to take all the decisions leading to the establishment of Federation itself. But by this time also, Jamaica had achieved internal self-government, and Federation, far from being a precondition for the island's political development as some might have thought in 1938 or 1947, now threatened, if anything, to become a brake on further constitutional advance. For while Manley insisted in 1956 that the Federation enjoy greater independence from imperial control, the Colonial Office was not inclined to concede Dominion Status to the Federation and West Indian leaders were not prepared to press the issue to the bitter end. The compromise which resulted thus gave the Federal Government greater authority vis-à-vis the British Crown but at the same time reduced the federal prerogative in relation to those of the unit governments. The Federation was restricted, then, to starting out at a level of constitutional advance below that already achieved by Jamaica.

The West Indian delegations also found themselves sharply divided, and at loggerheads, over the touchy issues of Customs Union and siting of the Federal capital. These divergences of interests reflected the long history of separate existence on the part of the constituent territories as well as the unevenness of their economic development and social progress, which, in turn, also mirrored differences in resource endowment and approaches to economic development. Jamaica, for instance, derived a fairly large percentage of public revenue from customs duties and was concerned to prevent a levy by the Federal Government on all local duties as they would require disproportionate contributions from Jamaica.

Bustamante, ever watchful of Jamaica's interests and sensitive to the possibility of increased taxation under any form of Customs Union, cabled to the J.L.P. Opposition spokesman at the 1956 Conference,

"Do not agree to one penny increase in taxation of any kind. We have our own economic distress here. It cannot be Federation at the expense of greater poverty." On the other issue, location of the Federal capital, Bustamante was known to have strong objections to the siting of the Federal capital in Barbados because of the existence, as he saw it, of two non-integrated Barbadian communities, differentiated on the basis of race and colour.

Had Norman Manley become Prime Minister of the West Indies or had the P.N.P. won the Federal Elections in 1958, it is quite possible that Alexander Bustamante might have bowed to Federation as the inevitable and would have been content to put up a vigorous fight to ensure protection of Jamaica's interest. As it turned out, Manley decided to stay at home and Bustamante's disappointment on this score, from a purely tactical point of view, gave way to guarded optimism as he saw in the J.L.P.'s federal electoral victory — a possible rekindling of the old Bustamante appeal, especially among the rural population. On the other hand, the prospect of Sir Grantley Adams who seemed to him to embody the "smugness" and "political cunning" of "small islanders" bent on "ganging up" against Jamaica, becoming the Prime Minister of the West Indies, was too much for Sir Alexander Bustamante. In a statement dealing with the appointment, he unleashed a fierce attack against the Prime Minister designate. "Adams has ruled over abject poverty for long years in Barbados, without visible improvement. How can this insular Adams, who lacks sufficient imagination, do any good for the ten federated States, having ruled over pauperized Barbados for so long, obviously without realizing the state of poverty there?"[12] Bustamante's unkind cut outraged feelings in the Eastern Caribbean and won sympathy for Adams not only there but in sections of the Jamaican community.

It should have been obvious to all, therefore, that Alexander Bustamante was fast becoming disenchanted with regional politics and with Federation. Nor did the mercurial Opposition Leader have long to wait for the next opportunity to feed anti-Federation sentiment in Jamaica. In August 1958, Trinidad objected to Jamaica's plan to set up an oil refinery under the protective umbrella of industrial incentives legislation. The Trinidad Government objected on the grounds that the proposal was not in keeping with the spirit of the agreement to establish a Free Trade Area in the short run and a Customs Union in the longer run. The Federal Government showed sympathy for the Trinidad position expressed by Premier Eric Williams, and Adams opined that he did not like monopolies, and presumably the Jamaican concessions were directed towards this very end. Bustamante was quick to take issue, and again pulled no punches. He warned that he would "rather this kind of Federation be smashed to nothing than for thousands of my people to be thrown out of work through a Customs Union by Trinidad dumping its manufactures here". What Bustamante was anxious to do, as Manley only too well realized, was to brand the P.N.P. in the eyes of the Jamaican populace as the party willing to compromise the national interest in order to satisfy a purely intellectual commitment to the goal of Federation and West Indian unity. So long, however, as Bustamante's caveats and warnings about Federation were based on vague misgivings or intuitive forebodings, Manley could afford to take a wait-and-see attitude even while giving reassurances that there were no grounds for apprehension as to Jamaica's continuing control of its domestic affairs and its rapidly expanding economic development programmes. There were fundamental issues which would be adequately safeguarded by Jamaica's delegation and negotiating teams.

Unhappily for Manley, a serious lapse in leadership on the part of Sir Grantley Adams at this very juncture served to bring already troubled waters to the boil. Dealing with the Jamaican oil refinery at a conference in Trinidad, Adams asserted, according to newspaper reporters, that the Federal Government, notwithstanding any tax holiday granted by Unit Governments, could levy its own income tax after five years and make it retroactive to the date of Federation. Of course, Adams went on to elaborate that he was not issuing a threat or warning, but was suggesting that Unit Governments would be well advised to consult with the Federal Government before conferring tax holidays or monopolies so as to avoid embarrassment in the future.

Alexander Bustamante, hard put to find an issue of substance with which to fight the P.N.P. in the General Election only months away in Jamaica, could not have wished for more. Federation had only recently become an issue of mass concern in Jamaica and fears and uncertainty as to the real import of Jamaica's participation in regional government were widespread, cutting across party lines. To Bustamante, Adams' threat presented a golden opportunity, not only to embarrass Manley personally, but to widen the crack of disunity within the P.N.P. on this very issue as well as to drive a wedge between Manley, Adams and Williams. For already, Adams was showing sensitivity to the fact that although he was Prime Minister, Norman Manley remained leader of the ruling West Indies Federal Labour Party, a situation likely to give rise to the suspicion, to say the least, of Manley being the back-seat driver.

Fully alive to these possibilities, Bustamante tauntingly cabled Adams: "You are reported as saying that notwithstanding any tax holiday granted by Unit Governments, the Federation can levy its own income tax and make it retroactive. You would only carry out that threat to Jamaica if Manley won the next elections." Is that possible? This opening salvo was followed up in the local arena with an eye-catching advertisement in *The Daily Gleaner* of 5th November 1958, in which Bustamante sardonically agreed with the position taken by Adams, arguing that to the extent that the Constitution was silent on the point the Federal Government technically might very well have the power to tax retroactively. Painting an equally grim and stark picture of the implied threat to Jamaica's political and economic status, Bustamante accused Norman Manley of typical "lawyers' evasiveness" and of misleading the public from the start about the real consequence of Federation to Jamaica. He then called for Jamaica's secession from Federation unless three conditions — the minimum for Jamaica's continuing membership — could be met. Firstly, the Constitution must be rewritten to ensure that the Federal Government would have no right whatever, without prior agreement, to impose any kind of taxation upon Jamaica. Secondly, representation in the Federal Legislature must be based on population, and finally, "any Customs Union must be such as not to hurt our workers or our economy." With a series of bold tactical initiatives, Alexander Bustamante had moved back into the political limelight — to become once more the actor dominating the Jamaican political stage. At the same time, secession was brought into the public arena as a matter for public discussion with the possibility also of it being made into a campaign issue in the 1959 General Election.

Norman Manley thus found himself once more having to react to Bustamante, the political maverick, as he had had to do so many times since 1938, and as his discomfort grew, Manley was forced to concede, "When the time comes for the Constitution to be reviewed, Jamaica will withdraw from the Federation unless the type of Federation devised and the Constitution is so changed as to suit the special circumstances of the West Indies and the maintenance and development of the life of Jamaica and the unit territories themselves." In one swoop, therefore, Bustamante had forced his political rival and one of the leading protagonists and architects of the West Indian Federation to take an unexpected and defensive "Jamaica first" orientation which was destined not only to

177

set him on a path of collision with his colleagues and associates in the Federation, but to adopt Bustamante's uncompromising conditions for Jamaica's continuing participation. Manley's first concern, however, was to defuse Adams' threat of retroactive taxation and to prevent it becoming an issue in the impending Jamaican General Election. Thus he began by seeking reassurance from the Prime Minister, but when this was short-circuited, he appealed to Adams to kill the issue by withdrawing what he had said. By this time, however, the tragi-comedy of errors already had begun to unfold.

Sir Grantley, convinced that he was being made the victim of political expediency in the electoral fight in Jamaica, or even worse, the victim of sinister conspiracy, turned to defiance and issued a much similar and equally offending statement, which confirmed that the Federal Government reserved the sole right to determine both whether its interests might be prejudiced by action of Unit Governments and the punitive measures which might have to be applied.

Bustamante, now convinced that he had found a campaign issue on which to challenge the P.N.P., moved to keep Manley "on the hook". At the Federal level, Robert Lightbourne, J.L.P./D.L.P. Opposition Member of the Federal Parliament, gave notice that he would call upon the Federal House, at its mid-November session, to approve of a new Constitution being prepared which would specifically exclude retroactive tax powers except by consent of units, and provide for representation on the basis of population. Lightbourne, incidentally, was a dynamic newcomer to the ranks of the J.L.P. who had returned from Great Britain after World War II with an established reputation as a successful and wealthy industrialist. He had also served as Managing Director of the Jamaica Industrial Development Corporation from 1952 to 1955.

Simultaneously, Bustamante proceeded along similar lines in the Jamaican House, enjoining the Government "to resist and defeat any and every attempt, proposal, measure, resolution or Bill relating to the compulsory acquisition of land in Jamaica by the Federal Government, to the imposition of taxation, retroactive or otherwise. . . . And that such means of resistance will include secession from Federation."

In January 1959, Bustamante was still baiting Manley, inviting him to instruct his five federal M.P.'s to join with the J.L.P./D.L.P. contingent in overthrowing Adams' Government. Manley would be allowed to choose a successor without J.L.P. interference although "if the next Prime Minister works against Jamaica's interest as Adams' Government is doing now, we would overthrow him too with the votes of your five members." Manley's response, very mild in the circumstances, was to appeal to Bustamante to "allow Jamaica to present a united front on this issue". In his anxiety to keep Federation as an issue out of the Jamaican General Election, Manley was led to bridge the gap and quickly at that, separating his position from that of Bustamante's and to accept the latter's three conditions for continuing participation or else secession. That this was indeed so, was confirmed by the Government's Ministry Paper No.18 issued three months later: The force of circumstances and continuing rivalry, seemingly had served to produce yet another "convergence" of differences between Jamaica's two contending political giants.

Bustamante's tactics, however, failed to stave off defeat in the General Election held in July 1959. Manley and the P.N.P. swept back into power for a second term, convincingly taking twenty-nine to the J.L.P.'s sixteen, in a House of Representatives which had been enlarged from thirty-two to forty-five constituencies. In a poll which saw 65 per cent of the eligible electorate voting, the P.N.P. obtained 54.8 per cent to the J.L.P.'s 45 per cent of the ballots cast. While the P.N.P. could be expected, as the party in office, to derive the advantage from the redefining of old, and the drawing up of new, constituency boundaries, the fact remained that the ruling party had significantly increased its popular support. Even more serious, however, for the future of the J.L.P. was the fact that the P.N.P., for the first time, made deep inroads into traditional rural J.L.P./B.I.T.U. strongholds. Incidentally, H.L. Shearer, second in command in the B.I.T.U., went down in defeat in Western Kingston, as did two other B.I.T.U. officers, Joseph McPherson and Arthur Smith, both conciliation officers who ran in Kingston constituencies. The B.I.T.U. representation in the House was thus reduced to Bustamante and L.G. Newland, General Secretary. For the J.L.P./B.I.T.U. combination, the writing was on the wall and its portent no less ominous. By disciplined and sustained organizational effort, the P.N.P. had steadily increased its electoral and parliamentary support emerging from a tiny parliamentary Minority in 1944 to become the Majority Party in seats as well as popular support, ruling with a very comfortable margin of seats. On the other hand, it was just as obvious not only that fortunes of the J.L.P. were on the wane but that the once-overwhelming personal appeal of Bustamante — the demi-god — was also on the decline.

As *The Daily Gleaner*'s political reporter observed, "The first and foremost lesson of the election is that no party in Jamaica is any longer as strong as its principal leader. The strength of Jamaica's parties, as of today, is in their organization."[13] The cult of the personality evidently was dwindling as a factor in Jamaican elections, and this had particular significance for the J.L.P. "The J.L.P. clearly needs to make itself an organization studious and serious and coherent instead of the unmarshalled collection of individuals which it tends to be at present."[14] It was not enough, as Bustamante seemed to think, to bring new blood into the Party. In a major advertisement in the press on the eve of the Election he had declared, "This is a new labour party — with new plans to attack the cost of living right from the start in order to make life easier for our people. We want benefits for all our people, not just a favoured few.

We have the plans,
We have the men."

The problem was that while Bustamante recognized as early as 1938 that the acquisition, as well as exercise of, industrial and political power called for organized and institutionalized support, he was not "an organization man". Rational or bureaucratic administration based on division of labour, specialization and differentiation of functions and formal authority or hierarchical structure to define the distribution of decision-making authority ran counter to his egocentrism, his autocratic bent and "intuitive" mode of operation. One redeeming feature, however, was that Bustamante had always shown a willingness to listen to others before making up his mind, and the Editor of *The Daily Gleaner* felt constrained to make this appeal: "Sir Alexander Bustamante owes it to his past and to the country to make as an absolute priority the creation of such a team (parliamentary opposition), the investing of its members with freedom from whimsical control and the provision for the parliamentary opposition of the study-group work and facilities which the complexities of government demand."[15]

Within the J.L.P. itself, the organizational reform-oriented group, of which D.C. Tavares and Mrs. Rose Leon were acknowledged leaders, found comforting support among the bright new men in the party, including John Gyles and Robert Lightbourne, both elected to the House of Representatives in 1959 and Edward Seaga, named to the Legislative Council (Upper House) by Bustamante, also in 1959.

Having decided that Manley and the P.N.P. might be vulnerable on the issue of Federation, Bustamante tried strenuously to make it the central issue in the General Election. In fact, the final J.L.P. election statement published in *The Daily Gleaner* three days before the Election, under Robert Lightbourne's signature and with the caption "Questions for Mr. Manley", dealt exclusively with Federation and its implications for Jamaica.

The J.L.P. thrust, however, lost much of its force when Manley assured that he would insist on constitutional safeguards in protection of Jamaica's national interests. In his counterpart statement, Manley asserted confidently, "The attempt to make Federation an issue in the campaign has rightly failed." As he saw it, "The major campaign issues were his government's record of accomplishment and the party's promise to go forward with the same plans which had advanced the country so greatly in four and a half years."

The verdict of the electors confirmed Manley's assessment but by the same token it also meant that they had accepted his assurances that he would demand absolute protection for Jamaica's interests, at the Conference scheduled for September 1959 to review the Federal Constitution.

At the other end of the Caribbean, the P.N.P. victory was hailed by Adams with relief. "The West Indies have to say, 'Thank God.' The future of the West Indies is now assured. All lovers of democracy must rejoice. I think the September Conference will go on smoothly." As one of "the lovers of democracy" and a partner in the Federal Union, Jamaica, however, had begun to have doubts about the wisdom of the marriage. Sir Grantley's optimism as one of the matchmakers of the Union, was understandable but hardly warranted. For confrontation, rather than compromise, was the logical consequence of the position taken by the Jamaica delegation. The proposals set out in Ministry Paper No. 18 bore the unanimous endorsement of the Jamaica Legislature, and the P.N.P., no less than the J.L.P., now stood committed to the principle of "representation by population". This formula would give Jamaica nearly half of the seats in the Federal Parliament, a significant increase above what the island had previously agreed to accept. Jamaica's position of "no compromise" left no room for retreat for the simple reason that the united front of both party leaders was based, paradoxically, not on concensus or genuine unanimity, but on disunity. Manley approached the forthcoming conference still confident that differences could be negotiated, while Bustamante held to the opposite view that Jamaica's demands would not win acceptance. Having set himself up as the champion of Jamaica's interests, Bustamante could be expected to react sharply to any detected softening of Manley's stand. Matters were made worse by the fact that Jamaica's was not the only position that was hardening. At the begining of September 1959, Dr. Eric Williams released the Trinidad Government's answer to the Jamaica Government's Paper No. 18. The "Economics of Nationhood" presented a Federation blueprint which collided head-on with Jamaica's, in philosophy, objectives and structure. It conceived of a tightly-knit unit Federation "adequately empowered at the centre to shape and direct the future of the Nation! — the centre should have a far wider range of powers than it at present possesses".

The September Constitutional Conference was not, therefore, a happy experience for the West Indian leaders who participated. The united front of the Jamaican delegation, especially on the issue of representation by population, was met with solid opposition from the Eastern Caribbean. On the second day of the Conference, Manley stated firmly that there was no room for horse-trading: "We are not buying anything; this is our stand; this is where we stay." In view of intransigence all round, the outstanding issues were referred to two Ministerial Committees. The Conference was disastrous. "The real misfortune . . . lay in the animosities which it had enlarged. Each leader came away expressing resentment against somebody or something. Those from the smaller units were alarmed by the truculence and unreadiness of Jamaica to concede a single point. The Jamaicans interpreted the furore over representation by population as a sign that their Eastern colleagues were determined to deny Jamaica her simple rights."[16]

The aftermath of the Conference in Jamaica was that the number of persons having second thoughts about Federation grew considerably. Speaking in the House of Representatives on 3rd November 1959 in support of his motion seeking approval of the stand taken by the Jamaica delegation, Manley urged that "Jamaica should remain in and try to make Federation work. . . . The remedy is to plan better and do better, not to destroy our original purpose." J.L.P. spokesmen were universally pessimistic and Bustamante made evident his complete disenchantment: "Jamaica should leave whether we get all material changes we want or not. Suppose we get all the changes we ask for, and we get nothing out of Federation, why should we take taxpayers' money here when the Premier himself has admitted that we have more hungry people here than in any other part of the West Indies to feed?" He did concede however that Jamaica might have to stay in Federation for the next two or three years having made an agreement to this effect. D.C. Tavares sprang the proposal that a referendum should be held to give the people an opportunity to express whether Jamaica should remain in Federation or not. He could hardly have been more prophetic for although his proposal was vetoed by the Government, only six months later the people of Jamaica were told in a dramatic announcement by Norman Manley that they would be afforded just such an opportunity.

Manley's decision came in response to a J.L.P. release in *The Daily Gleaner* of 31st May 1960 that the party would offer no candidate for the Federal by-election in St. Thomas to fill the Federal seat vacated ten months earlier by Robert Lightbourne when he ran, successfully, for the Jamaica House. The J.L.P. withdrawal flowed directly from the irrevocable decision of Bustamante and the J.L.P. to oppose Federation and to do everything within their power to secure Jamaica's withdrawal. The decision appears to have been wholly Bustamante's and grew out of an all-night meeting of the J.L.P. executive, which had been called the evening before to confirm the candidacy of Edwin Allen, one of the J.L.P. stalwarts who had been defeated in the General Election in July 1959, and to plan his campaign strategy. As the story goes the Executive was still trying, after long hours, to resolve the problem of finding J$3,000 to meet Allen's campaign expenses when Bustamante declared, "Allen will not run. We have no money."[17] This apparently did not please the majority of members present and D.C. Tavares, Secretary of the Party, protested, "But Chief, we can't say to the country and the world that we are not going to run because we have no money." A weary Bustamante is reported to have replied, "Well, tell them then that Jamaica is going to get out of Federation," and refused to discuss the matter further. There the decision rested. No one seemed bold enough or willing to defy the "Chief" and all that remained was for the Secretary of the Party to draft the withdrawal "statement" after Bustamante had left. It may be noted incidentally, that Bustamante's chief henchmen, Sangster and Lightbourne, were absent and abroad, not that their presence might have changed anything. Indeed, Robert Lightbourne, rumoured to be influential with the J.L.P. leader, was known to be even more critical of Jamaica's remaining in the Federation.

However tempting though it might be, it would be a mistake and a disservice to Alexander Bustamante to conclude that the consideration of as paltry a sum as fifteen hundred pounds, triggered the decision which eventually led to the dissolution of the West Indies Federation. By Jamaican (and West Indian) standards and on his own admission, William Alexander Bustamante was already a very wealthy man. It was not lack of party funds, then, but rather disillusionment and total disenchantment with Federation which formed the basis of this seemingly capricious decision. "Bustamante was in the position of a businessman who, discovering weaknesses in a project and seeing no hope of its viability, had reached the point of cutting his losses and abandoning it." This, according to the most authoritative of the contemporary historians of the Federation debacle, was the explanation offered by Donald Sangster, First Deputy Leader of the J.L.P. and successor as Prime Minister to Bustamante in 1967.[18] Sangster also confirmed that after the disastrous September 1953 Constitutional Conference and further deadlock at intergovernmental conference in May 1960, Bustamante and he had given up hope of the other delegations conceding Jamaica's position. The difficulty of raising the funds to finance the federal by-election campaign presented Bustamante then with an opportunity and a justification, within the party structure, to impose his will without even the slightest suggestion of consultation with any of his colleagues in Jamaica or his D.L.P. associates in the Eastern Caribbean.

The Opposition Leader's declaration of "total war" against Federation should be regarded as opportunistic, therefore, only from the point of view of its timing. As indicated earlier, Bustamante and the B.I.T.U., from the start, had not been part of the movement for Federation sparked by West Indian labour and political leaders under the aegis of the Carribean Labour Congress. Federation had never held, and did not hold, any deep emotional significance for him. He was not liked in the Eastern Caribbean and there was never any love lost between himself and the equally parochial and devious Sir Grantley Adams who was to become Prime Minister by default. Bustamante, moreover, had always had the suspicion that the British Government was attempting to use the Federation as a means of relieving the British Treasury of the obligation to assist financially, and otherwise, in the economic development of the West Indian Colonies. As early as 1947 it may be recalled, he had contended that Federation under the existing "pauperized" conditions was "nonsensical". As the Federal Union came closer to being a reality, Bustamante began to fear that Jamaican industries protected by high tariff structures would be undercut by Trinidad manufacturers. The 1958 Federal Election in Jamaica, in which he stunningly defeated Manley and the P.N.P., exposed that party's "Achilles' heel" and confirmed the strength of the anti-Federation feeling in Jamaica.

The blunder of Prime Minister Adams in threatening retroactive taxation, which gave Bustamante his "political opening" against Manley; the publication by Trinidad's Premier Eric Williams of the "Economics of Nationhood" which made explicit the assumption that the richer islands, and Jamaica in particular, should subsidize the poorer, which

184

served to alarm Bustamante even further; and the intervening constitutional and intergovernmental conferences which became increasingly more divisive and acrimonious — all these factors helped to carry Bustamante over the brink of his stand "no Federation unless on Jamaica's terms" to "no Federation on any terms".

His declaration of withdrawal and total war was opportunistic, however, in that it was made in full realization that Federation remained the one possible issue within the Jamaican political arena which might serve to arrest his party's declining fortunes and the threat which two successive electoral defeats posed to his style of leadership, and control of, the Jamaica Labour Party. After the 1959 elections, Bustamante had taken an extended holiday overseas and a number of the disheartened and disenchanted were sufficiently emboldened to launch a whisper campaign to the effect that the "Chief", then seventy-five years of age, was a tired old man and should step aside for younger leadership. Bustamante must have felt then that he was being hemmed in, increasingly, by his own party. In declaring that Edwin Allen could not contest the federal by-election because of lack of funds, Bustamante forced on his colleagues the choice of "put-up or shut-up". In a sense it was a choice between "the Devil and the Deep Blue Sea", for had any member of the Executive dared to put-up the money, it probably would have been construed as an act of defiance. By itself, however, Bustamante's declaration of war on Federation and his cavalier treatment of his colleagues might have been nothing more than another aberration or manifestation of "wilfulness", but for Norman Manley's unexpected and sensational response to the J.L.P. leader's challenge.

Within an hour after reading of the J.L.P. stand in *The Daily Gleaner*, Manley decided on a Federation Referendum. At a Cabinet meeting that same morning the Premier's proposal for a Referendum was ratified without a dissenting voice. Just as Bustamante had acted impulsively, on an instinct for survival, without consulting anyone, so Norman Manley, with the instinct of a fighter, reacted just as hastily without consulting anyone. Some have argued that the ways in which both decisions were taken merely served to underscore the personal dominance of Bustamante and Manley over Jamaican politics and government and that this personalism made a mockery of the politics of mass participation.[19] A number of considerations seemed to have prompted Manley's rather quick decision. For one thing, Bustamante, acting as though he was still a law unto himself, had thrown down the gauntlet and Manley, seeing it as a personal challenge, accepted it as such with alacrity. "Run away from a fight when you are challenged and you will never be able to look the world in the face."[20] What is more, he felt that he would be able to win the Referendum and thus silence Bustamante once and for all. The smashing victory in July 1959 had all but erased the memory and significance of the defeat suffered at the hands of Bustamante and the J.L.P. in the Federal Election in 1958.

On the other hand, while the P.N.P. had won a preponderance, 63·6 per cent, of the seats in 1959, it had won only 54·3 per cent of the votes. Thus a modest swing of 5 per cent in the popular vote, or 10 per cent of the P.N.P. vote, could bring a negative vote against Federation. To his Eastern Caribbean colleagues in the West Indies Federal Labour Party, Manley attempted to justify his decision on logical grounds, arguing in effect that Federation needed stability, and this could not be achieved with one of the two political parties in the major unit which for eleven years had supported Federation now committing itself to secession at the first opportunity. It was right therefore "that the people should be asked to decide the great issue". In choosing to fight Bustamante on the latter's terms, Manley must have thought that he would be striking his enemy at his weakest, but by the same token, he forced upon Bustamante and the J.L.P. a mortal battle for survival on the one and only issue on which the P.N.P. was vulnerable. In other words the ground chosen by Manley for the battle — namely Federation — was Bustamante's only strength. As a tactician, the Opposition Leader could not hope for more. The declaration of war on Federation began to pay-off immediately therefore for Bustamante. "It evoked a considerable section of popular sympathy; it embarrassed the Government who were known to be split on Federation. It recaptured the dynamism of the Jamaica Labour Party; it reinstated its leader's dominance and lifted party morale. Few within the party at the times recognized the full potential of their leader's action."[21] Bustamante was once more in pursuit of the one thing to which he was ever totally dedicated — the acquisition and exercise of power. But first, rifts within the party had to be healed and any incipient revolt crushed. The opportunity came with the Annual Conference of the J.L.P. which began in Kingston at the Success Club on 12th November 1960.

On the first day, at which Bustamante was absent, delegates proceeded to appoint officers, returning their "Chief" as President and Leader; Donald Sangster as First Deputy Leader; Edwin Allen as Second Deputy Leader; and as the only upset, D.C. Tavares as Third Deputy Leader in place of Robert Lightbourne. Mrs. Rose Leon, Chairman of the

186

party and a prominent member of the party reform group, was placed on the Executive. The climax of the Conference came, as usual, with the public session held the next day at the Ward Theatre, also in Kingston. Excitement ran high in anticipation of the arrival of Bustamante, the stellar attraction who would also deliver the main address. But the "Leader" never arrived. Instead he sent a prepared statement issued from his private residence, which was haltingly read by Mrs. Leon who then subsided in tears. In it Bustamante accused one member of the top Executive and a small clique of engineering forces and hooliganism at the Saturday session of the Party Convention so as to control and manipulate the Party to suit their own ends and ambitions. He charged that country delegates had been forcibly precluded from participating in the election of officers and that he would call a proper party meeting to deal with the situation and make proper appointments. In further statements to the press Bustamante vowed that he would no longer tolerate Party Secretary Tavares, "whose hunger for power goes back many years", holding any executive office in the J.L.P. Tavares was accused of promoting the view that "the new J.L.P. must be sustained by collective leadership rather than by one-man rule".

Here Bustamante was touching upon the matter which had really agitated him: "Ever since we've had this collective leadership, we've lost every election. It can't work." Tavares, in a conciliatory statement replied, "If Sir Alexander insists that I should not hold any office in the party, I will gladly resign and continue to work as I have always done for my party and country."[22] Actually what had happened at the first session of the Annual Conference was that Robert Lightbourne determined to make a bid to take over the First Deputy Leadership of the Party from Donald Sangster (and thus become the J.L.P. heir presumptive), but was thwarted by Tavares who, in a masterly fashion, organized the delegates against him in favour of Sangster. This had involved noisy demonstrations on the floor of the convention and led to Bustamante's allegation of "hooliganism". The truth of the matter was that the "Chief" had been long accustomed to lead his flock, brooking no opposition to his rule, and was quite unwilling to concede the slightest diminution of his position of pre-eminence within the Party. On this occasion, he was the more outraged that Lightbourne, a protégé "close to the throne", should have been outmanoeuvred. The tactic of publicly denouncing his lieutenants and accusing them of disloyalty, it may be recalled, was one which Bustamante had used with great effect against the caretaker administration of the B.I.T.U. in 1942, when the final break between himself and Manley and the P.N.P., as well as potential rivals within the B.I.T.U., had been effected. What it meant was that whenever he felt his leadership being threatened, Bustamante, ever sure of his personal popularity among the masses, would appeal directly to them and to rural delegates in particular, against the alleged threat or organized opposition within the Union or Party.

Having thus made a shambles of the will of the delegates at a properly constituted Annual Conference, constitutionally the supreme legislative authority within the J.L.P., Bustamante convened a new Conference in January 1961 and, in complete command of the Party and its proceedings, secured appointment of a panel of officers more to his liking. On this occasion, Mrs. Rose Leon, Chairman of the Executive Committee since 1948 and former Minister of Health and Housing 1953–5, became the sole casualty, when, after losing 106–269 to Edwin Allen in the contest for Second Deputy Leader, she challenged the honesty of the ballot, denounced Bustamante as a liar and severed connections with the J.L.P. She was subsequently welcomed into the ranks of the P.N.P. by Norman Manley, to whom she had been a "thorn in the flesh". In this case, politics — which "makes strange bedfellows" — was clearly the winner.[23]

Having closed ranks and restored unity in his usual masterly style, Bustamante then set about mobilizing the Party and its supporters for an all out assault on Federation. Before the January Convention was over he had donated fifty pounds to launch a "Referendum Enlightenment Fund", and two hundred pounds cash was collected on the spot. Within months, thousands of pounds were received in donations from sympathizers within and without the Party. Pressure was mounted on Manley to stop dragging his feet and announce the date of the Referendum. Manley, on the other hand, took the position that the Referendum could not be held until the Plenary Intergovernmental Conference had settled the pattern of the Federation which would be put to the public.

By March 1961, the J.L.P. anti-Federation campaign, and concomitantly its Referendum campaign, was at full blast throughout the length and breath of Jamaica and gaining momentum rapidly. The theme being hammered home was that there was widespread and terrible poverty obtaining in Jamaica, that the cost-of-living was oppressive and that Federation, which would certainly bring additional taxation, would only make matters worse, in effect, adding the economic burdens of the other islands to Jamaica's already heavy burden. The theme of poverty was dramatically reinforced and given wide currency in a celebrated "haves and have-nots" speech delivered in the Legislative Council by the J.L.P.'s Edward Seaga in a forceful attack upon the Government. By judicious selection and manipulation of statistics, and using 1958–9 as his sample years, Seaga argued that Jamaica's rate of economic growth, as measured by the G.N.P., had been losing momentum and in any event the island's alleged economic prosperity was lopsided, as 93 per cent of the population were in the underprivileged class — with the dividing line being an income of £300 per annum. "The Government is mobilizing the resources of the country to the disadvantage of the underprivileged. . . . This is a clear and personal indictment." Seaga then questioned the feasibility of Jamaica remaining in a Federation which could not hold out any prospect of economic advantage. Other J.L.P. spokesmen in the Legislative Council called for an early settling of the date for Referendum. Recapturing the earlier image of the J.L.P. as the party of the working man, Bustamante further dramatized the "haves and have-nots" theme by an "on the edge of volcano" speech in which, in simple but stark terms, he painted a picture of desperate hunger, crushing taxation, unemployment and inevitable revolt — conditions likely to be exacerbated by Federation. "The haves and have-nots slogan therefore gained political dimensions, throwing up new perspectives of protest and resuscitating the old preoccupations of class and colour."[24] In May 1959 there had been riots in Western Kingston, the depressed part of the city and the chief locale of the alienated Rastafarian cultist groups, so often at variance with the police and civil power because of their vocal and vigorous cries against social conditions as well as their use of ganja (marijuana) as a sacrament in their religion. Then in June 1960 a skirmish ensued between a combined police and military raiding party and desperadoes thought at first to be Rastafarians but who proved to be black Americans led by the son of Rev. Claudius Henry, a self-proclaimed "Messiah", who had earlier induced thousands to purchase "return tickets" to Africa. Henry's son was convicted for murder and hanged, and Henry himself later earned a ten-year sentence for sedition.

The net effect of Seaga's assault on the Government, reinforced by Bustamante's proven and formidable capabilities as fomentor of working-class unrest and agitation, was to short-circuit the Government's major electoral appeal — its record of economic and social achievements in six and a half years in office — even before the P.N.P. had launched its Referendum campaign.

The results of the Intergovernmental Conference held in Trinidad in May 1961 did little to relieve the pressure on Manley and the P.N.P. as concessions seemingly wrung by Manley from his Eastern Caribbean colleagues to ease his position in Jamaica still had to be confirmed and translated into a final constitution at the London (Lancaster House) Conference set up by the Secretary of State for the Colonies for 31st May 1961.

In Jamaica the Opposition continued its policy of harassment of the Government in the Legislature with J.L.P. spokesmen demanding that the Referendum be held at once and that the London Conference be postponed to await the verdict of the Referendum. The J.L.P. by their tactics were succeeding in heightening public impatience to "get it over with" and to put an end to the seemingly interminable series of conferences and related committees and working parties as well as the continuous bickering and crisis associated with them. By pressing for the early holding of the Referendum the Opposition also projected the image of a party full of confidence and anxious to be vindicated by the electorate.

By the time Norman Manley and his delegation returned, therefore, from the Lancaster House Conference in London on 17th June 1961 to launch effectively the P.N.P. Referendum campaign, the J.L.P. was near the peak of its anti-Federation crusade. An estimated 10,000 P.N.P. supporters assembled at the airport to give Manley a tumultuous reception, but some 4,000 J.L.P. supporters also marshalled for this occasion added an ominous and discordant note, and it required a very sizable police contingent to prevent the eager factions from getting at each other.

Weeks later, Bustamante returned to the attack in the House of Representatives with devastating effect. Having discredited Sir Grantley Adams as the first and inept Prime Minister of the West Indies, he now launched a similar attack to discredit Eric Williams of Trinidad. "If I or the Premier died, there would be no one to lead the West Indies in this Federation but that hideous [changed to 'contemptible' to meet the Speaker's objections] Dr. Williams . . . What Jamaican who is not a traitor to his country would want Dr. Williams to rule us?" In the tumultuous uproar which followed Bustamante's calculated attempt to play upon the fear of Eastern Caribbean domination of Jamaica, the J.L.P. then made the master stroke of its Referendum campaign which was to lay the basis of a new claim to immortality for William Alexander Bustamante. L.G. Newland, General Secretary of the B.I.T.U., carrying out a carefully planned strategy, moved an amendment to the motion introduced by Manley seeking acceptance of the Lancaster House White Paper on Federation, "rejecting the London report and requesting Her Majesty's Government to take the necessary steps to introduce legislation to grant Jamaica Independence on 23rd May 1962, and to seek admission for Jamaica in the British Commonwealth as a Dominion". "Though largely inspired by Referendum strategy, the J.L.P. surprise motion still stands as a landmark in Jamaica's political history. The future was to award Bustamante the credit for being the first to call for Jamaican Independence in absolute terms of immediacy — a claim consistently agonizing to Manley and the P.N.P. frontiersmen whose declared objective of full self-government had in the stormy days of 1938 been reviled by the Government as seditious and had placed them in danger of imprisonment."[25]

Tactically obliged to defeat the Opposition amendment, the P.N.P. administration was left in the unenviable position of having had to vote against a motion specifically setting a date for Jamaica's independence. It allowed Bustamante and the J.L.P. to set themselves up as the true repositories of the spirit of Jamaican nationalism, fighting to achieve and safeguard the country's freedom. It brought Bustamante into competition with Manley for the one title which had been unquestionably the latter's since the founding of the P.N.P. in 1938 — namely the "Father of the Nation". This must have been in Manley's mind when, at a mammoth political rally held on 3rd August, he announced that the Referendum would take place on 19th September 1961, the anniversary of the launching of the P.N.P. in 1938. Voters would be asked to decide "should Jamaica remain in the Federation of the West Indies". Manley also declared that if the Referendum was successful, he would seek to become the Prime Minister of the West Indies.

The J.L.P. appeal to the electorate rested quite unashamedly on isolationism. Federation was depicted as an unnecessary and undesirable burden, likely to aggravate Jamaica's endemic problems of poverty and unemployment. Seaga's theme of "haves and have-nots" made it that much easier to link Federation with local concerns. "Federation is bad for the poor and good for the rich". The P.N.P. countered with an appeal to the loftier and wider vision of West Indian unity and progress and the disadvantages of going it alone. Manley, however, had to carry the burden of the P.N.P. campaign. He addressed an unbelievable number of meetings, but could not fight on all fronts on which he was attacked without vigorous and wholehearted support from all his party colleagues. This he did not receive. Possibly many feared that in the guise of new converts to the cause of Federation, they would prove to be liabilities. The P.N.P.'s task of overcoming rural apathy was made that much more difficult. On the other side, Bustamante and his frontliners campaigned with an intensity and desperation born

191

of the realization that they had been given an unexpected chance. It was a question of fighting for survival and Alexander Bustamante was doing well what he was best at — mobilizing the rural voters of Jamaica. The rural J.L.P. vote was largely responsible for the "no" majority of 38,942 (8.2 per cent of the poll) which determined that Jamaica should secede from the West Indies Federation. Of the 453,580 persons who voted, representing only 60.87 per cent of the eligible voters on the list, 54 per cent voted "no" and 46 per cent "yes". In comparison with the 1959 General Election, both Parties suffered from abstentions. The P.N.P. however suffered its biggest loss in the rural areas where its vote fell by 71,000 while the J.L.P. rural vote rose by 10,000. Too much cannot be made of the argument, therefore, that West Indian nationalism lost out to Jamaican nationalism. If anything, "Federation was killed not by hostility but merely by indifference."[26]

· Following the Referendum, Manley announced that Jamaica would secede and become independent on its own. A government delegation would proceed to London to arrange these eventualities. He now had to contend, however, with a triumphant Bustamante. No discussions could take place in London without J.L.P. representation, "because on these matters you don't speak for Jamaica. I do." Obviously concerned to keep the initiative, Bustamante demanded the setting up of a bi-partisan Parliamentary Committee as a sequel to the Referendum. Manley also declared that a General Election would be held as early as possible, in advance of independence. To the J.L.P., anxious to follow up the advantage of the Referendum win, the General Election could not come soon enough.

In the third week in October 1961, a joint Parliamentary Committee was appointed "to prepare proposals for a Constitution for Jamaica to take effect on independence". The draft Constitution was taken to London for discussion, some significant alterations made, and was ratified by the Jamaica Parliament on 27th February 1962. The Constitution contained no radical departure from the Westminster model usually exported to ex-British Colonies. The disinclination of the leaders and members of both of the political Parties to break the link of continuity with the colonial era was explained by Manley: "We had a system which we understood; we had been operating it for many years with sense. It is a system which has endured in other countries for generations successfully. It is a system which is consistent with the sort of ideals we have in this country, and it was not difficult to decide that we should follow that familiar system with those modifications which we thought the circumstances of independence deserved."[27] The strength and maturity of bi-partism in Jamaica found expression in the Jamaica (Constitution) Order in Council 1962 which enshrined the position of Leader of the Opposition and required that he must be consulted in the making of certain political and key appointments.

Independence Day was set for 6th August 1962 and the pre-independence General Election was held in April 1962. The J.L.P. swept back into power and Sir Alexander Bustamante became Jamaica's first Prime Minister in independence. The J.L.P. won 26 seats and 50 per cent of the popular vote, the P.N.P. 19 seats and 50 percent of the popular vote, in a poll which saw 72 per cent of the eligible voters casting their ballots.

The victory of the J.L.P. and the defeat of the P.N.P. may be viewed as logical extensions and consequences of the Referendum. Notwithstanding the pro-Federation sentiment held by many of his colleagues, Bustamante unilaterally made the decision and then imposed it upon them as a party decision. Manley, likewise, reacting impetuously, decided upon a Referendum and then much to the discomfort of a sizable proportion of P.N.P. supporters, decided to stake the fortunes of the party on the Referendum. "Don't make any mistake. I have made it a party issue. I totally reject the proposition that this is not a party issue. . . . My life, my work, my leadership are all at stake in this issue. Your party's life, its leadership, its future are all at stake in the referendum. . . . I will stand or fall by this issue."[28] Manley's decision to call a General Election to determine who should lead the country into nationhood and independence was consistent with his position. After Manley had lost the Referendum, Bustamante would not allow him to re-establish his political credibility. Manley was portrayed by Bustamante and the J.L.P. as a man who had lost his historic purpose. "The Premier and some Government members were prime movers for independence and nationhood for Jamaica in 1938. That dynamic they have since lost in the mire of Federation. The people are therefore unable to see where they are going."[29]

In his celebrated speech before the Caribbean Labour Congress in Kingston in September 1947, Manley had spoken of Federation as a cause vital to the progress of the region and had observed, "If we federate, we must federate as self-governing units who voluntarily surrender some of the power which each has over his own to the common whole." The opposition of Bustamante to self-government as an immediate objective, and the tremendous authority he wielded over the masses, allowed him to slow-up the process, and Manley and the P.N.P. then had to concentrate efforts and energies on converting Bustamante to the cause of, as distinct from, the idea of self-government.

In the course of this enforced constitutional gradualism leading progressively closer to the norm of internal self-government, the P.N.P. was diverted from the goal which had brought the Party into being. By 1956, Manley and his party had decided to seek the final expression of self-government through the federal structure. No adequate explanation has yet been offered as to how or why this shift took place. "What happened to Jamaica's ambition to achieve Dominion Status? I think the answer is . . . that by supporting Federation we have elected to forego our own claims to Dominion Status and seek to achieve it as part of a Federal Government."[30] During the Referendum campaign, Manley did not deny that Jamaica could go it alone, but painted a grim and stark picture of what it would be like. He made it clear to listeners, including this writer, that it was an alternative that he could not contemplate with equanimity.

Alexander Bustamante, on the other hand, could concede, without harm to his cause, that initially he had opposed self-government but this had been consistent with his thoroughgoing conservatism and belief that one should first learn to creep, before attempting to walk. In 1946 during a debate in the House of Representatives on constitutional changes, he gave perhaps his most characteristic formulation of his philosophy: "Mr. Chairman, the Lord set an example for us. He could have taken one minute or even one second to build this world, but he did it in six days. I believe that when the Lord did this, and I do believe it, He was setting an example for us sinners. And so I prefer to follow the Lord's example by going a little slow.

"It takes three weeks, Mr. Chairman, for a hen to hatch an egg. The Lord could have made it possible for the hen to hatch that egg overnight."[31]

Admittedly also he had supported the idea of Federation, but here again he could argue that he had been led by events and by conviction to conclude that Jamaica could better fulfil its destiny and meet the aspirations of its people by achieving independence on its own. Bustamante could claim moreover that he was making up for his past hesitancy by seeking to put Jamaica again on the road to nationhood. On this he was on strong grounds, for the one thing that could not be questioned was his commitment to "Jamaica first". Although he had travelled very extensively, Bustamante remained insular in outlook, and his paternal concern for his people was sincere, as also his compassion for the working people. The alternative which he constituted and offered to the electors

194

was leadership free from regrets and ambivalence and a government which would seek to lessen the disparities between "haves and have-nots".

At seventy-eight years of age, then, Sir Alexander Bustamante began his third term in office, the Prime Minister of a politically independent Jamaica, witnessing the culmination of the process of decolonization which had begun with the social upheaval in May 1938 in which he had played a central role. If Jamaica had grown up, in political terms, so had Bustamante and the J.L.P. The new Cabinet boasted an impressive array of experienced "old guard stalwarts" and talented and bright new frontiersmen.[32] This was only right. The public administration had become more bureaucratic and sophisticated, and a measure of economic diversification had been achieved, although without any profound transformation in the structure of the economy.

Alexander Bustamante thus embarked on a new and equally exciting phase of his career, although under circumstances substantially different from those under which he had begun at the start of his public career in 1938.

7 THE NEW JAMAICA — POWER AND RESPONSIBILITY

Prime Minister designate Sir Alexander Bustamante did not herald the coming of political independence and nationhood with an outpouring of lofty and inspiring sentiments or with stirring emotional appeals to his countrymen to hail the dawn of a new era for Jamaica. This would have been out-of-keeping with his style and temperament. As one of his ablest political lieutenants explained, "One has to bear in mind that Jamaica came to independence fairly well prepared and therefore the trauma that usually accompanies a country which experiences independence and therefore heightens the difference between the post- and the pre-independence periods wasn't there. We had set up a range of institutions which were the necessary institutions to carry us forward into independence. We had set up the Development Corporations, the Central Bank, Administration of Justice; we had evolved the machinery and tried it and tested it and we had evolved a political maturity which also was tried and tested. So that when independence came, it wasn't as if there were a lot of things to be done then, that were different from what was being done before. It is true one could have used an approach towards heightening the national spirit which would have mobilized people for action, and we could have used some of the approaches which tend to almost border on gimmickry which have been used in this area and in other emerging nations and tend to give people the impression that there is something quite different and they must adjust differently and must act differently and so on. That wasn't done. Instead, we set about the hard facts of management of the country, build-up of further institutions, developing further capital flows, and so on."[1]

Nevertheless, when it came to the appointment of a new Governor General, Bustamante showed that he was very much alive to the need for, and importance of, symbolism in fostering national identity and a spirit of self-confidence. His recommendation that Clifford Clarence Campbell be appointed as the representative of the Queen in Jamaica, gave the new nation its first native-born and black Governor General.

196

In so doing, Bustamante, in one sense brought to completion the first phase of the "'mental revolution'" which he had helped to set in motion in 1938. For after he had emerged as the focus and pivot of a working-class protest movement that had the threat of racial confrontation, and was grapling to harness and give organized direction to that protest, Alexander Bustamante struck a radical note when he asserted that he would become Governor of Jamaica. Now, within the lifetime of many of his early followers, a black man — and not a brown man, or off-white — had become Governor General, the representative of the Queen (albeit of a white Queen) and the visible embodiment of the Head of State.[2]

Admittedly also, Sir Clifford was much more representative of the middle reaches of Jamaican society. Born in Westmoreland, the parish adjoining Bustamante's own birth parish, on 28th June 1892, he was the son of a civil servant. After completing elementary schooling, he spent two years at Mico Training College, graduating as a teacher in 1915. From 1916 until 1944 he served as headmaster (or principal) at three government schools in his parish. His political career began in 1944 when he was elected to the House of Representatives on the Busta-mante/J.L.P. ticket. Re-elected in 1949, he served as Speaker of the House from 1950 to 1954. In 1962, when the J.L.P. returned to power, he was appointed President of the Legislative Council (later the Senate) and then named Governor General a few months after.

Sir Clifford's success story, however, was not without significance for black lower-class Jamaicans. In a meaningful sense, the elementary teacher, especially in rural Jamaica, represented a choice of occupation and career which was not only an ideal, but a realistic hope of achievement for academically successful children of the poorer classes. In other words, teaching as a profession constituted an important avenue for social mobility and leadership on the basis of ascription.

"The teacher in Jamaica occupies a remarkable and powerful position. For not only is he a teacher in his school, and as such carrying the responsibility of moulding the mind and character of the coming generation, but he is also invariably the leader of life and thought and activity in the district where he belongs. . . . Whenever I go in any district which I regard as the real heart of Jamaica, and that is a district where small and middle-sized peasants and farmers predominate, I find them working their way slowly up to a higher economic level in this country. Those are the people I feel are carrying the future of Jamaica on their backs. Whenever I go into a real community of these people, I invariably find that the leader of thought in that community is the local teacher."[3]

197

Having, however, secured the appointment of a native-born Governor General, drawn from the majority segment of the population, Bustamante was equally concerned that there should be no doubt in the minds of the people as to who was the real political boss of Jamaica. He therefore determined that his government would build a new residence — Jamaica House — for the Prime Minister, on land which formed part of the estate of King's House, the official residence and establishment of former Colonial Governors but now of the Governor General. Bustamante's decision drew strong criticism within Parliament, from Opposition M.P.'s and especially from Norman Manley whose pre-independence government had earmarked Vale Royal as the official residence of the Prime Minister and had spent a considerable sum of money for its renovation. Bustamante retorted that in any event, Vale Royal was too small and inappropriate for the purpose. In irreverent fashion, he made the whole issue seem like "a storm in a tea-cup". "What hurts the Opposition Leader is because I declared I was going to make Vale Royal a maternity ward; but there is no place there for anyone to deliver. The Opposition Leader said I was going to send poor Campbell (Governor General) there but Campbell is going to King's House and poor Busta is not going to Vale Royal. I led you to believe that Campbell was going there to fool you [laughter]. Poor Campbell is going to King's House and poor Busta is not going to Vale Royal."[4]

On a subsequent occasion, however, the Prime Minister struck a more sober note: "Government is not building a home for Sir Alexander Bustamante. We are building a home for a nation. I have three first-class dwellings in the Corporate area without mortgage. I have recently built one on my property in St. Thomas. I do not need any house for Sir Alexander Bustamante."[5]

Of course, on psychological grounds, Bustamante could not be faulted. No one knew better than he the mentality of the Jamaican masses, and in locating Jamaica House — a busy venue of social and governmental activities — close to King's House, it could only serve to emphasize the purely ceremonial and perfunctory functions attached to the office of Governor General. Indeed, Bustamante had had occasion earlier to spell out the relationship between the two political offices. "The Governor General in his own judgement can send back my recommendation. But after it has been sent back, then I would advise him to do as I want. I am the Prime Minister of this country. In the first place he says I should recommend someone, in the second place I advise. An advice is a command. Even if the Governor General sent that back I would advise the Governor

General and send back to instruct him that this is my recommendation and it must go through. I am not a jelly fish Prime Minister. I know when to be soft and when to decide my right under the Constitution."[6]

It was thus as a veteran and self-assured politician that Prime Minister Sir Alexander Bustamante assumed direction of the island's political affairs. He also presided over a cabinet made up of proven and experienced parliamentary colleagues as well as talented newcomers. Many of the younger professionals and intelligentsia, who could see little prospect for rapid political advancement in the talent-rich People's National Party, had turned to the J.L.P. to provide an outlet for their talents and ambitions.

The new administration also showed itself far less inhibited by the philosophy of gradualism to which the J.L.P. had been so wedded in the past. For instance, the new Minister of Development and Welfare, thirty-two-year-old Edward Seaga, a Harvard-trained social scientist who proved to be an even more highly successful and effective Minister of Finance and Planning in the J.L.P.'s second five-year term, began work on a new Development Plan during 1962, and by July 1963, a Five-Year Independence Plan was completed and laid before Parliament. The Annual Budget presented by the Government in April 1963 in fact contained allocations for the first year of the Five-Year Plan. The Government also decided that television should be established on the island in 1963 and the franchise was awarded to the publicly owned Jamaica Broadcasting Corporation. As a number of new air services were established to facilitate travel between Jamaica and other countries, the Government carried forward plans for the establishment of a national airline. New initiatives in Agriculture led in 1963 to the launching of a Government Programme and establishment of an Agricultural Marketing Corporation. In October of the same year, a National Production Council was set up under the Chairmanship of Prime Minister Bustamante to stimulate greater effort and output from both the public and private sectors.

Even more importantly, from the point of view of moderating the divisive effects of rival political unionism, the Minister of Labour succeeded in setting up in 1962 a Committee made up of representatives of trade unions, employers and other interested parties to work towards drawing up a non-statutory Fair Labour Code, which would codify acceptable labour relations practices which had evolved over the years, including procedures for resolving rival union or representational disputes, a characteristic feature of industrial relations in Jamaica, and define unfair labour practices for trade unions and employers.[7] Unfortunately, after months of painstaking effort and genuine attempts at accommodation which proved to be quite productive, the Labour Code foundered on the issue of its applicability to public employees. The understanding was that the Charter would extend to public employees including Government servants in subordinate capacity but would exclude the police and defence forces. In November 1963, however, official spokesmen announced that Government intended to withdraw from participation in the Code and the whole effort collapsed. The Jamaica Employers Federation pointed out in a letter to the press, "It would be obviously absurd and inequitable to seek to impose certain moral standards on employers and employees in the private sector which Government was not prepared to honour in respect of its own employees."[8]

As far as his own ministerial duties were concerned, Bustamante retained responsibility for the Ministry of Defence and Ministry of External Affairs. In foreign affairs, his immediate task was to see to the establishment of formal diplomatic relations or links with former partners in the West Indies Federation, including Trinidad and Tobago, which had also gained Independence in August 1962, and to establish the country's relationships with the rest of the world. As Prime Minister and Minister of External Affairs of a newly independent and sovereign nation, Bustamante could not avoid being far more externally oriented than he had been in the past. Thus his role of elder statesman was given a new dimension, which he took readily within his stride.

Jamaica became the 109th Member of the United Nations, sought membership in its specialized agencies, established a permanent mission at the world body's headquarters, and Sir Alexander journeyed to New York to raise his country's flag at the traditional U.N. ceremony.

In September 1962, he attended the Commonwealth Prime Ministers' Conference in London, this time a Prime Minister in his own right. While the main topic on the agenda was the progress being made in negotiations in Brussels as to the conditions under which the United Kingdom might be admitted to the European Common Market, the atmosphere was embittered by the coming into effect on 1st July 1962 of the Commonwealth Immigration Act, enacted by the British Government to control immigration from Commonwealth countries, but particularly from non-white members of the club. The restrictions imposed by the Act had an immediate and drastic effect on the flow of emigrants from Jamaica. In the sombre mood of the Conference, Bustamante delivered a four-minute speech, acclaimed as one of the most impressive made

Fairfield University conferred the degree of Doctor of Laws on Sir Alexander Bustamante, 10th June 1963.

at the Conference, in which he scored the illiberality of the motives and principles which had not only given rise to the legislation but had been enshrined in it.

In July 1963, Bustamante also attended the first Conference of Heads of Caribbean Commonwealth countries, held in Trinidad, and reinforced his Government's willingness to continue the common (regional) services including the University of the West Indies, which had survived the break-up of the Federation, and to strengthen Jamaica's economic and cultural links with former partners and associated countries. Visits to the United States to receive an honourary Doctor of Laws degree from Fairfield University in Connecticut and to Washington for discussions with President John F. Kennedy were also highlights of Bustamante's activities during 1963. Prompted also by concern over the economic and trade repercussions which could result from Britain's entry into the European Economic Community (E.E.C.) Jamaica's relationship with countries of Latin America began taking a new direction. Early in 1962, Bustamante led a Jamaican delegation to attend the inauguration of the President-Elect of the Dominican Republic. In October of the same year, Jamaica accepted membership in the Latin American group in the United Nations and was accepted as a member of the United Nations Economic Commission for Latin America. Exploratory talks concerning Jamaica's entry into the Organization of American States (O.A.S.) continued.

As far as Bustamante was concerned, however, there could be no question of Jamaica adopting a position of ideological non-alignment or so-called "independent neutrality" in hemispheric relations. As between friends and enemies there could not be neutrality. This applied as much to Cuba as to the Soviet Union. In November 1962 he found occasion in Parliamentary debate to say, "I want to make a pronouncement. I don't hate the flesh of the Russians nor their person but I hate, I despise and I loathe communism. I would rather suffer death than live under the communist flag. That is why I declare in the United States, England and here that I am for the West and I am for the United States of America. . . .

"I have plenty of empty cells for communists to lock them up. . . . That is my policy, to lock-up communists. Communism is evil. It is deceptious. Anything that hates religion, I am against it. . . .

"I am for the West. I am against communism."[9]

Bustamante's uncompromising ideological stand also had a direct bearing on domestic politics. In due course, certain radical (left-wing) critics including a number of young Jamaican lecturers on the staff of the University of the West Indies, who dared to visit Cuba or hold up the Cuban experience when espousing land reform or dismantling of the remaining vestiges of the "plantation economy", either had their passports sequestered or suffered refusal of applications for new passports or revalidated passports. Of course, it should be noted immediately that seizure of passports and, where appropriate, exclusion orders against persons suspected of subversive intent or activities, had been instruments of control used by successive governments to protect national interests.[10]

The increasing number of cases in which the J.L.P. administration found it necessary to resort to seizure of passports in the post-independence period, gave rise first to suspicion and then the conviction that state power was being used to stifle criticism and opposition and effectively to infringe on the rights of citizens in the name of state security. The banning of certain literature, and later of the playing of certain protest records over the radio stations, only served to enhance the image of the J.L.P. as an authoritarian government. Was it going to be the case in Jamaica, as in so many former colonial territories, that freedom from colonial domination meant political domination by popular rulers? In the 1972 General Election, the J.L.P. found itself having to answer at the bar of public opinion.

Early in 1964, failing eyesight began to overtake Bustamante, and although he spent his eightieth birthday in office, within two months he had to relinquish his duties to Donald Sangster, Deputy Prime Minister and Minister of Finance who was appointed Acting Prime Minister. For the next three years, however, Bustamante continued to exercise very great influence over his party's administration of the country's affairs. For one thing, he was still President and unquestioned leader of the J.L.P. The arrangement was that Sangster was left to coordinate the day by day machinery and administration of government but with major decisions being taken at least with Bustamante's concurrence or after consultation with him. Conflict between Ministers or senior officials would, invariably, also be resolved by him. Many, therefore, were the pilgrimages that had to be made to the "Chief's" private residence at Tucker Avenue, overlooked by the Wareika hills, about five miles from the Office of the Prime Minister.

The arrangement worked smoothly because it was consistent with Bustamante's style of administration. Personal confidence was the basis on which he worked with people. And because he did not have to contend with any serious challenges or challengers to his leadership, delegation of authority and functions — the very essence of leadership — came easily to Bustamante. In fact, his willingness to let his Ministers run their own show and make mistakes — in good faith — helped to make his very firm rule tolerable.

Alexander Bustamante could never be made into a bureaucrat. For one thing, it is doubtful that he ever read anything long — be it book or document — in his life. It was his ears which provided the significant entrance into his mind, together with his observation of the expression on the face of the person who was dealing with him. This was in marked contrast to his cousin Norman Manley, who had a tremendous appetite and capacity for the written word and points of detail. Bustamante readily admits that he gave every encouragement to his lieutenants to speak their minds and to disagree with him, but when he thought it necessary to draw the line he would remind, "You have disagreed, now I have the last say. I object to all you have agreed to. Now goodbye."[11] A published anecdote recounts that when he became Prime Minister in 1962, the practice in Cabinet was for Ministers to present written submissions on matters on which they wished to have Cabinet endorsement. After Bustamante had heard from the senior Ministers as to the implications of particular proposals, he would announce his decision. This practice did not meet with the approval of one Minister who suggested that the democratic thing to do would be to take a vote. "Vote?" queried Sir Alexander. "A vote? Very well, we will have a vote. Those in favour say 'aye', those against, 'no'. Eleven ayes and one no — me — the no's have it, negatived; next matter."

Bustamante's intuitive trust in people who worked with him extended to his signing an important letter, after it had been read back to him by his Permanent Secretary (civil service head of a Ministry) or someone else working for him. In a sense, therefore, Bustamante lived by his memory, and in this Gladys Longbridge Bustamante played a critical role as his private secretary and confidante, and this role did not end when she became his wife. She was his "memory bank", so to speak.[12] In discussions, Bustamante would turn to her incessantly — "What was the sum of money we provided for that road in Lionel Town, Lady B?" — and such was her memory that she would recall what had been done three or four years previously. "What was the name of that man who came to see me last year when I was in New York, Lady B?" and again the name would be recalled. Gladys Longbridge Bustamante was therefore the complementary but unobtrusive other member of the team who made a tremendous contribution to the way in which

Bustamante was able to perform. He often expected others who worked with him to perform in the same way. One of Jamaica's very distinguished civil servants recalled that his telephone would ring, and it would be a summons from the Prime Minister. There would, however, be rarely any indication of what the Prime Minister wanted to see him about or wanted to discuss. On one occasion he protested to Bustamante's Secretary, pointing out that he would much prefer to be able to consult his files before giving advice that might be required. Apprised of this by his Secretary, Bustamante replied that he had no intention of letting his administrative officer know beforehand what he wanted to discuss, as he was more likely to get the truth if he took him by surprise, rather than allowing him to have an opportunity to think up a story or invent an explanation.

It is one of the paradoxes of William Alexander Clarke Bustamante that the very autocratic and egocentric tendencies which gave rise to his personalism or patriarchal rule also enabled him to satisfy the institutional requirements of leadership, namely, the ability to see the enterprise as a whole, to make decisions, to delegate and to inspire loyalty. He tended to see himself as belonging to all classes and all constituencies in Jamaica. This helped to sustain his sense of fairplay. He was a man of action who took decisions readily and there was never any doubt as to who was boss. In most emergent nations, the relationship between the political executive and the career civil service, constitutes a potential source of continuing tension. Jamaica has been no exception.[13] Yet, as far as Bustamante was concerned, his intuitive and unorthodox approach to administration led him to rely upon his civil service aides to do the administrative spadework and provide him with advice, and as a rule he enjoyed excellent relations with them. He demanded loyalty and he gave the same.

For almost three years, then, the J.L.P. governed Jamaica, led by an acting Prime Minister and a semi-retired Prime Minister. In February 1967, however, at eighty-three years of age, Sir Alexander Bustamante announced his intention not to run for office in the forthcoming elections. The electorate, however, gave him a happy send-off by returning his party to power with an increased majority of thirty-three to twenty. In February 1968, Members of Parliament officially paid tribute to the patriarch of Jamaican politics. Some of the more perceptive and significant of the tributes paid to him came from the Leader and veteran Members of the Opposition. Florizel Glasspole recalled how in 1959 he assured Bustamante that the P.N.P. would win the General Election but expressed the hope that he, Bustamante, would be re-elected. When the surprised J.L.P. leader queried, "What? Do you mean to tell me you want me to come back?" He replied, "Yes, good heavens, man, you are the salt and pepper on which we thrive in Parliament." This, coming from a political opponent who had fought him doggedly all along the way, must have pleased the old warrior.

8

THE MAN AND
HIS TIMES —
HERO IN FACT
AND FICTION

There are not many men who succeed in establishing themselves as legends before embarking upon a career of public service. But then not many men set out deliberately to create and propagate the legends which they feel are necessary to sustain their activities and careers. Alexander Bustamante was one such man. When he returned to Jamaica in 1934, he had been away for a period stretching over twenty-nine years, punctuated by at least four visits to his native land. Two of these visits were "flying visits", one in 1910 when he brought his fiancée home to get married, the other in 1922 which revealed him for the first time in the role of a "Cuban grandee" or successful man of affairs. The third visit in 1928 was intended by Bustamante to be his final return home to re-establish himself, but his venture into the dairy business proved unsuccessful and he took off again. Then in 1932 he was back again, to scout business possibilities, and when he left after a short stay, it was to head for the United States via Cuba.

As far as Jamaica was concerned, therefore, a blank curtain descended on the life and activities of Alexander Clarke during his long years of residence abroad and it was left to the returning *émigré* himself, under his newly acquired name of Bustamante, to fill in selectively some of the gaps.

The *Who's Who and Why in Jamaica*, which listed Bustamante for the first time in 1940, recorded that "at the age of fifteen, was adopted by a Spanish mariner and emigrated to Spain, where he received his education; joined the Spanish army, adopted the name Bustamante and became an officer; saw service in various disorders, Casa Blanca ... Spanish Morocco, until 1925 when he travelled to the Republic of Cuba and joined the police there". In the next issue (1941–6) the age of adoption and departure for Spain was lowered from fifteen to five. Bustamante has held to the story of his adoption with a tenacity which is remarkable in the light of very obvious and glaring inconsistencies. The 1941–6 edition of *Who's Who*, which placed him in Spain until

1925, also recorded the fact of his marriage to Mildred Edith Blanck in Kingston, Jamaica, on 12th December 1910. Clearly, the story of his adoption and Spanish upbringing is a fabrication by Bustamante for he left Jamaica for Cuba for the first time in 1905 at the age of twenty-one and a corroborative entry was made in the 1966 edition of the *Who's Who in Jamaica*.

One can only speculate as to why Bustamante thought it necessary to invent and promote the legend of his upbringing in Spain and military adventures in that part of the world. One possibility is that he might have been concerned both to justify the assumption of the name Bustamante and to project the image of a colourful adventurer and fighter who was not to be trifled with. It may be noted in passing that his cousin Norman Manley had returned to Jamaica a decorated war hero and Bustamante has always been very proud of the successful members and relatives of his family. In the many sharp clashes that he had with the late Norman Manley in the House of Representatives, Bustamante found many occasions to remind gleefully that "blood is thicker than water". On one occasion he noted, "It is said that when blood is fighting blood, the fight is thicker and harder. I am not fighting blood but fighting principles and policies. One thing I admire about my friend from Eastern St. Andrew (Norman Manley) is that when he is attacking me he can still laugh and remember that we are a laughing family." But he went on to add — "One thing I admire about my friend, the Member for Eastern St. Andrew, is that when he is attacking, when one looks at his facial expression, one sees that he does not mean it. What he is really saying in effect is 'Would to God Busta, I could come over to your side to assist you.' "[1]

Another possibility is that Bustamante may have been concerned to shroud his past as a family man, a role in which he had not been happily cast. By 1920 when he left Panama for Cuba, he was travelling alone. He appears not to have been very close to members of his family in Jamaica and his continuing aloofness from his mother and sisters after his final return home in 1934, possibly out of anxiety to preserve his freedom to slip out again as a foreigner if things did not work out, led to his estrangement from the family including Norman Manley, who took affront at his cousin Aleck's abdication of his family responsibilities. Yet, ironically, Bustamante's great personal appeal and popularity, when he assumed the role of "Messiah" of the working classes in 1938, derived much of its strength from the fanatical devotion and loyalty accorded him by working-class women, especially in the rural area. But at the same time, Bustamante never ceased to extol the virtues of,

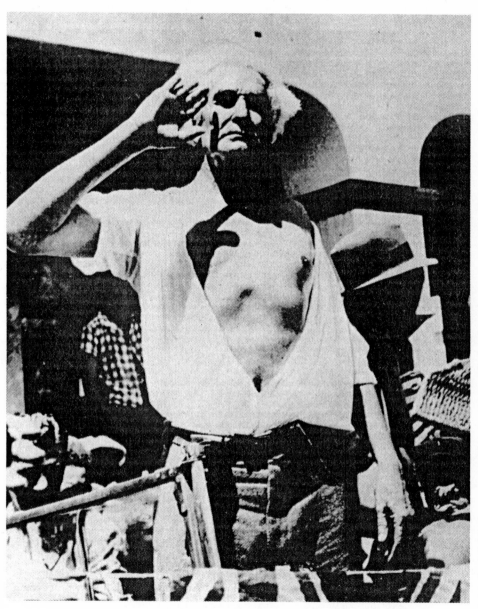

Hero in fact and fiction.

and show deep respect for, Jamaican womanhood, and his great charm and deferential respect at all times can be attested to by women of all walks of life and political persuasion in Jamaica. Indeed, his respect for women was taken to the point where it seemed almost exaggerated. For instance, immediately after he became Prime Minister, he gave instructions that "these frail ladies" should not work after 4 o'clock and his own secretary had to hide whenever she had work to do which would take her after that time, so that the Prime Minister would not see her there.[2] An eyewitness account also recalls occasions on which Sir Alexander would stop his car to take up women at a bus stop, because rain was threatening and he was afraid "that these frail creatures were going to get wet and something terrible would happen to them".

Throughout his career he also championed the cause of women in the public service. "There can be no good reason why in the civil service Government should not allow women to rise to as high and as far as their ability, education, and intelligence can carry them."[3]

Bustamante's gentlemanly concern for women was not lessened by retirement from active politics and at eighty-eight years of age, ever the genial host, he could still quip much to the satisfaction of female visitors of all ages, and to the amusement of his wife, "I love you honey" or to beaming husbands "You are lucky that I did not meet her before you married her".

Bustamante also exercised a strong fascination over children and young people who would flock around to see the tall bushy-haired and striking man whose name had become a by-word on the lips of many parents. On his part, Bustamante often expressed regret that he had no children of his own.

Finally, the possibility cannot be ruled out that Bustamante may have set out merely to "baffle" those around him, as a desirable technique of launching himself on a business career, and that the image of the well brought-up Spanish adventurer and world traveller along with the story of having made a fortune "playing the New York Stock Exchange" were intended to bolster and ensure his success by projecting himself as a worldly man of substance. Peculiarly enough, *Who's Who* in 1940 noted that he "baffled the public politically until May 1938", and well he should have, being listed as "Dietician, Money-lender, Politician (Republican Socialist), Trade Unionist, Publicist and Labourite".

Norman Manley in a recorded interview once described Bustamante as an "undifferentiated personality" with the capacity to be moulded by all the historic forces around him. Presumably what he meant to

The marriage of Sir Alexander Bustamante to Miss Gladys Longbridge, 6th September 1962.

convey by "undifferentiated personality" was that Bustamante was a man who had certain occupational or career interests and that he concentrated on their pursuit with such single-mindedness of purpose that he had little time for other (unrelated) matters. In this sense, Bustamante's recreational activities were both adjuncts to, and essential aspects of, his career as labour leader and politician. Thus *Who's Who* in 1940 listed his recreations as "conversations, standing drinks for friends and acquaintances [later changed to conviviality], motoring and speeches". This enumeration could only have come from Bustamante himself.

Later on in his career when he had acquired "Retreat", a large all-purpose farm and country hideaway along the seacoast in St. Thomas, farming, bee-keeping and swimming were added to the list of recreational activities and he was categorized as "Statesman, Planter, Penkeeper, Trade Unionist . . ." Non-vocational interests or pursuits, such as the arts and forms of entertainment including dancing, the cinema or sports, did not exercise much attraction for Bustamante who remained a wholly "political" being. People, rather than ideas or theories or things, was his business and preoccupation. His easy affability and his ability to talk their language made it easy for him to fraternize with workers and peasants, and, indeed, with his fellowmen at large. He readily accepted the shortening of his name to "Busta" and welcomed the familiarity as an indication of the esteem and affection in which he was held by the masses. Losing touch with the people was not likely to be one of Bustamante's besetting political sins. He also welcomed people around him and even during his declining years it was still left to callers and visitors to take their leave. At the same time, the interviewer or student of politics or unionism who came seeking to elicit from Bustamante profound philosophical discourses or statements or analyses of the social forces at work in Jamaican society was likely to be disappointed.

Bustamante tended to see his rise and role in Jamaican affairs in simple or elemental terms. His people were oppressed and downtrodden and needed a friend and leader. Moved by their plight to agitate on their behalf, he became the answer to their prayer, and everything else flowed from that.

While the interviewer might be rewarded with occasional flashes of his political or social insight, Bustamante himself was much more concerned to regale his audience with anecdotes and stories which were the stock-in-trade of the legendary Bustamante — his adoption at the age of five; his upbringing in Barcelona, Spain; his encounter with the immigration authorities in Canada when he attempted to enter that

212

country from the United States; the baring of his chest to the police in 1938, defying them to shoot him; the incident in which he threw one of his guns (variously a toy or unloaded gun or loaded with blanks) to a man who had threatened to shoot him thereby forcing the man to drop the gun and flee; his arrest in 1938 and detention in 1940 for seventeen months; and finally, his willingness to suffer deprivation for the masses. These were the things that one was certain to hear. The ever-present and solicitous Miss Gladys Longbridge, first as his private secretary up to 1962 and then as his wife thereafter, would gently correct the "Chief", reminding him that a statement of his was not altogether correct or that he was confusing particular dates and events and so on. He would reply that he could not have survived without her and how deeply touched he was by her utter loyalty and unfailing devotion to him since 1938.

The interpreter of Bustamante is left no choice but to attempt to piece together Bustamante's political, social or trade union philosophy from his letters to the press, debates in the Legislature, speeches at Annual Conferences of the B.I.T.U. and J.L.P. and responses given to specific questions or promptings in private interviews. There is the risk that by this process of piecemeal linkage and blending, the interpreter or analyst may attribute to Bustamante a degree of calculation or ideological consciousness and coherence which he himself would not recognize. Indeed, much of the charm and appeal of this "great man" lay precisely in his impetuosity, intuition, opportunism and manipulative intelligence. But whatever may have been the organizing principles or motivating forces which governed Bustamante's behaviour, there are a number of elements which cannot be gainsaid, such as his profound compassion for the working classes, his intuitive grasp of mob psychology, a powerful egocentrism, which left him with unshakeable belief in his natural right to, and capacity for, leadership, and an unswerving instinct and appetite for power. In many instances, therefore, to ask Bustamante to explain what were the factors which he took into account or considered in taking certain decisions or courses of action was to place him in a quandary and more often than not he would readily agree to the more "structured" hypothesis or reasoning suggested by the interviewer. The fact of the matter is that Bustamante was a man of the moment, reacting to situations and events as they happened. Consequently, he was impatient of those who seemed disposed to concentrate on the future or long run to the exclusion of the present and reacted strongly and negatively in parliamentary debates when the Opposition stressed the need for planning as the appropriate technique for solving Jamaica's problems. Bustamante

213

often accused them of waving the flag of planning as a kind of magic wand to achieve full employment and to put an end to so endemic an economic ill as unemployment. As far as he was concerned, this was tantamount to deception — Rome was not built in a day — and unemployment and poverty in Jamaica would not and could not be eradicated in generations much less within a lifetime. His duty as a leader of the people, therefore, was to try and improve their material lot, however modest, not in the distant future but in the present and within the limits set by the country's resources.

Thus, while education for the children of the poor and the working classes was important, higher wages or incomes, and derivatively, bread and butter for their parents and indeed for the entire family were more important in the short run. This same realism and pragmatism governed his approach as a labour leader. To adopt any other approach was to attempt to "fool the people", and Bustamante never hesitated whether in the Legislature or at the bargaining table to "tell it as it is". But by the same token, when he felt that workers' claims were just and reasonable, he would insist on those claims being met by strike action if need be, or failing that, would revert to the political power of the Government to ensure a satisfactory settlement.

As a labour leader, Alexander Bustamante exercised a truly remarkable authority over the B.I.T.U.'s rank and file. True, when it suited him he would be the first to advise workers that it was up to them to accept a particular settlement or not, but with rare exceptions, his recommendation was likely to carry the force of command. For there was never any doubt in their minds, or, for that matter, in Bustamante's mind, as to where his loyalty and sympathies ultimately lay. He was first and foremost a labour leader and champion of the underdog, and it was in this capacity that he was seen at his fiery best. Enraged, he was truly forbidding and no respecter of persons or of protocol. In January 1967, for instance, a dispute developed between the Jamaica Public Service Company, sole suppliers of the country's electric light and power, and its unionized work force — represented jointly by the B.I.T.U. and N.W.U. — over the dismissal of watchmen and subcontracting of certain services. Two illegal strikes occurred before the dispute was referred to an Arbitration Tribunal. Bustamante, still nominally Prime Minister, and of course still formal head of the B.I.T.U., electrified employers by sending a letter to the then Senator Hugh Shearer which was published in *The Daily Gleaner*. He charged, "The Jamaica Public Service Company's act in discharging watchmen, and from what I understand subcontracting the work to be done at cheaper rates, is outrageous and cannot be tolerated.

"When the employers are right I am with them, but when the workers are right I am even more with them. In this case there is not the slightest doubt in my mind that a diabolical advantage has been taken of the working man and I am completely with the workers in this struggle. The Union's request that the watchmen should be reinstated into the jobs and the Union's agreement to put the issue to arbitration while the men are in the job are reasonable."[4] This was typical of Bustamante and it mattered not that the Employers Federation and other public-spirited bodies deplored the fact that the Prime Minister had expressed sympathy with workers who had broken the law.

It was as a labour leader that Bustamante achieved his tremendous popularity and he was careful to sustain it on this basis. Thus at each B.I.T.U. Annual Conference he would set targets which were realistic, even in the short run, and then strive to attain them through industrial as well as political action. As far as the workers were concerned, therefore, Bustamante could always be expected to bring home the bacon. As a union negotiator, he was both admired and feared by employers. For one thing, they felt that, normally, once a bargain was struck with Bustamante, it would be kept. Moreover, it was preferable to do business with a labour leader who ardently espoused private enterprise and vigorously upheld the right of investors to a "fair rate of return" or profit. At the same time, however, whenever he rose from the bargaining table in righteous indignation or stalked from a conciliation meeting, it was as though a volcano had erupted or a hurricane had passed by. Employers or their representatives would be addressed peremptorily by surnames and cajoled or threatened as the situation demanded. They would be reminded who was the boss of Jamaica and how easily they could be broken by the workers. To illiterate and semi-literate worker delegates looking on, these carefully staged performances imparted a sense of power and gave deep psychological satisfaction.

Collective bargaining, as a process involving an element of "psychology, politics and poker", thus provided a setting in which Bustamante's personal endowments — shrewdness, quick wit, affability and supreme self-confidence — could be employed with great effect, and he was very much alive to the ritualistic aspects of collective bargaining. Thus, the tactical necessities of bargaining might require the union to ask, initially, for more than it was likely to obtain, or expected to gain, but this allowed the union negotiators to scale down demands or engage in trade-offs, depending on the strength of the employers' counter-argument and resistance as well as the willingness or unwillingness of both sides to risk an economic test of strength.

As a negotiator, Bustamante, however, was not interested in erudite presentation or verbal manipulation of the wage criteria used by labour and management to justify claims made or positions taken. He had the uncanny knack, which he carried over to his political administration, of being able to sift the chaff from the wheat and to get to the kernel of the matter. He knew what the workers wanted and the things which were really important to them. He knew better than any one else the limits of tolerance or zones of acceptance available to him, and especially so in those disputes which had left the workers involved thoroughly aroused. Moreover, as a businessman turned labour leader, Bustamante never doubted the extent of his own "reasonableness" (except of course in politically-inspired disputes) and so, once convinced that an employer could sustain the economic or payroll cost of the union's final compromise offer, he would move, impatiently, to bring matters to a head.

His rhetoric immediately would grow more strident, to herald escalation of the "war of nerves", culminating appropriately either in an ultimatum to the employer or a staged walk-out from the conciliation meeting, or both. One risk inherent in this type of stretegy, at least from the employer's point of view, was that workers would be carried away by the rhetoric and jump the gun by going out on strike in anticipation of the official strike call or in a show of support for the "Chief". In fact, this came close to being the normal pattern of labour-management relations in the sugar industry, the traditional stronghold of the B.I.T.U., and the scene of some of Bustamante's most famous and colourful labour-management encounters. In 1946, for instance, the B.I.T.U. was involved in a dispute with the Worthy Park Estate in St. Catherine, owned by the Clarke family, and Bustamante was led to say, "Mr. Clarke of Worthy Park thinks he is a tough man; but I want Mr. Clarke to know this; that that is my title. If there are two tough men in town, 'I am them two' as the Americans say; Mr. Clarke has no place in that definition and I am going to soften him up."

A few weeks later it was the turn of Robert Kirkwood (later Sir Robert), Managing Director of the West Indies Sugar Company and Bustamante's chief contender on the management side of the industry for two decades. "I will slap you . . . and pay for it." Bustamante also utilized some ingenious methods for disrupting production and exerting pressure on management when he did not wish to be accused of breaching collective procedures or of calling political strikes. For it must be remembered that the sugar industry, because of its predominant role in the economy, certainly from the point of view of employment and trade union membership, was also the scene of fierce struggles between the rivals — the union-party blocs. Accordingly, one of Bustamante's highly effective alternatives to the strike was the voluntary diversion of workers from work activities. The "Chief" would arrive in a sugar village or compound and like a magnet would attract around him a milling crowd of men, women and children. As he exchanged pleasantries, the word of his presence would spread like wild-fire to the fields nearby. He would then set out on foot along a strategic route, accompanied by the assembled group. At each stop point, the process would be repeated until, in effect, there was a near complete withdrawal of the work force and temporary "cessation" of work. Bustamante would be left free to decide whether he had come on a field visit, or out of anxiety to check on rumbles of discontent and thus prevent a dispute or grievance arising, or to visit ailing workers, or for a reason that best suited his purpose. Overseers would soon be reporting that work had ceased but that there had been no notification of a dispute or strike. At the same time, through the grapevine, management would learn the real reason for the "Chief's" displeasure. The employment of this technique was actually witnessed by this writer during the conduct of a representational poll at one of the sugar estates where the B.I.T.U. had objected that the list of workers eligible to vote was incomplete. Bustamante arrived at one of the polling stations and voiced dissatisfaction over the voting list. As supporters gathered around him, he set out for the next polling station, presumably on a legitimate visit of inspection, but this time being trailed, voluntarily, by supporters. By the time he had made a number of stops, the crowd had grown sufficiently large and intimidating for polling to be suspended until the lists could be corrected or amended.

Up to his retirement from active politics in 1967 due to failing sight and partial paralysis as a result of a stroke, Bustamante remained a man of tremendous energy, vitality and action. Almost without exception, he travelled by automobile in his many excursions throughout the country. This was his way of making his presence felt, for even if he did nothing more than wave (as he always did) when passing through a village or town, the word would spread that the "Chief" was in the area or out looking after the interests of the people. Travel by road also enabled Bustamante to visit out-of-the-way places and to arrive unexpected at trouble spots, for he believed not only in nipping problems in the bud but in personally confronting political foes or dissidents. Thus when-

217

ever he learned of disaffection, whether at the trade union or political level, Bustamante would appear on the scene, leaving his car if necessary to walk fearlessly into the hills or backwoods to "face-up" the disaffected. If he felt that the aggrieved had a case, he would promise redress. If not, he would uncompromisingly "lay down the law". Having thus made his position known, there would always be time for drinks to show that there was no rancour or to let "bygones be bygones".

In much the tradition of a benevolent despot, Bustamante also regarded himself as an original fount of justice or a court of last resort. A man with a very keen sense of fairplay, he would not hesitate to overrule any of his associates or subordinates in the Union, Party or Government, if he felt that they had made a bad decision or had acted unjustly. Thus there was always the sentiment, among the rank and file and aggrieved persons, that if they could state their side of the case to Bustamante personally, there could be hope of a fair or favourable decision. This expectation was reinforced by the easy accessibility of Bustamante to his followers and his willingness to see virtually anyone (supporter or not) from whatever walk of life. The result was that Bustamante enjoyed a fair measure of immunity against criticisms of his leadership, and no one realized it or appreciated it more than he did. It accounts for his penchant for "washing his dirty linen in public" and for his habit of publicly denouncing alleged challenges to, or usurpations of, his authority, whether within the B.I.T.U.or the J.L.P. What was involved each time was an appeal directly to his supporters at large, but particularly to rural devotees against the party machine or bureaucracy. The response on every occasion was a strong vote of confidence in the "Chief" and endorsement of the action he had taken or proposed to take, to put matters right. To many of his loyal followers, Bustamante's reassertion of his absolute authority would by itself be an act of explanation as to why the Union's or Party's affairs had appeared not to be going right. It signified that the "Chief" had not been getting the full support of his team. Here then was the case of a powerful charismatic leader using popular, and often imperfectly institutionalized support, to sustain his absolute control over party and union hierarchies.

At no time, therefore, during his active career as labour leader and politician was there ever the slightest possibility of Bustamante being persuaded to function as "the first among equals". From his senior lieutenants no less than from the rank and file, the "Chief" exacted absolute loyalty and obedience. They were first of all followers, and then colleagues or friends, as the case might be. Such, however, was the capacity

218

of Bustamante to charm and grow upon those around him, that he often inspired the total loyalty which he demanded. In any event, however much the more organization-minded of his colleagues might have been inclined to chafe at his autocratic tendencies and "one-man rule", they were forced to concede that when it came to the pursuit of political power, more often than not, their leader was proven right in his instinctive assessments and arbitrary decisions. For if results are the measure of a politician's success, then Alexander Bustamante was eminently successful. He and his party were in office for fifteen of the twenty-two years that he was active in public life.

For Bustamante, party politics meant total commitment and loyalty on the part of supporters or sympathizers, whether they were card-carrying members of the party or not. Nowhere was this made more evident than in the dispensing of appointments, or patronage, if you will.

With the exception of the established Civil Service where he deferred to the British and European model of a professionalized or career civil service subject to the minimum of political interference in appointments, Bustamante leaned towards the American patronage system, certainly when it came to appointments to statutory corporations and boards or other quasi-public bodies. Not only was it a matter of "to the victors the spoils", but there was little room or scope in such agencies for so-called independent or politically neutral public-minded citizens, more so if it meant that Bustamante's wishes, or those of the responsible Minister, would not be the final guides to action and decision-making. To Bustamante and J.L.P. colleagues, "fair play" did not extend to appointing or retaining persons known to be or suspected of being P.N.P. sympathizers. Neither, for that matter, were purely administrative personnel exempt from the loyalty test. The quasi-public sector thus emerged as the main rewarding feature of the political system, with two very unhappy consequences. In the first place, by the end of the J.L.P.'s first two terms or ten years in office, political victimization and discrimination had become deeply imbedded in Jamaican politics, so imbedded that. the change of administration in 1955 merely served to confirm the pattern of "ins" and "outs". For in the matter of political patronage, the differences between the J.L.P. and the P.N.P. proved to be differences of degree rather than of kind.

Bustamante defended himself and the J.L.P. administration by arguing that he was not acting against P.N.P. sympathizers because of their political loyalties but because they allowed political considerations to intrude upon, and influence, the performance of their duties. Furthermore, where such persons occupied positions of strategic importance or influence in the society, as for example, government school teachers or field and extension officers whether of the Ministry of Agriculture or of quasi-public bodies such as the Jamaica Agricultural Society, it was only reasonable for the party constituting the government to act in self-protection. Nevertheless, although Bustamante subscribed fully to the maxim that (political) self-preservation is the first law of nature, and was rarely inclined to give help or comfort to his political opponents, this did not prevent him, on occasions, from intervening to end harassment or avert dismissal of persons known to be staunch and active supporters of the P.N.P., on the grounds that "although he is P.N.P. and supports my cousin Norman, he is a good man and is doing a good job."[5]

The second of the unhappy consequences of the application of patronage in the "grey area" or "fourth arm" of government so to speak, was (and is) that Jamaica could get no nearer to solving the fundamental problem of agriculture — that of marketing — because patronage took precedence over technical and administrative competence, as far as production, marketing and credit boards or corporations were concerned. This legacy has carried over to the present time.

Bustamante's decisiveness in dealing with political opponents, both within and without his party or union, stemmed, however, from his obsession with power, rather than anything else, and relatively few of his political opponents could accuse him of acting out of rancour or vindictiveness. In fact, at the purely personal level, Bustamante remained on very amicable terms with most of his inveterate political foes. The stakes were high and he played hard within the rules of the game, even if he did set many of the rules himself.

One of the advantages enjoyed by Bustamante throughout his career, strangely as it may sound, was that his political opponents, including Norman Manley, could not be sure whether he was being serious or not, and even better, from Bustamante's point of view, whether to take him seriously or not. Much the same problem exists, of course, for the writer or historian attempting to interpret or explain Bustamante as the dominant figure on the Jamaican political scene for over thirty years. Part of the explanation lies in the fact that William Alexander Bustamante was every bit of a showman and gloried in showmanship. It was evident in his practice of always making a late and dramatic entrance. When Parliament paid tribute to Sir Alexander on his retirement from active politics, Florizel Glasspole recalled the occasion on which he saw Bustamante for the first time. "It was a Sunday night way back in 1937. I was attending church service at the Coke Methodist Church. Midway the service Mr.

Speaker, the eyes of the congregation were turned on a figure who stepped into the Church . . . and walked straight up the aisle and sat way up, Mr. Speaker, in the very front pew of the Church . . . If you had seen him walking up that aisle, a gaunt figure, the famous walk in those days, staggering from side to side . . . On that occasion I looked at him as a wild-eyed man. And then he sat down and listened from a very uncomfortable pew. . . .

"At the end of the sermon, he simply got up, walked down the aisle . . . and disappeared entirely."[6]

Bustamante was the complete extrovert. On another occasion he was en route to Trinidad aboard an aircraft which carried a group of American college girls on tour. One of the girls, looking through a *Life* magazine which carried an account of the Queen's visit to Jamaica, thought she saw a resemblance between the man sitting in the aircraft and the person shown in one of the photographs. She approached Bustamante, showed him the photograph and asked, "Is this you Sir?" This so tickled Bustamante that he got up, stood behind the door leading to the pilot's cabin and began describing to the delight of all the passengers, his conversation with the Queen, what he thought of her, and what she wore. The steward was then summoned, asked how many bottles of champagne he had, and ordered by the exuberant Bustamante to serve everyone champagne at his expense.[7]

Yet there were occasions when Bustamante was genuinely anxious to hide his generosity. Robert Lightbourne, Minister of Trade and Industry, recalled for Members of Parliament an incident which he witnessed while waiting to see Bustamante on one occasion. "Sir Alexander came out of his green Buick. A little boy rushed in the yard. The police ran the the boy out of the yard. The boy was obviously begging. Sir Alexander said — 'No, no sonny, you can't come in here' and then he quietly went round to the back there and gave the boy a pound. Then he saw that I had witnessed what had happened. And I will never forget it, Sir. These were his words: 'Well what am I to do? The boy is hungry.' "[8]

There were, of course, other incidents totally devoid of political significance, such as occurred on one of Bustamante's visits to Barbados. There a man broke through the crowd and said something to Bustamante who suggested that he come and see him at his hotel. A witness to this episode who also happened to be in Bustamante's suite when the man arrived, saw Bustamante make his visitor a substantial gift of money to help him out of a predicament. This remained an incident known only to the parties until recounted to this writer.[9]

221

The real key to the enigma of Bustamante lies in his personality and his appreciation of the role he was called upon to play. His egocentrism, his flamboyant style and penchant for dramatization, his brashness or braggadocio if you will, and his unbounded energy and vitality, were attributes which left Bustamante well equipped to play the part of agitator. His natural sympathy for the underdog and his emotional link and identification with the underprivileged in Jamaican society, involved him in agitational politics in an environmental setting which provided maximum scope for his skills and qualities, and at the same time, determined the nature of his appeal and the form of his dominance as a "Messiah". For Bustamante's appeal, which by its very depth placed him in the tradition of Bedward and Garvey, lay with the black population, deeply religious and superstitious and of low educational, vocational and social status, who constituted both the majority and the base of Jamaican society.

Bustamante's seeming excesses and eccentricities were the very things which appealed to the traditionalist agro-proletariat and peasantry who proclaimed him as their hope of a better life on this earth. His attack on the existing social structure and order enabled Bustamante to adopt a posture of radicalism which met the yearnings of his followers for human dignity and self-assertion without his having to espouse reconstruction of the economic system or the main prop of the offending social order.

By temperament an autocrat, Bustamante also satisfied the predilection of a colonial and plantation society for authoritarian and paternal rule and guidance. In fact, so in tune was the "Chief" with the ethos and expectations of the masses, especially in rural Jamaica, that he allowed himself to be as much moulded and guided by their sentiments. It is in this sense that it may be said that Bustamante avoided the more difficult and challenging task of reshaping the attitudes of his followers and of hastening the process of decolonization.

Norman Manley, when he wanted to refer pejoratively to Bustamante from the political platform, called him "Busta'nansi". Anansi is a spider, the Jamaican trickster folk hero of animal tales. In humanized form, he is the "Sam-fie man" — the Jamaican counterpart of the supreme confidence man in North America or the Spanish rogue (*picaro*) "who lives by his wits and treats outrageously anyone upon whom he has the chance to impose his superior cunning". Occasionally, retributive justice may intervene and Anansi falls into the pit he has dug for another, but as a rule Anansi manages to come out on top. "Anansi trick them all; nobody can trick Anansi, only Brar (brother) Death!"

As the story goes, at a political meeting in the parish of Clarendon during the Referendum campaign, Manley warned listeners, "Busta'nansi fooling all of you." A few days later, Bustamante was passing through the same district and was told of Manley calling him Anansi. In his speech, Bustamante replied: "My cousin Manley says I am Anansi — but I am going to wrap him up in my web." The result of the Referendum — a victory for Bustamante — was taken as confirmation that Bustamante had indeed "wrapped up" his cousin Norman Manley.

The insinuation of Bustamante's fearfully prophetic powers began as early as 1937. A published anecdote recounts that in that year, during an election campaign in the Corporate Area, Bustamante was stopped by Lewis Ashenheim, city solicitor and one of the two leading contestants, and asked: "Mr. Bustamante, what are you doing in this election?" Bustamante retorted, "Mr. Ashenheim, I am doing everything for you to lose," and continued his stroll. The anecdote concludes: "Mr. Ashenheim did lose the elections." More ominous and portentous, however, as far as the masses were concerned, was the "attack", also in 1937, launched by Bustamante, then money-lender and budding popular agitator, against the Governor, Sir Edward Denham. Denham had proposed that the Usury Act be revised and tightened up to prevent abuses by money-lenders. Bustamante reacted strongly to what he construed to be a threat to himself and his profession and spearheaded from the public platform a "Denham must go" campaign. When, a year later, in the course of the riots the Governor died after an abdominal operation, it was seen as fulfilment of Bustamante's charge that "Denham must go".

Bustamante, on his part, not only accepted the jibes of political opponents and ego-deflaters with good grace and unshakable aplomb, but sought always to turn them to his advantage with his ready repartee. Perhaps the greatest of all the anecdotal classics about Bustamante arose out of his visit to Washington not too long after he had become Prime Minister. There, it is claimed, at the National Press Club a very cynical reporter observed: "Sir Alexander, it is being said in Washington that you were born in a little thatched hut which you built with your own hands." Replied Bustamante mischievously: "That's not me my son — that was your President Lincoln. I was born in a manger." But to many of Bustamante's ardent followers who could look back to the 1938 era and the road along which they had travelled, this was not just humour, but a permissible and meaningful analogy.

In an interview with the writer during 1970, a J.L.P. Member of Parliament of rural working-class background, who had risen through union and party ranks to become a Minister of State in the J.L.P. government, was asked to respond to the question: "What does Bustamante mean to you and to Jamaica?" He prefaced his remarks with the declaration: "The Saviour for humanity on earth after the death of our Lord and Saviour Jesus Christ — William Alexander Bustamante". He went on to explain that the women of Jamaica should kneel on broken glass bottles, if necessary, at the very mention of the name Bustamante. For, before the advent of Bustamante, women in the public services, including post mistresses, teachers and nurses, could not marry and retain their jobs. At the same time, as single women, they were eligible for maternity leave and were thus encouraged to live in concubinage and bear children out of wedlock. Bustamante had changed all that. Other economically depressed categories of female workers, including domestic servants and women undertaking the arduous task of breaking stones by the roadside, had had their wages raised substantially over the years. Thus he "lifted up the unfortunate into fortunate". Speaking of himself, the Minister of State said: "But for Bustamante, I would be nothing. I wouldn't know anything about unionism or politics." It was thus Bustamante, the man, rather than the Bustamante Industrial Trade Union or the Jamaica Labour Party, who symbolized the hopes and achievements of black working-class Jamaicans and more particularly of the illiterate and lowly sugar and agricultural labourers.

Sir Alexander himself sat quietly and listened intently while the two-hour interview was recorded, occasionally breaking his silence to murmur, "What would have happened to Jamaica if I had not come along?"

Bustamante received tribute and homage as natural and proper and without ever any pretension of humility. But then he managed to achieve just about everything that he said he would. As he was wont to say, "I deal only in firsts." Thus he became Jamaica's first Chief Minister and and first Prime Minister. He also served as Mayor of Kingston and St. Andrew in 1947, in the wake of the first municipal election based on adult suffrage. The only boast he did not make good was to become Governor or Governor General of Jamaica, and this eluded him simply because he could not be Prime Minister and Governor General at the same time. In any event, he would hardly have contemplated a choice between an office endowed with a plenitude of political power and one burdened with largely symbolic and ceremonial duties.

The greatest honour of all to overtake Alexander Bustamante, that of being proclaimed a National Hero during his lifetime, was probably the one honour he did not envisage. The institution of a Jamaican system of national awards to replace the traditional British and Imperial Honours and Awards, followed the enactment of the National Awards Act of 1969, one of the few deliberate and significant acts of decolonization undertaken by the Jamaican Parliament. The National Heroes Awards Committee, appointed by the J.L.P. administration in August 1969, under the Chairmanship of the Minister of Home Affairs, unanimously recommended to Prime Minister Hugh Shearer, that the opportunity should be taken at the conferment of Jamaica's first national honours, to confer the title of National Hero, the highest in the new system of awards, on Sir Alexander Bustamante, in life, and posthumously on Norman Manley (who died on 2nd September 1969), in recognition of the outstanding services both men had rendered to the nation.

"The trajectory of Jamaican history can be defined as the struggle of the majority of our people to transform ourselves from being the object of the history of other nations, into being the agent and creative subject of our own. The National Heroes of Jamaica — those already honoured, and those still to be so — are all defined by the fact that at some time in their lives, they made the choice to dedicate themselves to this transformation. At some time in their lives they refused to continue to accept their colonial status as a part of other people's history. With this refusal they began the process of creating their own."[10] Thus begins the opening paragraph of the argument prepared for and submitted by the National Awards Advisory Committee to the Prime Minister in support of their recommendation.

The report, however, contained no justification or discussion of the desirability of proclaiming persons as National Heroes during their lifetimes. Of course there is something to be said for honouring worthy recipients while they are alive and able to appreciate it, rather than heaping encomiums upon them when they have passed from the scene and only posterity can derive satisfaction.

As it turned out, Alexander Bustamante and Norman Manley, great rivals in life, were proclaimed National Heroes at the same time so that not even death was able to put an end to the pairing of the cousins or the political rivalry which had characterized their relationships during the three decades that they dominated the political life of the country.

As far as Alexander Bustamante is concerned, there is every reason to believe that the verdict of later generations and their historians will be much the same as that arrived at by contemporary society and contemporary historians. Leaders, whether heroes or not, are both a product and a reflection of their times and environment. "The hero is as old as human

memory. To all peoples, at all times, the hero has symbolized their particular ideal of behaviour. And yet the hero cannot be accused of perfection.
His weaknesses are often as pronounced as his virtues. Like Achilles, he
may have courage, and be a great warrior, but he is also arrogant and
selfish. Like Ulysses and like Anansi, he survives through a kind of cunning
which is none too scrupulous. What then distinguishes the hero? The
Greeks had a word for it. They called this quality of the hero his *arete*.
The *arete* — the essential quality — of a knife, for example, is its cutting
edge, not its carved handle; that of a horse is its speed, not its flowing
mane. . . . Among oppressed people, this conscious decision to choose
between alternatives, and to choose the improbable one of standing up
to the strong is the *arete*, the essential quality of the hero. It is of the essence
of the colonial situation, that the colonized should accept his status as
given, as one pragmatic fact."[11]

Bustamante, then, made a choice or number of choices which were
of critical importance not only for his own future but that of Jamaica.
Bustamante's appraisers have argued that the decision or choice which
he made in 1938 to build an island-wide Union was, in the context of the
time and circumstance, a revolution against the given facts. "To attempt
to establish a Union in the Jamaica of 1938 was not only to challenge the
Jamaican employers. Jamaica was a political colony of Great Britain and,
through powerful companies like the West Indies Sugar Company, and
the United Fruit Company, was also an economic colony of Great Britain
and the United States. The *raison d'être* of these companies operating in
these underdeveloped areas was built on the basic tenets of available
supplies of cheap labour. The principle of trade unionism in Jamaica
therefore, meant the negation of the tenet of cheap labour."[12] To suggest,
as this passage does, that Bustamante's role in the shaping of modern
Jamaica and the place of honour his country has accorded him stems from
his decision to form a trade union, and the threat which it posed to the
existence of the supply of cheap labour, is to place the cart before the
horse and to obscure the real nature and significance of his contribution.
Firstly, neither the decision to form an island-wide trade union, nor the
spadework which saw the actual beginnings of such an organization,
originated with Bustamante. Secondly, the Jamaica Workers and Tradesmen Union launched by A.G.S. (Father) Coombs as early as 1936 and
in which Bustamante served his apprenticeship, was an established and
rapidly expanding organization, with the potential of becoming an
island-wide labour organization. Furthermore, even without Bustamante,
there was nothing to prevent the other trade union leaders of the stature

226

of Glasspole, Campbell, Nethersole and the four H's, aided by Manley, from establishing a viable and cohesive labour movement in Jamaica. Thirdly, the British (Colonial) administration was in no way as opposed to the establishment of trade unionism in Jamaica as the ruling classes in Britain had been to the formation of trade unions by British workers during the latter part of the eighteenth century and most of the nineteenth century.

On the contrary, the Trade Union Act passed in 1919 was designed to foster the growth of trade unionism in Jamaica by conferring legal status on properly constituted and registered unions and affording them protection against criminal prosecution as conspiracies or unlawful combinations operating in restraint of trade. Admittedly, other important immunities were omitted, but trade unions remained relatively few and weak and ineffective, not because of the Trade Union Act, but simply because there was little scope for conventional (craft) trade unionism in a backward agrarian economy.

Finally, the B.I.T.U. did not present any immediate threat to the supply of cheap labour. Far from that, decades later and indeed even in the post-independence era, the relatively low levels of wages obtaining among workers in all but the high-earnings extractive and processing industries, such as bauxite, oil refining, petroleum distribution and cement manufacture, have been counted among the inducements which Jamaica has to offer to foreign investors. The fact of the matter is that because of its essentially conservative social and economic philosophy, the B.I.T.U. pursued a wage policy of piecemeal and gradual improvement in money wages and fringe benefits.

No, the major contribution of Bustamante derives from his willingness to identify and make common cause with the working classes and this led him to attack the bastions and sacred cows of colonialism — inept public administration and social and economic privilege which were linked directly to considerations of race, colour and class. The demand for higher wages and earnings (or conversely the existence of low wages and earnings) was not the only source of the social discontent and upheaval in 1938, for then it would have come much earlier. The fact is that the Jamaican labour force of 1938 did not constitute a true wage-earning class or proletariat. Jamaican workers were part wage-earners, part small farmers or peasants, and as such, constituted an agro-proletariat. Hunger and demand for land featured, therefore, along with the demands for better wages and working conditions. The ambiguous status of the agro-proletariat represented both a cause and an effect of their impoverished economic condition. Because the work force was not wholly dependent on wage employment and the income it provided for sustenance, employers were relieved of the full weight of pressure which would have been forced upon them, had the workers of necessity been left no alternative but to engage in desperate struggles with the capitalist class to ensure their survival.

Although it might not have been expressed in specific terms, the workers and peasants desired also, and possibly above everything else, to be accepted as human beings and to be raised from the status of outcast in their own country. This emotional and social liberation required not just improved wages and conditions of employment but an end to racial and social discrimination and the perversion of justice. It meant, therefore, challenging one of the basic rules that had served to cement and keep the social system intact, namely, deference or submissiveness on the part of the socially inferior to their superiors, inferiority and superiority being determined by racial heritage and occupational status. At the same time, after years of conditioning within that very social system, the working classes, convinced of their own inferiority, had become suspicious of those from their own ranks who aspired to leadership and who might have been able to articulate their grievances and demands.

It is the measure of the man Bustamante that he was able to become the focus of, and crystallize, working-class discontent and, having done that, to institutionalize it in the form of political unionism or the politics of protest. He was able to do this because he shared certain emotional experiences with the underprivileged he sought to defend. In terms of broad social and economic stratification, he had been born into, and brought up as a member of, the planting class. But at the same time, his father Bobby had compromised himself, by marrying a dark-skinned woman of the soil who "worked ground". Aleck Clarke Bustamante would have had ample opportunity to observe the force and significance of colour, for good and for ill, in his country.

In spite of his "natural advantages", Alexander Clarke Bustamante had failed to make the grade in his native land. Nor had his pilgrimages overseas taken him much further along the route to economic success, at least up to 1932. His repeated visits to Jamaica had served, if anything, to confirm him as the adventurer of the family, "a rolling stone who had gathered no moss". When, therefore, he returned to Jamaica in 1934, he could not afford to fail. Nor could he be satisfied with being a money-lender catering to low-income groups, for although he might make good financially, he ran the risk of being dubbed a loan-shark or usurer and of remaining socially on the fringes of Jamaican society. He also would have realized that without the higher education or professional training such as his cousin Norman, for example, had managed to obtain by winning scholarships, he would have to prove his "respectability" — no mean achievement in a society governed by rigid social stratification based on a complex hierarchy of race, colour, educational upbringing, occupational status and money-making.

Seeking an outlet for his abounding energy, he turned to public affairs and polemics, and then to agitation, as he began to sense the mood of simmering discontent among the have-nots. Indeed, as a lender of money to these groups, he would have heard endless tales of misery and woe. Bustamante felt himself on trial and was therefore as restless and rebellious as the workers who became the objects of his concern. Having been brought up on a plantation he could understand the yearning of the workers and peasants for a measure of dignity and human comfort. As he was to comment in October 1938, "There are certain officers working with that Company (West Indies Sugar Co. Ltd.) who belong to the old school of overseers who believe that they can treat the people today as they did in days gone." Alexander Bustamante was thus a maverick, but a maverick with a difference.

Seemingly endowed with overwhelming self-confidence and great personal courage, he would not allow himself to be cowed or intimidated. His impressive physical stature, his braggadocio, his exaggerated and often violent rhetoric, his shrewdness, his earthliness and, above all, his foreign experiences, constituted his appeal to the masses who "glorified in him the poses and perquisites they felt they could never obtain for themselves".[13] In other words he seemed but a larger projection of his followers.

The critical decision, then, which Bustamante (and also Manley) took and which started him on the road to notoriety, power and finally fame and glory as a National Hero, was the decision to identify himself politically with a social section other than his own.

The next decision, not only to launch an island-wide trade union but to bestow his name upon it, was also of critical importance, but it followed logically from the politics of agitation. Discontent had to be institutionalized so that the politics of agitation and protest could be transmuted into the politics of accommodation, for the masses had shown that reform, not revolution, was what they wanted. The B.I.T.U. emerged as a vehicle uniquely placed, both to satisfy psychological and material needs of workers, and to give vent to the ambitions and personalism of its leader.

The perceptiveness of a quite extraordinary man combined with the peculiar circumstances operating on the sugar estate and plantation gave rise to the remarkable achievement of enduring trade union organization among agricultural workers. In the process, the pattern of trade union growth which had obtained in the industrially advanced countries, and which had become the accepted norm, was inverted.

The "peculiar circumstances" of the sugar plantation have already been referred to but they can bear repeating at this point. The abolition of slavery had produced a free labour force and created a wage relationship, but the implications of this change had not been fully grasped or made real to workers. The shift from status to contract had been effected legally, but psychologically and socially, the old regime lived on. The sugar estate with vestiges of serfdom, if not of slavery, remained for the rural labourer, the only complete community he knew. These relationships were ordered by the mores and customs of the plantation way of life. He gave his allegiance to a hierarchy of authorities and in return enjoyed a certain degree of, albeit impoverished, security; physically, that his subsistence needs would be met; emotionally, that his social relationships were ordered according to a predictable pattern. The troubled 1930's produced changes which endangered the stability of established relationships and expectations, unsatisfactory though they might have been. When this came about, workers were thrown more and more outside or on the fringe of the operation of a social system which traditionally had governed their way of life. In the B.I.T.U., the worker found a means of enforcing his demands for improvement in keeping with awakened aspirations. But no longer would he rely as much on the deference expected of him as a social inferior to lift himself from the morass of economic and social stagnation. The familiar medium of protest, the strike, assumed a new potency as it was whetted by direction and organization.

But perhaps the most momentous of the decisions taken in sequence by Bustamante was the decision to launch the Jamaica Labour Party as the political arm of the B.I.T.U. In 1943, it led to the triumph of Bustamante and the working class at the polls in the first General Election in December 1944 and ushered in the era of political unionism. It brought the masses, or at least unionized labour, into the focus or centre of organized politics and made the support of labour the primary yardstick of legitimacy for any political party that wished to survive.

Of course, it can be argued that this particular decision of Bustamante's also led to fragmentation of both the labour movement and the political and nationalist movement, and eventually yielded a two-party, two-union system so dominated by the cousinhood of Bustamante and Manley that "it left the Jamaican masses as nothing more than the darkened theatre audience that alternatively applauds and hisses the actors on the national stage."[14] In assessing the validity of this verdict or caricature of Jamaican politics, it is necessary, however, to distinguish between ideological bias and empirically justifiable generalizations. On fairly objective grounds, it may be argued, for instance, that although structured on a mass basis, both the P.N.P. and J.L.P. are mass parties in name only. Both have formal pyramidal structures which, unlike the authoritarian business firm, are supposed to embody the premise of democractic government that authority flows from the base up, while accountability flows from the top down. At the base, "branches", in the case of the J.L.P., and "groups", in the case of the P.N.P., are intended to give the people of the country an opportunity — through membership in the party of their choice — to participate in the affairs of government. The groups, formally, are co-ordinated by constituency organizations which hold their own Semi-Annual or Annual Conferences and, in the case of the P.N.P., play a significant part in the selection of candidates for local and national elections. Groups and constituency organizations also send delegates to the Annual Conference, the supreme legislative body of both parties and also elect members to serve on the National Executive Council and Executive Committee, in the case of the P.N.P., and the Executive Committee, in the case of the J.L.P.

It will be readily conceded, however, that the groups or branches have never attained the degree of effectiveness originally expected of them, more so in the case of the J.L.P., and have served primarily as electoral or vote-getting devices. This applies with equal force to parochial or municipal politics where the basic elements, whether group or branch, engage in important "pump or priming" activities. The group and constituency organizations probably have been most successful in meeting the psychological need for group and party identification, and least successful in carrying out the critical function of political education. Similarly, the Annual Conference has evolved into a ritualized form of communication, allowing for restatement of basic party creeds and partisan distortion which "has become a hallowed tradition of the era of mass politics".

If the Annual Conferences normally serve as acclamatory rather than deliberative bodies, in election years they are readily geared to the electoral function and are used by the party leaders to signal campaign issues and approaches.

Given then the realities of party politics and government described above, one can agree that participation of the rank and file or masses in the political decision-making processes has been limited in respect of procedural forms, substance and continuity. But by the same token it can be argued that the regimes which have tended to achieve very high levels of working-class electoral participation have been totalitarian or authoritarian regimes which have insisted that the working classes exercise the right to vote and choose their rulers even while denying them freedom of choice between competing leaders or notables.

It can be argued also and conceded that the splitting of the labour movement in Jamaica has had a number of unfortunate consequences for the masses. It not only shattered the unity of the labouring class but bred violence and hate as the agro-proletariat and unemployed turned in against themselves and fought, worker against worker and peasant against peasant, to give allegiance and fealty to basically middle-class leaders.

Admittedly also, much of the dynamism of incipient nationalism, initially generated by the P.N.P., was spent in the fratricidal struggle between rival union-party blocs. Thus, instead of being able to capture the swell of racial consciousness which had crested in the revolt of the labouring poor during 1938, and to harness it to the cause of a vigorous anti-imperialist and nationalist movement aimed at achieving a Jamaican identity and consciousness based on pride and racial self-respect, Norman Manley and the P.N.P. were forced to devote all their energies and organizational talents to converting Bustamante (and the traditionalist agro-proletariat) to the cause of self-government even while seeking to wrest political power for themselves. Furthermore, Bustamante was won over to the cause of self-government only when he became convinced that the P.N.P. did not intend to establish a socialist or communist state. The P.N.P. by force of circumstances thus was led to abandon whatever radical policies it had initially espoused while retaining the (captive) rhetoric of socialism, a dubious advantage at best.

Undoubtedly, also, the price paid by the community at large was that the march towards self-government and political independence became so gradual that it ended up being a damper rather than a stimulus to the spirit of innovation and national regeneration. When the final constitutional step was taken in August 1962, Jamaicans were not impressed or convinced that a new era had dawned or was about to dawn or that they stood on the threshold of a new exhilarating experiment in living. Unlike their counterparts in many African or Asian countries, the Jamaican populace had not been welded together by armed resistance or civil disobedience directed against the colonial power. They had not been electrified by any threatened assertion or declaration of independence, nor had they participated, except in a purely formal or perfunctory sense, in the more mundane but no less exalted task of devising an independence constitution. "It was hardly surprising, then, that the island entered its independence stage in a mood of half-hearted, simulated enthusiasm, hardly filled with any real passion for its achievement. Colonialism, for Jamaicans, ended not in a bang but a whimper."[15]

Of course, what matters is not whether colonialism goes out with a whimper or a bang, but whether the achievement of political independence and nationhood serves to deepen the resolve of a people to create a way of life which will make citizenship a meaningful existence and experience for the members of society and to release the creative energies and talents which are needed to realize that objective. In this social equation, leadership can be a factor of critical importance, if for no other reason than that the dedication and inspiration of popular leaders can do much to raise the levels of effort and sacrifice on the part of members of the society.

By his electoral victory in 1962, Alexander Bustamante earned the right to lead Jamaica formally into independence, but the independence ceremonies constituted an emotional let-down for the sizable urban and rural-urban segment of the population who were supporters of the P.N.P. or admirers of Norman Manley. They were crest-fallen and bitter at the seeming travesty of history which made Bustamante, rather than Manley, the one to accept the constitutional instruments bestowing political sovereignty. For many also, again primarily among the middle classes, pride of achievement such as there was could not but be tempered by the realization and haunting sense of guilt that Jamaica's independence had been won at the expense of the West Indian Federation.

Of course Alexander Bustamante was not bothered by any such misgivings. If he and his party had been instrumental in slowing down the constitutional train, the P.N.P. in turn had brought it to a dead-end by diverting it unto the Federation siding, and it had been left to him, Bustamante, to set the constitutional drive back on the rails and redeem the situation for all concerned, including himself. Nevertheless, there are many Jamaicans, irrespective of their "political affiliation" who have shared the assessment later given by Manley in 1969 that Bustamante was more successful as a politician than as a nation-builder: "The fact is that during the short period when Jamaica was really and truly under his leadership as our first Prime Minister, he had no vital interest in the development of national spirit; it is at least arguable that he had always been more concerned with political power than with nationhood and he had a continued concern with the status and preservation of his own improvement."[16]

If, however, the "national spirit" had not been sufficiently developed and manifest by Independence Day, 6th August 1962, it was because Norman Manley and the P.N.P., and Alexander Bustamante and the J.L.P., and indeed the populace of Jamaica, had embarked upon a rabid form of bi-partisan politics which can only be described as "political tribalism". An otherwise culturally "detribalized" society (detribalized in the sense that the vast majority of the population were descended from slaves who had been forcibly displaced from their homeland, culturally disinherited and, in due course, converted into Anglicized colonials or pseudo-Europeans living in an Afro-Asian environment) had indeed resolved themselves into two great political groupings of P.N.P.-ites and J.L.P.-ites, each with some semblance of a distinctive political culture reflecting the ethos of its dominant leader. Hard-core followers of each party, bound together by strong "in-group" sentiments, would from time to time engage in forays against traditional enemies, and each election campaign would issue in the politics of revenge or reckoning as the winning "tribe" attempted to assert its physical as well as political superiority over the vanquished. The net effect, as already indicated, was to shift attention from national policies and remedial measures to the rationing of limited employment opportunities and the dispensing of rewards.

Nevertheless, when all is said and done, the forging of a stable two-party system, which has completely monopolized electoral loyalties, represents an outstanding achievement by Bustamante, Manley and their respective colleagues and associates. Nor can it be denied that in the course of doing so, both Bustamante and Manley, certainly in their early impetus, challenged a lot of the colonial presuppositions about Jamaican society, such as the assumed servility of the working classes and the inability and disinclination of Jamaicans to govern themselves. The Bustamante Industrial Trade Union and later the Jamaica Labour Party became the institutionalized expression of working-class discontent and protest, while the People's National Party embodied Manley's belief in the efficacy of organized politics and the ability of the Jamaican people to determine their own destiny. In a celebrated speech on the occasion of his seventy-fifth birthday banquet at which he anounced his decision not to stand again for election as President and Leader of his party, Norman Manley spoke of the mission of his generation: "My generation had a distinct mission to perform. It was to create a national spirit with which we could identify ourselves as a people for the purpose of achieving independence on the political plane. I am convinced, deeply convinced, that the role of this generation is to proceed to the social and economic reform of Jamaica."

However much Alexander Bustamante may have been preoccupied with power, he cannot be excluded from that generation which had a "distinct mission to perform" and his contribution cannot be ignored. The creation of a nationalist spirit in Jamaica would have been unthinkable if the bulk of the population, in this case the labouring classes of workers and peasants, had not been made to feel conscious of themselves as a class and had not been provoked to militancy and organized action. "The class militancy of the Jamaican crowd unleashed by 1938, although thus somewhat muted, has basically remained as a permanent element in Jamaican society. The old habit of class deference has gone for ever, as testified, indeed, by the way in which bitter complaint about 'bad manners' and 'abusive' language of the street populace has become, over the years, the stock in trade of the middle class and its communications media."[17] Bustamante in his insistence that the common man and indeed his countrymen at large be treated with respect, allowed no exceptions. Who else but Alexander Bustamante could say to a harried British Colonial Secretary who sought to limit him, as the leader of a Jamaican delegation, to a twenty-minute audience, "I did not travel all the way from Jamaica to talk to you for twenty minutes!"[18] The working classes have been made very much aware of their power, although it is better appreciated and more frequently exercised at the industrial level where there is never any inhibition about disrupting the production or flow of goods and services. If at the political level, as has been suggested, the militancy and political power of the masses have been challenged or transmuted into a political framework or order, the implied objective of which is to create a "middle-class Jamaican civilization", that is quite another matter. It is one of the ironies of politics and social life that it has been the preoccupation of middle-class intellectuals and revolutionaries, from Lenin in the East to Fidel Castro in the West, to create or articulate on behalf of the masses what they conceive to be both the ethos and objectives of a "working-class civilization". It seems that left to themselves, the working classes are concerned both through trade union and political action to place themselves within that very orbit of coercive comparison — "the middle-class civilization". Thus, if the P.N.P. and J.L.P. and their respective leaders are to be criticized, it is that they failed indeed to create mass awareness of the realities of the challenges facing Jamaica — challenges which, if they were to be met so that the working classes could be afforded greater mobility, would have meant bold and resolute action to effect some restructuring of Jamaican society and the Jamaican economy.

If also, the two mass parties failed to involve the masses as fully and meaningfully as they might have in the decision-making processes of politics and government, it is an exaggeration to say that the Jamaican working classes or masses have been relegated to the role of "the darkened theatre audience that alternatively applauds and hisses the actors on the national stage". In spite of the admitted weaknesses of the basic elements of party structures and government and the convergence of the P.N.P. and J.L.P. in terms of social objectives and policies, it remains the inescapable fact that there has been no falling off in the level of mass electoral interest. Moreover, in the post-independence era, the electorate has continued to demonstrate its preference for orderly change of governments alternating the parties, on what many observers are convinced, is a ten-year or two-term electoral swing. The pre-independence pattern of rabid partisanship among the black working classes has not diminished either. An average of over 65 per cent of the registered electorate has turned out at each general election since 1944 to vote for one or other of the two main political parties. Indeed, in February 1972, the P.N.P. won a landslide victory over the J.L.P., taking thirty-seven seats to the J.L.P.'s sixteen in an election which has been described as "a social revolution via the ballot box".[19] The P.N.P.'s victory has been interpreted by most competent observers as a mandate to effect fundamental economic and social change or a social and economic "revolution", if one prefers the more emotive term which is now part of the conventional wisdom.

Some of the factors which have accounted for the partisanship and abiding political attachment of the masses to the P.N.P. and J.L.P. as two middle-of-the-road and essentially middle-class-led parties have already been discussed. Included are the initial personal appeal of Bustamante and Manley; the development of political unionism which saw the forging of alliances between the two parties and their associated trade union blocs often through intense and violent rivalry; the dispensation of political patronage and the dependence of employment and economic opportunities upon political and trade union allegiance; and finally, the emergence of a pervasive regime of political tribalism. There are of course additional factors, such as the reinforcement of the political culture through the processes of socialization, embracing the family, school, village or community, church, trade union and communications media, which have helped to perpetuate the structure of politics among the younger generations.

Another important consideration which is often overlooked is that participation of the masses in the decision-making processes of party and government in Jamaica must be judged not by the yardstick of conventional party politics, but in terms of the totality of involvement and experiences in the system of political unionism. A worker may be a functional member of a trade union such as the B.I.T.U. or N.W.U. (or other union) and may feel that he makes an input, direct or indirect, into the policy-making processes of his affiliated party through the voice of the elected union representative or representatives who sit on the Executive Committees or councils of the party. As a consequence, the worker may be content to remain a supporter, as distinct from a member, of the political party.

At the end of 1971, the combined union membership of the Bustamante Industrial Trade Union and the National Workers Union was reported to be 301,300 out of a total of roughly 315,500 organized workers. Admittedly, this membership includes a sizable proportion of non-dues-paying adherents who, strictly speaking, are supporters rather than members of the Unions. But the fact remains that 40 per cent or more of the Jamaican labour force are unionized or as much as 16 per cent of the total population, if one wants to express it that way. Now the number of electors officially listed as being eligible to vote in the General Election held on 29th February 1972 was 603,614. Organized workers and their dependents must constitute, therefore, a significant proportion of the electorate, and to many of them it could be a matter of indifference, an "either/or proposition", whether they make an input into the political decision-making processes through the trade union or through the political party. Jamaican unions and parties, then, are opposite sides of the same coin.

There is no denying, however, that both major political parties in Jamaica, and more so the J.L.P., have a long way to go if they are to be made into, and function more appropriately as, mass parties. But it does not point us in the direction of a solution to say that both the P.N.P. and the J.L.P. "are fundamentally bourgeois in spirit". For a shift to the other end of the ideological spectrum or continuum, and the acceptance of socialism (or Marxism) as the appropriate ideology of the working classes or the *raison d'être* of a mass party, will not by itself guarantee that the ruling groups or leaders will welcome expanded participation. Indeed the result could be oppression. Whether this is likely to be so or not must depend upon the values of the dominant groups or leaders, the degree of social consensus about political forms — whether, for instance, representative government is highly valued — and the extent to which those who have achieved political power are determined to keep it.

The presumption appears to be also that a mass party is something less if it does not espouse radical (socialist) ideology and seek to effect radical (socialist) reconstruction of society. There is of course some historical justification for this bias. The mass party, or as Duverger describes it, "the exterior party", that is, a party having a life outside of parliament, required acceptance of the broadening or redefinition of political power to the point where it could encompass the idea that the mass public must participate in the political processes or be controlled.[20] The practical implications were that the masses must be taken into account by the political élite either by rational participation or control.

The extension of the franchise and the adoption of universal suffrage brought about the expansion of socialist parties in Europe and later in many of the emergent nations and so-called underdeveloped countries. To the extent also that socialism (Marxism) emerged as the appropriate ideology for the working classes or masses, there appeared to be an organic link between the mass party and socialism, so much so that it could be suggested that one of the key distinguishing features of a mass (and presumably socialist) party was the lessening of its dependence on capitalist sources of financing.

"Mass party technique replaces capitalist financing of electioneering by democratic financing. Instead of appealing to a few big private donors, industrialists, bankers or important merchants, the mass party spreads the burden over the largest possible number of members, each of whom contributes a modest sum."[21] But other doctrinal and non-doctrinal parties have felt obliged likewise to broaden the base of their appeal and to enlist working-class support.

Ideology by itself cannot therefore be the overriding criterion for assessing the purposiveness or efficacy of a mass party. More important are the degree of sensitivity or responsiveness to the masses and the extent to which they participate in the political decision-making processes. "For to bring the masses into the political system means to encourage parties that are not mere aggregates of local and personal interests, but parties that give or profess to give to the man in the street a voice in politics that he cannot have, if all he is given as a political choice is between one group of notables and another."[22]

At the same time, in the post-World War II era, pre-independence conditions and the necessity for extremism, along with the post-independence challenge of national integration, have constituted a strong

238

impetus towards, as well as the rationale for, one-party states particularly in Africa, the Middle East and Asia. Some of these are one-party authoritarian, others one-party totalitarian. To the extent also that externally created mass parties often develop a total formula or ideology for society, they tend to be intolerant of opposition. More often than not, therefore, when radical left-wing intellectual critics bemoan the lack of participation of the masses in party politics, they are responding primarily to tactical considerations, for the logic of their own ideological position would suggest that mobilization or controlled participation rather than free and effective participation in the political decision-making processes is the type of involvement envisaged for the masses.

As far as Jamaica is concerned, one must reject any suggestion or even implied assumption that the masses are completely pliable or malleable and as a result have been duped or constrained by middle-class leadership to abandon class militancy and to accept the bourgeois ethic or the ethic of capitalism. On the contrary, the Jamaican masses have shown themselves to be highly politicized and quite capable of dealing with leaders and politicians of either party who are deemed to have lost contact with the people or to have offended sensibilities of the electorate. What is more, the working classes and the electorate in general have been content to await the political day of "reckoning" and to pass judgement via the medium of the ballot box.

The General Elections of 1944 and the most recent, twenty-eight years later, provide an interesting contrast and food for thought. In 1944, Norman Manley and the P.N.P. were rejected and almost annihilated at the polls by the working classes, in spite of the fact that Manley had been a true and proven friend of labour. The P.N.P. lost because it was largely a party of the urban middle classes and came perilously close to being identified with the traditional enemies of the working classes — that is to say with the plantocracy and their coloured and black middle-class allies. Sensing the distrust of the blacks for the light-skinned and brown-skinned middle classes, Alexander Bustamante set out to, and succeeded in, transferring this distrust to Norman Manley and the P.N.P. The P.N.P. campaigned on the basis of socialism, and a commitment to planning and rational administration as the means of achieving economic and social progress. The 1944 elections represented, then, the triumph of tradition and emotionalism over reason and administrative intelligence. By 1955, the P.N.P. had succeeded in achieving mass support through the development of its trade union wing — first with the T.U.C., then with its successor the N.W.U. The P.N.P. victory of 1955 was clearly predictable, as also its rout of the J.L.P. in 1959, although there were indications, beginning with the Federal Elections of 1958, that the P.N.P. had begun to lose touch with grass-roots supporters. Carried away by the obvious superiority of its administration and record of achievement, the Party was being lulled into believing that technical competence and statistically measurable rates of growth and progress would be sufficient to assure re-election. The Referendum and Federation debacle brought the P.N.P. prematurely to the polls and the Party was given little time to mend its fences.

Victory at the polls in 1962 brought Bustamante back into power to lead the J.L.P. into its state of political maturity, so to speak. The J.L.P. also survived Bustamante's retirement from active politics to win in 1967 by a very comfortable majority of thirteen seats, but this reflected the efficacy with which constituency boundaries were redefined and new constituencies gerrymandered. There was not even the slightest overall swing to the J.L.P.

By 1972, Shearer and the J.L.P. were in much the same position as the P.N.P. in 1962 — but without the intrusion of any external issue such as Federation. The J.L.P. could boast of a record of very impressive achievements. The administrative and financial infrastructure needed to facilitate modernization of the economy had been well laid; the manufacturing sector had been expanded; significant urban development and physical construction was underway; a food processing industry had been established and a measure of economic diversification achieved. The J.L.P. had embarked upon a programme of acquisition of sugar-estate lands devoted to cane cultivation, a "radical" posture indeed for the J.L.P. to adopt. Even more significant and radical, however, was the reform of tax collection and administration to curb widespread and massive corporate and personal income tax evasion. At the industrial level, the B.I.T.U. had broadened its traditional rural base to include pockets of urbanized and clerical categories of workers. As high-income-earning groups were brought within its orbit of representation, the B.I.T.U. began to lose some of its traditional agrarian working-class image. In both J.L.P. and B.I.T.U., therefore, the thrust was towards self-confidence and "respectability". In union as in party, the activities of university trained and professional cadres were highlighted, and Prime Minister Shearer was projected as the impeccably dressed and dignified statesman. The J.L.P. approached the General Election confident that the Party would, on the basis of its record of performance, regain office although with a smaller majority, as the P.N.P. had been considerably revitalized under Michael Manley's leadership. The P.N.P., on the other hand, after three years of intense organizational activity, spearheaded by Michael Manley and new blood, projected itself as the party of the sufferers and the common man.

Exercising a powerful charismatic appeal, very much in the tradition of Alexander Bustamante of the 1940's and 1950's, and utilizing demagogic and rhetorical techniques also reminiscent of the "Chief", Michael Manley succeeded in projecting the image of a modern-day "Messiah" — Joshua — with his "rod of correction". Interestingly enough, Moses Bustamante was being succeeded by Joshua Manley, and there was Moses' "rod" — actually an ornate and elaborate miniature walking stick presented to Michael Manley by Emperor Haile Selassie I of Ethiopia on the occasion of the P.N.P. Opposition Leader's visit to that country — being brought into play to confer legitimacy on Joshua. This writer witnessed extra-ordinary scenes of adulation as working-class Jamaicans, in urban and rural areas alike, thronged the P.N.P. leader to touch him and the "rod of correction". In a style of politics also reminiscent of Prime Minister Pierre Trudeau of Canada, the P.N.P. leader seemingly never tired of kissing enthralled female enthusiasts of all stations and walks of life.

As part of the reversal of leadership and party roles, Michael Manley also appealed to the traditional religiosity of the Jamaican people which had been a characteristic posture of Alexander Bustamante and the J.L.P.[23] Denouncing the pervasiveness of gambling in Jamaican society, including the National Lottery established by the J.L.P. administration in the face of stiff opposition from all the Churches, Michael Manley called for moral reconstruction of Jamaican society and for the Church to provide initiative in creating a society in which peace, love and brotherhood would replace political hatred, violence and tribalism.[24] A desperate last-minute bid by the J.L.P. only days before the General Elections to make capital of a seemingly blasphemous pamphlet issued by self-proclaimed "Repairer of the Breach" Rev. Claudius Henry, which pictured and referred to Henry, Emperor Haile Selassie I and Michael Manley as the leadership of the "Trinity of the Godhead", found the leaders of all the significant denominational Churches united in their support of Michael Manley. In a full-page statement published in *The Daily Gleaner*, the powerful Church leaders asserted: "We consider that the use of the 'Henry Pamphlet' to attack the leader of the P.N.P. and his party represents a departure from our standards by being an example of personal abuse and deplorable dragging of the name of God into the election fight for party advantage.

"In the light of the repudiation of this pamphlet by the P.N.P. leadership (by letter to the Heads of Churches and by public broadcast) we condemn the use made of this pamphlet in J.L.P. advertisement and call upon those

241

concerned to stop using it."

Stressing also the "time for a change" theme, the P.N.P. promised to put an end to mounting criminal violence, including armed robbery, rape, murder and gang warfare, which had thoroughly aroused the entire populace and especially rural inhabitants. Crime and violence were effectively linked to unemployment and the lack of employment opportunities for the youth who were becoming increasingly alienated from, and at war with, society, as they turned to crime and violence. Law and order, then, was perhaps the most critical issue in the General Election, reinforced by P.N.P. allegations of political corruption and graft on the part of the J.L.P. It was also insinuated that because the country's political rulers were able to derive pecuniary advantage from the exercise of public office and were able to do so cleverly and with impunity, the deprived and disadvantaged constituting the criminal element were encouraged to help themselves and take their spoils by violent means.

The P.N.P. also argued very tellingly that the J.L.P./B.I.T.U. alliance had embarked, especially during the period 1967–72, on a policy of political victimization and job discrimination which had been pursued in such a thorough and systematic way as to render the P.N.P./N.W.U. alliance irrelevant as a political force. The very survival of Jamaica's two-party system was therefore at stake.

The 1972 General Election was fought on a wave of emotionalism only matched by that of December 1944. In 1972 the fight was, however, between the two trade union leaders. On the one hand, Hugh Shearer, seeking to draw on what remained of the Bustamante magic, was projected as the responsible and very proper leader of a party which had taken Jamaica into independence and could claim a truly impressive record of performance.

On the other hand, Michael Manley, having all the social credentials lacked by Shearer, adopted quite the opposite posture. Here was Joshua, with his rod of correction, coming to attack privilege and wrong-doing and to lead his people into the promised land. In direct contrast to the impeccably dressed Hugh Shearer, Michael Manley instituted the "bush-jacket" and casual wear as the symbolic dress of a liberated people and a manifestation of the determination of the P.N.P. to achieve a unified and more egalitarian society.

For the first time in Jamaica's political history, popular music and recordings by largely working-class artistes and the Rastafari, with deeply religious overtones, were directed against the party in power, expressing deep-seated yearnings of the masses for social justice. This mood of dis-

242

enchantment and then of anger which was expressed through the media and entertainment came through spontaneously at first, but was then harnessed by Manley and the P.N.P. to build the popular swell and revulsion against the J.L.P. The result was a massive rejection by the masses, including agricultural workers and peasants, and the middle classes, of the J.L.P. The P.N.P. won 37 seats to the J.L.P.'s 16 and gained 56 per cent of the popular vote to the J.L.P.'s 44 per cent. Close to 80 per cent of the eligible voters cast their ballots in an election which saw the electorate responding to the P.N.P. slogan — "Better must come". The P.N.P., however, made few specific promises as to economic or social changes which would be implemented, and now faces the challenge of translating the mood of the country, via the route of Michael Manley's much-touted politics of participation, into programmes and policies and of mobilizing working-class and general support for the changes which seemingly must be made.

In a sense, therefore, the working classes have served notice on the other classes, as they did in 1944, that they must be brought into the mainstream of the country's economic life. The new Prime Minister sees three challenges facing his government: the creation of a national spirit and national unity; the achievement of a more egalitarian society with the establishment of forms of social and economic organization that will make this possible; and the development of a spirit of self-reliance so that the challenge of external ownership and control of Jamaica's resources can be dealt with effectively.

The emotional release and state of euphoria which followed in the wake of the P.N.P.'s victory of liberation has raised some interesting problems already. Michael Manley has adopted the position that to put an end to the old style politics of the Bustamante-Norman Manley era, the P.N.P. must abandon the traditional politics of tribalism, in which vengeance is taken of the vanquished and to the victors go the spoils. Having fought an election in terms of good and evil, of "good guys" and "bad guys", die-hard P.N.P. members, and indeed a broad spectrum of supporters from all classes, have insisted that the "bad guys" be brought to heel and punished. One of the first acts of the P.N.P. administration, therefore, has been to set up a commission to investigate and bring to light malpractices or breaches of trust or conflicts of interest, more so where they might have issued in graft and corruption, as well as the incidence of political and job victimization, with particular reference to preferential hiring or award of public contracts. At the same time, however, the P.N.P.'s rank and file has not responded favourably to the plea for a politics of reconciliation and the question remains whether the leader of a victorious party in the wake of a highly emotionally-charged election can reasonably expect to call for, and embark on, a politics of national unity and reconstruction, without similarly issuing the call for a coalition government.

A change in the substance as distinct from the style of Jamaican politics would require, at least where the P.N.P. is concerned, the revitalization and building up of the party into a dynamic and effective instrument not only for education of the masses and their involvement in the formulation and implementation of governmental policies, but also as an effective instrument for mobilization of the masses by the leaders of party and government. In April 1972, the P.N.P. set up an Appraisal Committee to advise it on all aspects of the Party's organization and functioning, including the relationship between party and government and the society at large.

The J.L.P., on the other hand, has been shattered by the election, and Alexander Bustamante thus lived to see his worst fears realized as his party sank to its lowest ebb since its formation in 1943. In 1970, he confided to this writer his fears that as soon as he was removed from the scene, the J.L.P. would disintegrate under the pressures of factional rivalries and internecine warfare. Although retired from active politics, Bustamante, as titular head of both J.L.P. and B.I.T.U., continued to exercise considerable influence. As he himself said, "Although everyone might think that I am old and my day is done, yet I like to think that I still exercise some influence from up here."[25] Up here, incidentally, was his home perched on the brow of the Irish Town hills overlooking the plains of Kingston, St. Andrew and coastal St. Catherine.

Events in the weeks preceding the General Election held on 29th February 1972 demonstrated how well Alexander Bustamante knew his colleagues and protégés. Serious disagreement erupted publicly between Edward Seaga, Minister of Finance and the J.L.P.'s economic "miracle man", and Wilton Hill, Minister of Housing, over the constitutionality and propriety, from the point of view of fiscal accountability, of the Minister of Housing assuming legal control of his Ministry's Housing Fund. The Minister of Finance, to give vent to his displeasure, retired from his Ministry Office to the sanctuary of his official home, and it was not until the Annual Conference of the J.L.P. held during November 1971 that the "active" Leader of the Party, Hugh Shearer, was able to achieve the appearance of a rapprochement or reconciliation. At the same time, it was common knowledge that Robert Lightbourne, the dynamic

Minister of Trade, was disenchanted with Shearer's leadership and had decided not to seek re-election. Although he was persuaded to run under the J.L.P. banner and won re-election, Lightbourne promptly resigned from the J.L.P. after the Party's defeat to become an independent Member of Parliament. In letters to the press he alleged that he had resigned because the J.L.P. "proposes to change its ideology and principles from those on which the party was founded, to others which the party has long regarded and proclaimed as repugnant".

Political commentators suggested that influential factions within the J.L.P. had taken the position that survival of the Party dictated that it move ideologically to the left of the P.N.P. so that it could capture the mood for change and become a viable alternative to the P.N.P. Although he was careful to pay tribute to Sir Alexander as the founding father of the J.L.P. whose guiding principles were in danger of being jettisoned, Lightbourne's supporters aroused Bustamante's ire by issuing a call in the form of a resolution passed by a caucus of thirteen J.L.P. parish Councillors in St. Thomas, that an emergency meeting and island Conference be held to select new leaders of the Party, in view of the great disunity in the top leadership of the Party. Sir Alexander, in a statement to the press, commented tartly, "The Resolution has been brought to my attention, and as there have been no exceptions stated, I take it to include me." He went on to reject the call and to advise, "The Councillors concerned would be well advised to look after the interest of the people who put them there, instead of being influenced by people who are seeking to gain their own self ends. Let me remind them that this party was built on the blood, sweat, sacrifice and hard work of the working-class people of this country and not on treachery.

"Anyone who wishes to leave the party is at liberty to do so, as there are no chains attached to them."[26]

In a post-election visit in March 1972, Sir Alexander confided to the author that he was surprised by the strength of the electoral swing against, and defeat of, the J.L.P. Lady Bustamante also confirmed that party leaders generally had anticipated a victory.

That the J.L.P. leaders could have remained convinced up to the eve of the election that they would return to office is an indication of the extent to which they had lost contact with grass-root sentiment. Certainly, had he been active in the field, Alexander Bustamante could hardly have misjudged the situation so completely. To any observer taking the pulse of grass-root sentiment in rural areas, and attending meetings of both parties throughout the island, and approaching the task with even a modicum of objectivity or detachment, there could be hardly any doubt about a P.N.P. victory. The only uncertainty was the size of the P.N.P. majority. It was obvious from the mood of the country that the P.N.P. had become the focus of both popular discontent and expectation and that throughout Jamaica, and especially in the heart of Bustamante-land, Michael Manley, acclaimed as Joshua, had captured what remained of the old Bustamante magic. It is perhaps one of the contradictions or paradoxes of Jamaican politics that at a time when nearly everyone seemed convinced that the era of Manley-Bustamante politics had come to an end, a member of the political dynasty, embodying the intellectual attributes of his father Norman Manley and the flair and popular charismatic appeal of cousin Alexander Bustamante, should have swept into power with the real possibility of becoming a very powerful and dominant leader. For while it is true that the P.N.P. as a party sustained a truly creditable organizational effort involving a veritable army of dedicated party workers and volunteers to win the election, there is no denying that Michael Manley, as the new leader of the P.N.P., spearheaded the revitalization of the Party and by his popularity transformed a ground-swell into a veritable political tidal wave.

The personalism of the Bustamante-style politics, nevertheless, can be said to have come to an end, in the sense that while in 1938 and after there were many working-class Jamaicans who were prepared literally "to follow Bustamante 'till we die'" and to die for the "Chief", few, if any, workers and peasants in the Jamaica of the 1970's would be disposed to make such a commitment to Michael Manley or any other new political leader. On the contrary, as the levels of educational attainments of the masses, and of the youth in particular, rise and the electorate becomes more sophisticated, the tendency of the younger generations to be more skeptical and critical of political leaders, which is already clearly evident, is likely to become more pronounced, diminishing, in the process, the irrational element in Jamaican politics.

As far as the Jamaica Labour Party is concerned, one may question the wisdom of Bustamante remaining titular head of the J.L.P. and the B.I.T.U. in spite of his retirement from public office and from the political hustings. In the first place, although Prime Minister, Hugh Shearer was limited to being "active" as distinct from formal and legitimate head of the J.L.P. and B.I.T.U., and was thus denied the exercise of full authority, resting as he did in the pale of the gray eminence of Bustamante. It must be remembered also that Shearer became Prime Minister, not as a result of leading the J.L.P. to victory at the polls, but because he emerged as the winner, and by a narrow margin at that, in a ballot conducted by the J.L.P. parliamentary group to choose a successor to Donald Sangster (posthumously made Sir Donald Sangster) who had died in office.

In these circumstances, Shearer attempted to bolster his authority and hegemony over his colleagues by seeking to establish that as protégé and heir apparent, he derived his legitimacy from Bustamante whose "blessing" and support he enjoyed. Like Elisha, therefore, the seal or mantle of leadership was supposed to have been passed to him. This was evident in J.L.P. political advertisements in the press, and in party publications, by the twinning, invariably, of photographs of Bustamante and Shearer. The Prime Minister frequently spoke also of carrying on the work and policies of his leader and mentor. The net result was that Shearer became identified with a Bustamante style and era of politics which he could not emulate on the basis of his own personal appeal, and which, moreover, was coming to an end. Bustamante's intuitive approach to decision-making and politics, his flamboyance, his exploitation even of the "Anansi-mentality", were aspects of the Jamaican political culture which Shearer and the J.L.P. should have been concerned to put behind them. Indeed it was incongruous in the light of the rationalistic approach to politics and administration practised by Edward Seaga and Robert Lightbourne, the bright new-wave J.L.P. politicians who headed respectively the key ministries of Finance and Planning, and Trade and Industry.

In contrast, Michael Manley suffered the loss of a father and confidant, but was left free to make his imprint upon the P.N.P. and to rebuild it into an effective electoral machine so that he could win his first electoral battle and humble his traditional rival Hugh Shearer. Another consequence of Bustamante's continuing hold and influence over both the J.L.P. and B.I.T.U., reinforced of course by the influence of Lady Bustamante in the Party and especially within the B.I.T.U., where she holds the office of Treasurer, was that the threat and baneful effects of factionalism were merely delayed, not avoided. Had Sir Alexander bowed out altogether from the scene, it would have been easier for Shearer and his colleagues to have worked out an accommodation when the sweets of office and power could be more readily appreciated. As it has turned out, the J.L.P. will find it extremely difficult to survive the humiliation of a massive rejection of the party leadership by the electorate if factionalism is not brought under control. The immediate hope of the J.L.P. is the still-powerful and stable B.I.T.U., but even so the B.I.T.U. faces a formidable challenge in recapturing popular support for its political affiliate.

In these circumstances one is led to wonder whether the B.I.T.U./J.L.P. may not be handicapped in the task of rebuilding by yielding to nostalgia and deferring to Sir Alexander's wish to remain titular and symbolic head of both organizations during his lifetime. Asked by this writer in March 1972 whether it was not his duty to give up titular leadership of both institutions, Sir Alexander replied firmly: "No, my people would feel that something has gone wrong, if I gave up the leadership." This may sound like vanity, and it probably is, but it is not an unexpected response from a man who made few concessions to his age and took it as his natural lot to be a leader of men. Indeed, the one thing for which Alexander Bustamante is likely to be long remembered is the decisiveness of the leadership he gave as a great labour leader, if not the greatest, and one of the country's most successful politicians.

Much has been said and made of the intuitive nature of Bustamante's judgments and decision-making. But this does not mean that he was not concerned to have all the facts, information and implications laid before him. His party colleagues attest to the fact that he invariably sought their advice on important issues and that most of his key decisions were taken when his senior lieutenants were present.

In spite of his popular image, as a temperamental and autocratic leader, if not dictator, Bustamante was famous for having "second thoughts" on matters.[27] His senior lieutenants in union and party learned not to take his initial or off-the-cuff reaction as the final word. Indeed, the ranking and influence of secondary leaders depended on their respective abilities to get back to Bustamante and to put the issue in which they were interested, or concerned, in a different light so that they could get a reversal of the decision or a go-ahead. For having made sure that his leadership was beyond question and challenge, Bustamante never hestitated to admit to error and was known to write to colleagues and say, "I told you such and such or I made such a decision, but I was wrong. Proceed as you suggested." Similarly, although he had no taste for detailed organizational work or effort, a good deal of committee activity flourished below Busta- mante and was facilitated by his willingness to hear verbal reports, arrive at a judgment and make decisions. But by the same token, when Busta- mante felt strongly about any issue and made a firm and final decision, this was evident to his colleagues and associates, and there the matter rested. The "Chief", therefore, exercised firm but benign leadership, more so during the latter stages of his career and in his role of elder states- man. In this regard, the role and influence of Gladys Longbridge Bustamante cannot be over-emphasized. As an utterly devoted and loyal

Her Majesty the Queen and Prince Philip paying a courtesy visit to Sir Alexander at his home in 1966.

colleague, confidante and wife, who deliberately eschewed political office and public acclaim, she was able to fill the role of intermediary with great success. Bustamante readily admits that he talked over all important matters with her, and she was thus able to insinuate or reintroduce points of views or other considerations which may have been ignored or overlooked by Bustamante in making a snap decision or in adopting a certain position. Miss Gladys, or Lady Bustamante as she eventually became, invariably was present at most if not all private or personal interviews granted by Bustamante, and her gentle reminders and proddings often helped to keep the "Chief" on the rails, so to speak. She was and has been his eyes, his ears and his memory, choosing to forego political office and avoid the political limelight, so that she could devote all her time, talent and energy to his well-being and to his causes.[28] That Gladys Longbridge Bustamante does not figure more prominently in this study, is not to deny her influence as the power behind the throne, or the contribution which she has made, in her own right, as staff officer of the B.I.T.U. and an influential voice in the councils of the J.L.P. If anything, it reflects the very success with which she filled the role of the unseen hand which she set for herself.

Although a man "by nature and temperament autocratic" and with "very strong and firm opinions of his own", as his cousin Norman Manley noted, Alexander Bustamante was willing to listen and learn and then to act. He served his country well and has been richly rewarded in all respects. The distinction of being Jamaica's only living National Hero has brought him homage from his countrymen and visitors of distinction to the island, all of whom without exception have driven tortuously up the hills of Irish Town or queued on the lawn of Jamaica House to pay respects. But one suspects that all this may not have altered Bustamante's wish to end his days in the saddle, still the top man in the Party and Union.

POSTSCRIPT

Practically two years have elapsed since the manuscript for this book was completed and handed over to the publishers. A number of mis-adventures, including the temporary loss of photographs which could not be replaced, combined to upset production schedules. In view of the publication time-lag, therefore, it seemed appropriate to add a post-script.

Sir Alexander Bustamante is now in his ninety-first year, and is still holding his own. It is fair to say, however, that the curtain has rung down on his personal era of politics in Jamaica.

At the Annual Conference of the Jamaica Labour Party, held in November 1973, the honorary post of "Chief" was especially created for and conferred upon Sir Alexander, so that he will remain uniquely "the Chief" of the Party which he created, led, and completely dominated for a quarter century or more.

Hugh Lawson Shearer, Leader of the Parliamentary Opposition and "active" leader of the Jamaica Labour Party, in turn was elected Leader of the Party, thus leaving him free, if he wishes to do so, to remove himself from the shadow of eminence cast by the legendary William Alexander Bustamante. Whether Shearer will be able to earn, rather than invoke, the support, esteem and loyalty of his colleagues is another matter. He has been given room in which to manoeuvre.

In October 1973, Edward Seaga, formerly J.L.P. Minister of Finance and Planning, announced that he would be taking a two-year "breather" or leave of absence from his duties in the Party, to do some writing among other things.

Robert Lightbourne, formerly J.L.P. Minister of Trade and Industry, who resigned from the J.L.P. to sit as an Independent Member of Parlia-ment, announced in 1974 the formation of a new political party — the United Party (U.P.) under his leadership. The launching of the U.P. came in the wake of the island-wide Local Government Elections which saw the P.N.P. sustaining its overall popularity with the electorate, gaining

251

54 per cent of the ballots cast to the J.L.P.'s 43 per cent. The P.N.P. also gained political control of twelve of the fourteen Parish Councils, with the J.L.P. retaining one and Lightbourne's group of Independent candidates, all six of whom were elected, taking control of the St. Thomas Parish Council from the J.L.P. It is still too early to say whether the Lightbourne-led United Party will be able to "get off the ground" and become a force of political significance. It is, however, most unlikely as the U.P. does not have a trade union base and thus does not meet the yardstick of legitimacy for political parties in Jamaica.

In the meantime, Prime Minister Michael Manley and the P.N.P. have been attempting to translate the 1972 "Mandate for Change" into the "Politics of Change" and "Participation". In his book *The Politics of Change — A Jamaican Testament*, released early in 1974, Manley has expressed his belief that democracy can, and must, offer to the electorate a feeling of power over their destiny, allowing them to participate actively in the decision-making processes which influence their lives. A prerequisite for the achievement of participatory democracy, however, is the inculcation of the spirit of self-reliance, that is "the ability on the part of the people of a country to make common efforts towards the general development and welfare of the group" (page 42). Enjoined with democracy are the principles of equality and social justice. Together they constitute the "touchstone of political morality".

An egalitarian society, according to Manley, must first of all ensure equality of opportunity, and consequently every developing society must aim at free compulsory education as its highest national priority. Tuition-free secondary education became effective in Jamaica as of September 1973, and tuition-free university education is to follow for eligible Jamaicans. In return, those benefiting will be required to give two years of service in a National Youth Service which will be put on a compulsory basis just as soon as the administrative machine has been geared up. The "free" education policy, seen in the context of human resource development, was preceded a year earlier by the launching of a massive literacy campaign, aimed (perhaps too optimistically) at eliminating functional illiteracy within four years.

Property owners also learned that the new educational thrust would be financed primarily from additional revenue to be derived from substantially higher levels of property taxation under a rationalized scheme designed to collect more from those who have the ability, or the means, to pay more. Taxpayers have thus been given a practical lesson in the economics of egalitarianism.

Seemingly fundamental also to the present Government's philosophy of change are recognition of the need, and a determination, to counteract the deeper or psychological consequences of colonialism — the so-called "dependence syndrome" and the related inferiority complex, the predilection for things "foreign", distaste for manual work and the "free-ness" or "anansi" mentality, all of which have served to inhibit the development of national self-confidence and a commitment to the ideal of sustained effort and excellence.

If there is anything new then in Jamaican politics, it may well be the concern on the part of the present regime to address itself systematically to the task of psychological reorientation of Jamaican society.

As far as Manley and the P.N.P. are concerned, one of the first major acts of psychological disengagement came with the decision of their administration to break with the traditional pattern of celebrating Labour Day, which up until then (May 1972) had seen the two major political parties and their respective affiliated and rival trade union blocs sponsoring separate mass rallies and marches which often ended in street clashes — or menacing confrontations. Instead, citizens of all walks of life were invited and led by the Prime Minister and Ministers of Government to come out on Labour Day and to give a day's free work to the nation involving some project of social utility but with the emphasis on manual labour.

Another gesture deemed to be of symbolic significance by the P.N.P. regime was the introduction of the "Kareba", a variant of the Afro-Asian "bush jacket" or "safari jacket" as an appropriate mode of dress for Jamaicans and an alternative to the traditional European jacket and tie.

Both the new Labour Day format and the new mode of attire appear to have gained widespread approval and have been quickly institutionalized.

Apparently on the assumption that one way of instilling self-confidence in a people is to give them confidence in the integrity of their leaders, legislation has been introduced requiring all Parliamentarians to declare their income and assets annually, on a confidential basis, however, to a Parliamentary Commission which has wide investigatory powers. Similar legislation is to be introduced for holders of public office in governmental and quasi-governmental services. Incidentally, salaries and allowances of Members of Parliament and senior civil servants were substantially increased when the Integrity legislation was introduced.

In the economic sphere, also, developments have unfolded which seem to portend new directions in Jamaican politics and social philosophy.

In the *Politics of Change* Manley has intimated that commitment to egalitarianism in a post-colonial society such as Jamaica's also means that the Government must subscribe to a set of economic policies as being fundamental to the building of a just society. One implication that emerges is that "clearly political independence and national sovereignty are inconsistent with a situation in which 'the commanding heights' of the economy are foreign owned and controlled". (page 104).

The logic of this dictum has very recently been brought to bear on the bauxite and alumina industry, which along with public utilities, banking and the sugar industry have been deemed by Manley to constitute the "commanding heights" of the Jamaican economy and as such clearly belong in public ownership and control.

On 15th May 1974, the Prime Minister in a statement read in the House of Representatives announced that negotiations between the Government and the bauxite and alumina companies concerning a new formula for determining increased revenue payments had not been concluded within the time-table set by Government, and consequently Government would be introducing legislation to provide for the imposition of a Production Levy on bauxite mined for export and for local processing, as well as for an increase in royalty payments, both to be effective from 1st January 1974.

The Production Levy is based on a percentage value of the realized price of primary aluminium and will range from 7.5 per cent in 1973–4 to 8.5 per cent by 1976–7 of the imputed value of each ton of bauxite ore.

The legislated settlement reflects not only a new and dramatic Third World outlook in Jamaica's strategy for economic development, but also the extent to which Jamaica's foreign policy will be used as a means of furthering the country's perceived self-interest. Manley reasserted his theme that the developing countries can no longer continue to supply raw materials to the developed world on a basis of passive acceptance of prices set by these countries or other agencies, and that methods must be devised to link the values received by developing countries for their raw materials to the values of final goods produced by the industrially advanced countries. The value-added formula was introduced in the bauxite negotiations against a background of the unprecedented increases in prices that had taken place during 1973 in international markets for a number of staple foods, intermediate goods, and crude oil and petroleum products. The Consumer Price Index in Jamaica by the end of 1973 had increased by 19.2 per cent in Kingston as against 5.9 per cent in 1972, and in rural areas by 20.4 per cent in 1973 as opposed to 5.5 per cent the previous year.

As part of its strategy of dealing with the bauxite and alumina companies, the Jamaica Government took the initiative in establishing early in 1974 the International Bauxite Association, including all the major bauxite and alumina-producing countries, presumably so that the multi-national corporations involved could not use the leverage of threatening to restrict production in Jamaica and to expand elsewhere.

Much more significant than the revenue claims, in terms of the longer-run implications for restructuring of the Jamaican economy, were other items on the Government's "shopping list" on which negotiations are to resume in the near future. Jamaica served notice of its intention to reacquire all the lands now owned by bauxite and alumina companies so that surface rights may pass from the companies into national hands, in order to reacquire control of the bauxite which constitutes Jamaica's greatest single natural resource; and negotiate arrangements for Government's participation in the ownership of bauxite and alumina operations in Jamaica.

It may be noted appropriately that the policy of economic nationalism adopted by the P.N.P. administration in respect of the bauxite industry has received support in principle from the Opposition J.L.P. and such reservations as have been expressed are not inconsistent with the role of an opposition party in bi-partisan politics.

Finally, the "new frontiersmen" of the "politics of change" have found themselves being haunted by one of the preoccupations of the Bustamante-Manley era — the maintenance of law and order — which has led the incumbent administration to adopt new initiatives and measures to combat crime, the originality and authorship of which the J.L.P. Opposition might be happy to concede to the P.N.P.

Faced with a rising tide of crime, involving the indiscriminate use of fire-arms and daily killings, at first concentrated among the working class but eventually extending to leading businessmen in the community, and convinced also that the availability of and access to guns in the island were linked to the traffic in narcotics (ganja or marijuana and cocaine) as well as other activities on the part of "organized crime" in Jamaica and North America, Manley announced on 19th March 1974 anti-crime measures which are in many respects unprecedented in the history of peace-time administration in Jamaica. The measures introduced include:
1. The Suppression of Crime Act, which enables the Government to declare any area of Jamaica a special area for purposes of the Act for

a period up to thirty days subject to extension by affirmative resolution of the House of Representatives. Within the special area the police have full authority to search any person, enter any building, arrest and detain any person on reasonable suspicion that he or she is committing or about to commit a crime, and set up road blocks;

2. Amendment to the Juveniles Act which will make juveniles (persons of fourteen years or more) subject to the same punishment as is available in the law to deal with adult crime. The Act also will give power to wardens who must guard juvenile offenders, as is available to warders of the general prisons in the island. The major consideration here was the fact that much of the gun crime was being committed by juveniles;

3. The Gun Court Act which provides that a person apprehended on a charge of illegal possession of a fire-arm will be placed on trial within seven days. There are no preliminary enquiries and cases are heard by a single magistrate appointed for the purpose. If an accused is guilty of other offences, that person must first answer the charge of illegal possession of a fire-arm. Conviction carries a mandatory requirement of indefinite detention. One appeal only by a convicted person is allowed to the Court of Appeal of Jamaica and no bail is available at any stage. The public is debarred from entering the Gun Court — but accounts of what took place are made available to the press and media. A Review Board alone will be empowered to advise whether a detainee may be released;

4. Accused persons and detainees under the Gun Court Act are kept in a special prison in the same locale as the Gun Court.

The new measures have aroused considerable concern among the legal professions, some of the leading members of which have expressed the view that existing instruments available to the Government (for example, declaration of a State of Emergency) could have been used. Other persons, including civil rights exponents, have queried the constitutionality of the measures adopted.

The measures, particularly the Gun Court Act, appear, however, to have widespread support from the masses and society at large, especially as a number of prominent middle-class personalities have been convicted and detained under the Act.

The continuing apprehension and seizure of a number of aircraft, including a converted bomber, as well as the attendant forfeiture to the Government of Jamaica of at least three twin-engine aircraft and a like number of marine craft, all caught in the narcotics trade, have led to popular satisfaction that "Mr. Big" and not just the "small man" can be made to feel the force of the law.

The anti-crime measures must be viewed, however, as a diversion from the main task of national reconstruction. The intensification of crime and violence is but a symptom and a reflection of problems which are endemic to the structure of the Jamaican economy and society:

— population pressure and mass unemployment of close to 25 per cent of the labour force, concentrated moreover among the youth who are likely to remain inexperienced unemployed;

— serious under-employment, substantiated by National Insurance Scheme statistics which indicate that in a particular year — 1971 — 44 per cent of the persons who made contributions worked for thirteen weeks or less in the year;

— uneven distribution of wealth and wealth-earning opportunities;

— mal-utilization and under-utilization of resources, human and otherwise.

The quest for social justice and greater equality of opportunities is not without its ironies. A fairly comprehensive set of labour laws is being placed on the statute book and new financial institutions have been and are being devised to offer an increasing measure of security of employment and income to those who are already employed and who moreover enjoy the protection of trade union representation. For instance, the launching of the Workers' Savings and Loan Bank in August 1973, an early success story, represents in a sense a joint government, trade union, and worker venture in workers' capitalism. The Termination of Employment Act, originally brought forward by the previous J.L.P. administration, and enacted in June 1974, requires minimum periods of notice for termination based on years of service and determines the right, as well as the eligibility, of employees for redundancy payments.

Impending National Minimum Wage and Equal Pay for Equal Work legislation will likewise offer added protection for all wage-earners. Another piece of legislation — the Labour Relations and Labour Disputes Act — taken over from the previous administration, will break new ground and require, among other things, compulsory recognition of trade unions, thereby strengthening the bargaining position of those who have an income-earning propensity.

The legislative programme referred to above is consistent with the expectations and traditions of political unionism and "welfare labourism" initiated by Alexander Bustamante in 1945, and in this sense, the continuity of the Bustamante era remains unbroken.

But what about the ever-increasing numbers, especially among the youth, who remain outside the mainstream of economic life? The task of bringing them into productive relations is so formidable and so urgent that it may not lend itself to piecemeal labour welfarism. It is in this sense that the Jamaican society may have to seek more innovative solutions than in the past. For the technology of protest has become more sophisticated and deadly. Automatic weapons and home-made shot-guns have replaced machetes and sticks and stones. At the same time, the lure of crime has also grown stronger, for the stakes appear to be much higher. What may be involved, therefore, in the search for more effective solutions, is not just a tinkering with the system as it is, but a rapid dismantling of the structures of privilege and a restructuring of the economy itself within a much shorter time horizon. It is the philosophical as well as practical implications of embarking on either or both of these two courses of action that Jamaicans must now consider as a matter of urgency.

* * *

It is the author's hope that Jamaicans — especially those of the current and younger generations who perhaps have heard or read of the struggles of the recent past, and who may be inclined to take for granted or to debunk for ideological reasons "the story of how the active plan to win independence for our people came into being and was finally achieved" (the late N.W. Manley) — will be no less impatient about the changes, social, economic and political, which they are anxious to make or have made in the quest for a better Jamaica but at the same time, will be more tolerant of the achievements and failures of the founding fathers and their own parents. It is only proper that the peak achievements of one generation should be the starting point of the next, and that past action should not be accepted uncritically as a guide for present or future action. But a country deemed to have only an "inglorious" past is not likely to have a great future.

G.E.E.
July 1974

ABBREVIATIONS

B.I.T.U.	Bustamante Industrial Trade Union
C.D. & W.	Colonial Development and Welfare
D.L.P.	Democratic Labour Party
E.E.C.	European Economic Community
I.S.E.R.	Institute for Social and Economic Research
I.C.F.T.U.	International Confederation of Free Trade Unions
J.B.P.A.	Jamaica Banana Producers Association
J.D.P.	Jamaica Democratic Party
J.G.R.W.U.	Jamaica Government Railway Workers Union
J.L.P.	Jamaica Labour Party
J.W.T.U.	Jamaica Workers and Tradesmen Union
J.I.C.	Joint Industrial Council
K.S.A.C.	Kingston and St. Andrew Corporation
M.H.R.	Member of the House of Representatives
M.L.C.	Member of the Legislative Council
M.P.	Member of Parliament
N.L.P.	National Labour Party
N.W.U.	National Workers Union
O.A.S.	Organization of American States
P.N.P.	People's National Party
S.M.O.	Senior Medical Officer
T.T.G.W.U.	Tramway Transport and General Workers Union
T.U.C.	Trades Union Congress (Britain)
T.U.C.	Trades Union Congress of Jamaica
T.U.C.	Trade(s) Union Council (Jamaica)
U.N.I.A.	Universal Negro Improvement Association
U.W.I.	University of West Indies
W.I.F.L.P.	West Indies Federal Labour Party
W.F.T.U.	World Federation of Trade Unions

NOTES

CHAPTER 1   *The Early Days*

¹Actually in some parts of the island, as for example in the parish of St. Mary, banana rather than sugar-cane cultivation constituted the more significant crop, being cultivated on a relatively large scale on the estates of the landed gentry as well as the properties of the professional classes and the plots of peasant cultivators. Mr. H.P. Jacobs has drawn my attention to the fact that as late as 1926 the value of banana exports was £2.1 million and that of sugar £750,000; while 71,000 acres were under bananas and only 44,000 acres under cane. Nevertheless, however much the cultivation and processing of sugar-cane may have declined, even in the parish of Hanover during Bustamante's youth, yet sugar cultivation remained much more significant in terms of employment, and the sugar plantation was the dominant social enclave.

²Eric Williams, *Capitalism and Slavery*, University of North Carolina Press, 1944, p. 86.

³Philip Curtin, *Two Jamaicas*, Atheneum, New York, 1970, p. 46. (Originally published by Harvard University Press, 1955.)

⁴See Philip Curtin, *Two Jamaicas*, Chapter I.

⁵B.A. Kerr, "A Priceless Heritage", *The Sunday Gleaner*, 16th November 1969.

⁶N.W. Manley, "My Early Years", an autobiographical fragment in *Manley and the New Jamaica: Selected Speeches and Writings 1938–1968*, edited with notes and an introduction by Rex Nettleford, paperback edition, xcvi.

⁷N.W. Manley, in *Manley and the New Jamaica*, ed. Nettleford, xcvi.

⁸N.W. Manley, in *Manley and the New Jamaica*, ed. Nettleford, xcvi.

⁹N.W. Manley, in *Manley and the New Jamaica*, ed. Nettleford, xcvii.

¹⁰*Jamaica Hansard*, 18th August 1946.

CHAPTER 2   *The Wanderer Returns*

¹*The Daily Gleaner*, 29th June 1922.

²Cited by C. Paul Bradley, "The Rise of Mass Parties in Jamaica", *Social and Economic Studies*, I.S.E.R., U.W.I., Vol. 9, No. 4, 1960.

³G.E. Eaton, "Trade Union Development in Jamaica", *Caribbean Quarterly*,

U.W.I., Vol. 3, Nos. 1 and 2, 1962.

[4]See William J. Makin, *Caribbean Nights*, Robert Hale Ltd., London, 1939.

[5]Quoted by C. Paul Bradley, "The Rise of Mass Parties in Jamaica", *Social and Economic Studies*,Vol. 9, No. 4, 1960.

[6]W.J. Makin, *Caribbean Nights*, Robert Hale Ltd., London, 1939.

[7]M.G. Smith, *The Political Implications of Jamaican Social Structure*.

[8]Personal interview with Lady Gladys Bustamante, 23rd March 1972.

[9]Details provided about Bustamante's siblings in this section are based on information provided by Frank Hill, journalist and radio commentator.

[10]*Plain Talk* served as a kind of "popular" weekly from 1935 to 1939. It sold for one penny and catered to the *petite bourgeoisie* (shopkeepers, independent artisans, etc.), municipal politicians, rate-payer groups, social reformers, and so on, as well as working-class readers. It carried articles on labour conditions, trade union endeavours, particularly of the Jamaica Workers and Tradesmen Union (J.W.T.U.) as well as the activities of the Universal Negro Improvement Association (U.N.I.A.) founded by Marcus Garvey. Bustamante was given extensive coverage by *Plain Talk*, which carried many of his letters, and in January 1937 he offered to buy shares in *Plain Talk*. The weekly was published by T.H. Kitchener, Managing Director and Treasurer. Secretary and Editor-in-Chief was no less a person than Alfred Mends, civic and political reformer who had also been active as a trade union organizer, and an associate of Bain Alves, who had organized Kingston Waterfront workers in 1918 into the Longshoremen's Union No. I. Alves continued to be active as a trade union leader up to 1924 when he was elected a (municipal) Councillor for Kingston. By this time, Alves had also managed to bring in a number of organized artisanal groups (e.g., bakers) under the banner of his Jamaica Federation of Labour. Alfred Mends became President of the Jamaica Reform Club in 1924 and held this position for a number of years, commenting on labour issues, giving strong support to the Jamaica Federation of Labour and espousing socialism as the appropriate political ideology for Jamaica. Ironically, in 1927, Mends was the subject of a libel suit brought against him by his erstwhile friend and associate — Bain Alves.

CHAPTER 3   *The Call to Leadership*

[1]See the "Report (with Appendices) of the Commission appointed to enquire into the Disturbance which occurred on Frome Estate, Westmoreland, 2nd May 1938", Government Printer, 1938. See also the "Report (with Appendices) of the Commission appointed to enquire into the Disturbances which occurred in Kingston in Jamaica between 23rd May and 11th June 1938", Government Printer, Kingston, 1938. And see O.W. Phelps, "Rise of the Labour Movement in Jamaica", *Social and Economic Studies*, I.S.E.R., U.W.I., Vol. 9, No. 4, December 1960.

[2]William J. Makin, *Caribbean Nights*, p. 69.

[3]Personal interview with N.W. Manley, 1969.

[4]Personal interview with N.W. Manley, 1969.

[5]Personal interview with N.W. Manley, 1969.

⁶ *The Jamaica Standard*, 30th May 1938.
⁷Personal interview with N.W. Manley, 1969.
⁸William J. Makin, *Caribbean Nights*, p. 63.
⁹N.W. Manley, "Inaugural Address" at the launching of the People's National Party, September 1938.
¹⁰N.W. Manley, "Inaugural Address" at the launching of the People's National Party, September 1938.

CHAPTER 4   *Labour Leader Triumphant*

¹ *The Jamaica Standard*, 8th September 1938, p. 6.
²This idea formed the basis a decade later of a doctoral dissertation: G.E. Eaton, "The Development of Trade Unionism in Jamaica in the Perspective of the Role of Trade Unions in Developing Countries", McGill University, Montreal, Canada.
³Recorded interview with N.W. Manley, 1969.
⁴Recorded interview with Kenneth G. Hill, 1969.
⁵Recorded interview with N.W. Manley.
⁶Recorded interview with N.W. Manley.
⁷Recorded interview with N.W. Manley.
⁸Recorded interview with Ken Hill, 1969.
⁹Recorded interview with N.W. Manley.
¹⁰See *The Daily Gleaner*, 21st February through 27th February 1942, for details of the split and controversy.
¹¹Recorded interview with the late O.T. Fairclough, 1969.
¹²*Labour and Capital*, September 1943.
¹³Full articulation of the concept and characteristics of political unionism as the typical pattern of unionism in underdeveloped countries will have to await publication of my forthcoming book, *The Development of Trade Unionism in Jamaica*. Many Caribbean readers, however, would have heard me expound on the model and implications of political unionism in lecture rooms, trade union and management training courses and public forums throughout the Caribbean since 1959. Of course the forms and patterns of trade unionism in so-called under-developed or developing countries, have also been the subject of books published by other authors.
¹⁴This interpretation was first suggested to the author by Professor George Crumper, University of the West Indies.

CHAPTER 5   *Tutelage in Politics and Nation-building*

¹Nettleford, ed., *Manley and the New Jamaica*, p. xxi.
²N.W. Manley, in *Manley and the New Jamaica*, ed. Nettleford, p. 98.
³N.W. Manley, in *Manley and the New Jamaica*, ed. Nettleford, p. 111.

[4]N.W. Manley, in *Manley and the New Jamaica*, ed. Nettleford, p. 100.

[5]Quoted by N.W. Manley, in *Manley and the New Jamaica*, ed. Nettleford, p. 98.

[6]Gordon Lewis, *The Growth of the Modern West Indies*, p. 104.

[7]*Jamaica Hansard*, 3rd March 1946, p. 95.

[8]*Jamaica Hansard*, June 1945, p. 176.

[9]*Jamaica Hansard*, June 1945, p. 174.

[10]*Jamaica Hansard*, 12th April 1945, p. 46.

[11]*Jamaica Hansard*, June 1945, p. 175.

[12]N.W. Manley, *Manley and the New Jamaica*, ed. Nettleford, p. 20.

[13]Nettleford, ed., *Manley and the New Jamaica*, p. ix.

[14]The Conference was held at the London School of Economics and Political Science in May 1967. For a report of the proceedings see the journal *Government and Opposition*, Vol. 3, No. 2, Spring 1968. The definition ran as follows: "Populist movements are movements aimed at power for the benefit of the people as a whole, which result from the reaction of those, usually intellectuals alienated from the existing power structure, to stresses of rapid, economic, social, cultural or political change. These movements are characterized by a belief in return to an adaptation of more simple and traditional forms and values, emanating from the people, particularly the more archaic sections of the people who are taken to be the repository of virtue."

[15]This generalization is based on the findings of unpublished research undertaken by the writer in Jamaica during 1962–3.

[16]*Jamaica Hansard*, 3rd January 1946, p. 2. The Industrial Relations Committee had been set up by the Government in April 1943 to review the system and pattern of labour-management relations and to make recommendations. It issued an Interim Report in October 1943 which embodied a Fair Labour Code, and a Final Report in 1945. The Committee recommended enactment of a Comprehensive Industrial Relations Law to provide, among other things, for Central Trade Boards and a Central Agricultural Board to review wages and working conditions, and an Arbitration Court.

[17]Increasingly as the P.N.P. grew stronger in Greater Kingston and environs, so did its readiness to meet J.L.P. provocation with organized force and violence. Thus for instance in August 1949, inter-party conflict involving the top brass of both parties marred a municipal by-election in one of the hill constituencies of Eastern St. Andrew. In a riotous fracas in Gordon Town a J.L.P. supporter was killed. Colourful and fiery Wills O. Isaacs, the P.N.P.'s counterpart of the flamboyant Bustamante, threatened to come to blows with Bustamante. Bustamante narrowly escaped being hit by a rock thrown at him and was cut over one eye by a knife-wielding P.N.P. supporter. Bustamante, protecting Miss Longbridge, retreated to the safety of his car and made a getaway in the course of which a number of persons were struck by the still-open car doors. A one-man Commission of Enquiry, conducted by Sir Hector Hearne, Chief Justice, found Wills O. Isaacs, then 3rd Vice-President of the P.N.P., responsible for the "saturnalia of hatred, intimidation, insult and abuse, violence and even death at Gordon Town". Isaacs resigned as 3rd Vice-President of the P.N.P. and was charged with incitement to riot. During the course of his defence he uttered the remark for which he will long be remembered: "What are a few broken skulls in the making of a nation?" Experience since 1945 has shown that once the masses are spurred on to violence, it

often becomes difficult for leaders to restrain them. Thus in the General Election of 1959, the J.L.P. supporters suffered violence at the hands of P.N.P. supporters at a time when the P.N.P. was clearly dominant and "on top of the J.L.P.", and thus had little excuse for calculated harassment of the J.L.P.

[18]Banning of public meetings because of confrontations and violence occurred in 1946, 1947, 1949 and 1951.

[19]N.W. Manley, "P.N.P. Presidential Address", 11th August 1945.

[20]*Jamaica Hansard*, July 1947, pp. 390–1.

[21]*Jamaica Hansard*, July 1947, pp. 393–4.

[22]Nettleford, ed., *Manley and the New Jamaica*, p. xiii.

[23]Nettleford, ed., *Manley and the New Jamaica*, p. xxi.

[24]*Jamaica Hansard*, 22nd November 1949, p. 412.

[25]*Jamaica Hansard*, 22nd March 1949, p. 94.

[26]*Jamaica Hansard*, 22nd March 1949, p. 95.

[27]*Jamaica Hansard*, 18th July 1950, p. 268.

[28]*Jamaica Hansard*, 5th February 1952, p. 39.

[29]N.W. Manley, in *Manley and the New Jamaica*, ed. Nettleford, p. 50.

[30]Nettleford, ed., *Manley and the New Jamaica*, p. lvi

[31]*Jamaica Hansard*, 12th July 1950, p. 263.

[32]Nettleford, ed., *Manley and the New Jamaica*, p. xiv.

[33]*Jamaica Hansard*, 22nd July 1953, p. 293.

[34]*Jamaica Hansard*, 29th July 1953, p. 41.

[35]*Jamaica Hansard*, 8th June 1949, p. 172.

[36]Recorded interview with Arnold S. Jackson — then M.P. (J.L.P.) for Hanover East, at Irish Town, 1970.

CHAPTER 6   *From Defeat to Triumph 1955–1962*

[1]*National Plan for Jamaica* 1957–1967, p. 27.

[2]Austin Peck, "Economic Planning in Jamaica", *Social and Economic Studies*, Vol. 7, No. 4, December 1958. For extended discussion see G.E. Eaton, "The Development of Trade Unionism in Jamaica in the perspective of the role of trade unions in underdeveloped countries", Ph.D. Dissertation, McGill University, 1961. Compare also Owen Jefferson, *The Post-War Economic Development of Jamaica*, I.S.E.R., U.W.I., Jamaica, 1972.

[3]*Jamaica Hansard*, May 1956, p. 234. For Bustamante's contribution to the debate and the quotation cited in the text, see pp. 225–6.

[4]*Jamaica Hansard*, 16th April 1957. Compare also with earlier and contradictory statements by Bustamante: "I was able to exist, or thirteen of us were able to exist, because our father was a very small cultivator in Blenheim Hanover" (*Jamaica Hansard*, 19th January 1949). "My father was one of Hanover's largest planters; he was not rich but was comfortably situated. Misfortune came — and he lost nearly all he possessed. Deserted by wealthy friends — white, black and brown.

As a child I never forgot that his workers stood by him" (*Plain Talk*, 4th September 1937, p. 2).

[5]*Jamaica Hansard*, 12th June 1957, p. 356.

[6]*Jamaica Hansard*, December 1958, p. 600.

[7]In a book, *The Politics of Constitutional Decolonization, Jamaica 1944–62*, published and released by the Institute of Social and Economic Research, U.W.I., even while this chapter was being written, the author, Trevor Muroe, in a highly critical interpretation of Jamaican politics, commented: "Late in the day, the Federal issue therefore became of immediate significance to the manner and timing of Jamaican independence. Of equal importance, however, was the fact that the issue dramatized much that was inherent in the political life of the country after 1944. Through it many of the less obvious features of the political process found their clearest expression — for example the continuing role of the Imperial Power, the almost complete absence of popular participation, the considerable agreement among the colonial and Imperial political elites, the irrelevance of the masses except in conditions where this unanimity was broken and so on." See Chap. 4 "Federation and the Politics of Non-Participation 1947–1961".

[8]This chapter draws heavily on Sir John Mordecai's *The West Indies: The Federal Negotiations*, London, 1968, which is the most comprehensive and authoritative of the studies on the creation and break-up of the West Indies Federation.

[9]Sir John Mordecai, *The West Indies: The Federal Negotiations*, p. 85.

[10]Report of the Committee on Industrial Relations, Government of Jamaica, 1945.

[11]Mordecai, *The West Indies: The Federal Negotiations*, p. 46.

[12]Mordecai, *The West Indies: The Federal Negotiations*, p. 93.

[13]*The Daily Gleaner*, 2nd August 1959.

[14]*The Daily Gleaner*, 30th July 1958.

[15]*The Daily Gleaner*, 30th July 1959.

[16]Mordecai, *The West Indies: The Federal Negotiations*, p. 182.

[17]Taken from the account given by Mordecai, *The West Indies: The Federal Negotiations*, p. 220–1.

[18]Mordecai, *The West Indies: The Federal Negotiations*. Also confirmed to this author by Mr. Edward Seaga in personal interview.

[19]Compare Trevor Munroe, *The Politics of Constitutional Decolonization, Jamaica, 1944–62*, Chapter 4.

[20]N.W. Manley, "Presidential Address, P.N.P. Conference", 21st May 1961.

[21]Mordecai, *The West Indies: The Federal Negotiations*, p. 222.

[22]*The Daily Gleaner*, 15th November 1960.

[23]Mrs. Leon was elected on a P.N.P. ticket in the General Election held on 29th February 1972 and was appointed Minister of Local Government.

[24]Nettleford, ed., *Manley and the New Jamaica*, pp. 191–2.

[25]Mordecai, *The West Indies: The Federal Negotiation*, p. 397.

[26]Mordecai, *The West Indies: The Federal Negotiations*, p. 414.

[27]*Jamaica Hansard*, 23rd January, 1962.

[28]"Presidential Address, P.N.P. Conference", 21st May 1961.

[29]D.C. Tavares (deceased) in parliamentary debate, in *Jamaica Hansard*, 6th July 1961. Bustamante also struck much the same note: "It is an undeniable fact that for years and years when some of us were against independence for Jamaica, for

we thought that the time had not yet come, it was the Premier who went over the streets and valleys and mountain sides proposing independence for Jamaica within the British Commonwealth of Nations. But today, he has changed just like the Arabians" (*Jamaica Hansard*, 11th July 1961, pp. 379–80).

[30]N.W. Manley, in parliamentary debate, *Manley and the New Jamaica*, ed. Nettleford, p. 138.

[31]*Jamaica Hansard*, March 1946, p. 57.

[32]The old guard included: Sir Alexander Bustamante, Prime Minister and Minister of External Affairs; Donald Sangster, Deputy Prime Minister, Minister of Finance and Leader of the House; Edwin Allen, Minister of Education; L.G. Newland, Minister of Labour; and Leopold Lynch, Minister of Local Government. The later and talented group included: Robert Lightbourne, Minister of Trade and Industry; David C. Tavares, Minister of Development and Welfare; Dr. Herbert Eldemire, Minister of Health; John P. Gyles, Minister of Agriculture and Lands; Roy McNeil, Minister of Home Affairs; and Kenneth Jones, Minister of Communications and Works.

CHAPTER 7   *The New Jamaica — Power and Responsibility*

[1]Personal interview with Edward Seaga, M.P., August 1972.

[2]For instance: "We say this and I say this, I want to be the first Governor of the colony and I am going to be the first Governor in this colony, but this must come slowly by degrees — degree by degree" (*Jamaica Hansard*, June 1945, p. 76).

[3]N.W. Manley, "Education and the new national spirit", in *Manley and the New Jamaica*, ed. Nettleford, p. 104.

[4]*Jamaica Hansard*, 7th November 1963, p. 88.

[5]*Jamaica Hansard*, 12th December 1963, p. 145.

[6]*Jamaica Hansard*, 16th June 1963.

[7]The writer served on that Committee as a representative of the University of the West Indies and played the role of mediator and expert adviser.

[8]*Jamaica Hansard*, May 1964, p. 188.

[9]*Jamaica Hansard*, 7th November 1962, p. 87.

[10]One of the first persons to be made the victim of an exclusion order under the New Constitution of 1944 was none other than Adolphe Roberts, a distinguished Jamaican-born novelist and historian. A fervent nationalist and one of the founders of the Jamaica Progressive League in New York in 1936, Roberts embarked upon a lecture tour in Jamaica during 1937 to preach the theme of self-government for Jamaica. He also contributed articles to *Public Opinion*. Roberts was denied entry as a nationalized American by order of the Executive Council. Florizel Glasspole raised the matter in the House of Representatives and sought to have the exclusion order reconsidered, but the P.N.P. Opposition was outvoted by the J.L.P. Majority.

[11]Personal Interview with Sir Alexander Bustamante, March 1972.

[12]Observation of G. Arthur Brown, Governor of the Bank of Jamaica, in personal interview, November 1972.

[13]See B. St. John Hamilton, *Problems of Administration in an Emergent Nation*, Praeger, 1964.

Notes

CHAPTER 8   *The Man and His Times — Hero in Fact and Fiction*

[1]*Jamaica Hansard*, September 1950, p. 455.

[2]Personal interview with G. Arthur Brown, Governor of the Bank of Jamaica, 12th November 1972.

[3]*Jamaica Hansard*, June 1949, p. 169.

[4]*The Daily Gleaner*, 7th January 1967.

[5]The main criterion used by Bustamante to determine whether he could work with anyone was confidence. Nowhere was this better exemplified than in his relationship with James (Jimmy) Lloyd. From 1945–9 Lloyd's brother, Dr. Ivan Lloyd, was the leader of the P.N.P. five-man Opposition contingent in the House of Representatives. Bustamante as the leader of the Majority Party and Minister of Communications soon discovered that Jimmy Lloyd was the top civil servant in what subsequently became the Ministry of Local Government. There probably would have been many of Bustamante's colleagues who would have warned him to have nothing to do with Ivan Lloyd's brother. Yet there developed the closest relationship and confidence between Bustamante and Jimmy Lloyd during the entire period that the latter's brother remained a prominent member of the P.N.P.

[6]*Jamaica Hansard*, 28th February 1968, pp. 495–6.

[7]Personal interview with G. Arthur Brown, 12th November 1972.

[8]*Jamaica Hansard*, 28th February 1968, p. 497.

[9]Personal Interview with G. Arthur Brown, 12th November 1972.

[10]Sylvia Wynter, *Jamaica's National Heroes*, p. 1.

[11]Sylvia Wynter, *Jamaica's National Heroes*, p. 24.

[12]Sylvia Wynter, *Jamaica's National Heroes*, pp. 25–6.

[13]Gordon K. Lewis, *The Growth of the Modern West Indies*, McGibbon and Kee Ltd., 1968, p. 181.

[14]Gordon K. Lewis, *The Growth of the Modern West Indies*, p. 190.

[15]Gordon K. Lewis, *Growth of the Modern West Indies*, p. 186. The reaction of Jamaicans residing overseas to the fact of independence was quite the opposite to that of Jamaicans at home. "The jubilation of the local populace appeared to be exceeded by that of Jamaicans resident abroad at the knowledge that they belonged to a country that could now take its place by right on international bodies": B. St. John Hamilton, *Problems of Administration in an Emergent Nation: A Case Study of Jamaica*, Praeger, 1974, p. 175.

[16]N.W. Manley, "Farewell Address, P.N.P. Annual Conference", 1969.

[17]Gordon K. Lewis, *Growth of the Modern West Indies*, p. 179.

[18]*Jamaica Hansard*, 22nd February 1968, p. 496. As the story goes, Bustamante went to London for sugar negotiations. The then Colonial Secretary, Sir Oliver Lyttleton, arrived at the Conference after the proceedings had started and reportedly said to Bustamante, "Well, Mr. Bustamante, will you say what you have to say as quickly as possible because I can only spend twenty minutes here." Bustamante is reported to have made his now famous retort and then stalked out of the room.

[19]For a concise and very readable analysis of the General Election of 29th February 1972 see Olive Senior *The General Elections 1972 — A Perspective*, Kingston Publishers, 1972.

[20]Maurice Duverger, *Political Parties*, Methuen & Co. Ltd. See the "Introduction: The Origin of Parties".

[21]Duverger, *Political Parties*, p. 63.

[22]D.W. Brogan, "Foreward", in Duverger, *Political Parties*, p. vii.

[23]Compare Bustamante's campaign ad in *The Daily Gleaner*, 25th July 1959, speaking of Manley and the P.N.P.: "You and your party have chosen your weapons — Stones and the Clenched Fist. I and my party have chosen ours — God and the People of Jamaica."

[24]Compare also Bustamante's campaign ad in *The Daily Gleaner*, 26th July 1959: "Love is the Word — is my message." It is similarities like these which led this writer to say during a panel discussion on General Election night, 29th February 1972, that Michael Manley was in many respects Bustamante reincarnate.

[25]Personal interview with Sir Alexander Bustamante, Irish Town, 1970.

[26]*The Daily Gleaner*, 17th April 1972.

[27]Personal interview with Edward Seaga, M.P., 1972.

[28]Actually, Gladys Longbridge contested once for a seat in the House of Representatives, when she ran on 10th July 1951 as a J.L.P. candidate against F.L.B. Evans, the P.N.P.'s colourful candidate, who was nicknamed "Slave Boy", in a by-election in a constituency of Westmoreland. Results: Evans, 8,245; Longbridge, 2,463.

INDEX

Index

9 789766 101916